Effective Early Literacy Practice

DATE DUE

The Library Store #47-0119

Effective Early Literacy Practice

Here's How, Here's Why

edited by

Andrea DeBruin-Parecki, Ph.D.

Old Dominion University

Norfolk, Virginia

a division of High/Scope Educational Research Foundation

Baltimore • London • Sydney

a division of High/Scope Educational Research Foundation

Paul H. Brookes Publishing Co.
Post Office Box 10624
Baltimore, Maryland 21285-0624
USA

www.brookespublishing.com

Typeset by Spearhead Global, Inc., Bear, Delaware.
Manufactured in the United States of America by
Versa Press, Inc., East Peoria, Illinois.

The individuals described in this book are composites or real people whose situations
have been masked and are based on the authors' experiences. Names and identifying
details have been changed to protect confidentiality.

The excerpts and artwork appearing in Chapter 5 are from *The Early Literacy Skills
Assessment: Dante Grows Up* by Andrea DeBruin-Parecki. Copyright © 2005 by
High/Scope Educational Research Foundation. Reprinted by permission.

Library of Congress Cataloging-in-Publication Data

Effective early literacy practice: Here's how, here's why / edited by Andrea DeBruin-
Parecki.
    p.   cm.
    Includes index.
    ISBN-13: 978-1-55766-940-7
    ISBN-10: 1-55766-940-6
    1. Children—Language. 2. Literacy. 3. Early childhood education. I. DeBruin-
Parecki, Andrea. II. Title.

LB1139.L3E35 2008
372.6–dc22
                                            2007040093

British Library Cataloguing in Publication data are available from the British Library.

2012   2011   2010   2009   2008

10   9   8   7   6   5   4   3   2   1

Contents

About the Editor

Andrea DeBruin-Parecki, Ph.D., Associate Professor, Early Childhood Education, Child Study Center, Old Dominion University, Norfolk, VA 23529

Andrea DeBruin-Parecki is nationally recognized for her work in the field of family literacy. She developed the Adult/Child Interactive Reading Inventory (ACIRI), a reliable and valid tool that measures the interactive reading skills of an adult and a child during storybook reading (available from Paul H. Brookes Publishing Co.). She has designed family literacy programs and has acted as a consultant across the country. In addition to the ACIRI, she created the Early Literacy Skills Assessment, a comprehensive, reliable, and valid tool in the form of a children's storybook that measures phonological awareness, the alphabetic principle, comprehension, and concepts about print. She has expertise in the areas of emergent literacy, assessment, literacy within at-risk and minority populations, and the motivation of at-risk populations. She was a Fulbright Senior Specialist in Guatemala. Her work related to literacy development in young children and families has been published and presented at national, regional, and state conferences.

About the Contributors

Patricia A. Edwards, Ph.D., Professor of Language and Literacy, Teacher Education Department, Michigan State University, 304 Erickson Hall, East Lansing, MI 48824

Patricia A. Edwards is a professor of language and literacy and the recipient of the prestigious Michigan State University 2001 Distinguished Faculty Award. From 1997 to 2002, she was a senior researcher at the Center for the Improvement of Early Reading Achievement. She is the author of two nationally acclaimed family literacy programs: *Parents as Partners in Reading: A Family Literacy Training Program* and *Talking Your Way to Literacy: A Program to Help Nonreading Parents Prepare Their Children for Reading*. Her books include *A Path to Follow: Learning to Listen to Parents* (1999, Heinemann); *Children Literacy Development: Making It Happen Through School, Family, and Community Involvement* (2004, Allyn & Bacon); and two forthcoming books, *A No Nonsense Strategic Guide for Launching Successful Parent Involvement Initiatives* (Scholastic) and *It's Time for Straight Talk: When White Teachers Work in Multicultural Settings* (Heinemann). She served on the board of directors of the International Reading Association (1998–2001) and was the first African American president of the National Reading Conference (2006–2007).

Billie J. Enz, Ph.D., Interim Associate Dean, School of Educational Innovation and Teacher Preparation, Arizona State University–Polytechnic Campus, 7001 East Williams Field Road, Building 140, Mesa, AZ 85212

Dr. Enz is the Interim Associate Dean at the School of Educational Innovation and Teacher Preparation at Arizona State University. Dr. Enz is the author and co-author for several books on new teacher development and mentor training, including *Trade Secrets for Primary and Elementary Teachers* (2002, Kendall/Hunt Publishing Company); *Trade Secrets for Middle and Secondary Teachers* (1999, Kendall/Hunt Publishing Company); *Ready, Set, Teach: A Winning Design for Your First Year* (2003, Kappa Delta Pi Publications); *Teachers! How to Win the Job You Want* (2000, Kendall/Hunt Publishing Company); and *Life Cycle of the Career Teacher* (1999, Corwin Press). Dr. Enz is a member of the early childhood education faculty and teaches language and literacy courses. She has co-authored two textbooks in this area: *Teaching Language and Literacy: From Preschool to the Elementary Grades* (1996, Allyn & Bacon) and *Helping Young Children Learn Language and Literacy: From Birth Through Preschool* (2007, Allyn & Bacon).

Linda M. Espinosa, Ph.D., Professor of Early Childhood Education, University of Missouri–Columbia, 211 Townsend Hall, Columbia, MO 65211

Dr. Espinosa is Professor at the University of Missouri–Columbia and former Codirector of the National Institute for Early Education Research. Dr. Espinosa's practical experience and research interests focus on the design and evaluation of optimal learning environments for young children who are at risk for school failure. An expert in the area of young English learners, Dr. Espinosa has worked extensively with low-income Hispanic/Latino children and families throughout California. From this and other work, she has published many articles and training manuals on how to establish effective educational services for low-income, minority families who are acquiring English as a second language. Presently, Dr. Espinosa's work focuses on professional development and teacher preparation systems and their relationship to effective early childhood teaching practices.

Cynthia P. Gehrie, Ph.D., Director, Video Documentation Partnership, Post Office Box 1305, Highland Park, IL 60035

Dr. Gehrie is an urban ethnographer who works on research, evaluation, and public education projects using holistic observation techniques and video documentation. Dr. Gehrie was the methodologist in The Urban Principal Research Project at University of Illinois–Chicago (National Institute of Education) and is a co-author of the book *Principals in Action: The Reality of Managing Schools* (1984, Glencoe/McGraw-Hill). She established research protocols and video interview prompts for a study of Chicago school principals featuring in-service training for teachers in math and science instruction. She has created more than 90 educational videographs. She served as a documenter/delegate for a U.S. State Department women's delegation to Afghanistan, representing 500 California women's organizations in the spring of 2003. She has also been published in national journals. Currently she is combining staff development and video documentation/evaluation for three Early Reading First grants.

Maureen R. Gerard, Ph.D., Coordinator, Office of Professional Field Experience, Arizona State University West, 4701 West Thunderbird Road, Phoenix, AZ 85069

Dr. Gerard is Coordinator, Office of Professional Field Experience, at Arizona State University West. Her research interests include early literacy development and language acquisition. Her publications include the co-authored book *Environmental Print in the Classroom: Meaningful Connections for Learning to Read* (2004, International Reading Association). Dr. Gerard is a member of the International Reading Association, serves on the Arizona Governor's School Readiness Board Professional Leadership Implementation Team, and serves as Chair of Elementary Education at Grand Canyon University.

Myae Han, Ph.D., Assistant Professor, Individual and Family Studies, University of Delaware, 111 Alison West, Newark, DE 19716

Dr. Han is an assistant professor of individual and family studies at the University of Delaware, where she teaches courses in early childhood education and early literacy. Her research interests are children's play and early literacy development. She is currently a codirector of a Delaware Early Reading First project.

Elizabeth Landerholm, Ed.D., Professor, Early Childhood Education, Northeastern Illinois University, 500 North Saint Louis Avenue, Chicago, IL 60625

Dr. Landerholm is a professor of early childhood education at Northeastern Illinois University, Chicago. She has been a principal investigator of Project ROLL, an Early Reading First grant funded by the U.S. Department of Education. She has also directed an Even Start grant and other grants related to early childhood education, parent education, and teacher education. Her publications/conference presentations are in the areas of early childhood education, parent education, and the Reggio Emilia approach to early childhood education.

Miriam Martinez, Ph.D., Professor, The University of Texas at San Antonio, 1 University Circle, San Antonio, TX 78249

Dr. Martinez is a professor of education at The University of Texas at San Antonio. Her research and publications have focused on the nature of children's literary meaning making and responses to literature. She has also conducted research on instructional interventions that impact children's responses and on classroom libraries with colleagues. Dr. Martinez is a co-author of *Children's Books in Children's Hands* (2005, Allyn & Bacon). She is also a co-editor of *What a Character!: Character Study as a Guide to Literary Meaning Making* (2005, International Reading Association) and *Book Talk and Beyond* (2005, International Reading Association).

Lea M. McGee, Ph.D., Professor, Reading Recovery and Early Literacy, The Ohio State University, College of Education and Human Ecology, Teaching and Learning, Ramseyer Hall, 29 West Woodruff Avenue, Columbus, OH 43210

Lea M. McGee is the Marie C. Clay Professor of Reading Recovery and Early Literacy at Ohio State University. She has published four books, numerous books chapters, and many articles in *The Reading Teacher, Language Arts,* and *Reading Research Quarterly,* among others. She is a past president of the National Reading Conference, has directed two Early Reading First grants, and frequently works with teachers in their classrooms.

Gwendolyn Thompson McMillon, Ph.D., Associate Professor of Literacy, Department of Reading and Language Arts, Oakland University, 490G Pawley Hall, Rochester, MI 48309

Dr. Gwendolyn Thompson McMillon is an associate professor of literacy in the Department of Reading and Language Arts at Oakland University, where she teaches undergraduate reading methods and graduate research methods courses. Her research focuses on examining the literacy experiences of African American students at school, church, and other learning environments, and developing ways to help students, parents, and teachers become "border crossers"—successfully negotiating cultural boundaries. She earned a Ph.D. in 2001 from Michigan State University and was awarded the Spencer Dissertation Fellowship for Research Related to Education. Her work has been presented at numerous conferences and published in leading journals, including *Language Arts, Reading Teacher,* and the *National Reading Conference Annual Yearbook.* Dr. McMillon is the principal investigator for the Michigan Department of Education Title II Improving Teacher Quality Grant. She has served in various capacities, including co-chairperson of the National Reading Conference Ethnicity, Race, & Multilingualism Committee and reviewer for the *Michigan Reading Journal.*

Lesley Mandel Morrow, Ph.D., Professor of Literacy, Chair of the Department of Learning and Teaching, Rutgers, The State University of New Jersey, 10 Seminary Place, Department of Learning and Teaching, Graduate School of Education, New Brunswick, NJ 08901

Dr. Morrow is a professor at Rutgers, The State University of New Jersey. She is a professor at the Graduate School of Education, where she is Chair of the Department of Learning and Teaching. She began her career as a classroom teacher, then became a reading specialist, and later received her doctorate from Fordham University in New York City. Her area of research deals with early literacy development and the organization and management of language arts programs. Her research is carried out with children and families from diverse backgrounds.

Alison H. Paris, Ph.D., Former Assistant Professor of Developmental Psychology, Claremont McKenna College, 850 Columbia Avenue, Claremont, CA 91711

Dr. Paris is a former assistant professor of developmental psychology at Claremont McKenna College. While currently on family leave, she continues to perform research on learning, motivation, and educational practices, including children's early reading development, assessment, and instruction; the development of reading comprehension skills and genre-based thinking in young children; and engagement and self-regulation in school contexts.

Scott Paris, Ph.D., Professor, University of Michigan, 530 Church Street, Ann Arbor, MI 4810

Dr. Paris is a professor of psychology and education at the University of Michigan, where he served as Chair of the graduate program in psychology for 6 years. He was a principal investigator in the Center for the Improvement of Early Reading Achievement and a member of the board of directors of the National Reading Conference. Dr. Paris's research has focused on cognitive development, reading, metacognition, and self-regulated learning. He has created educational materials to help children acquire reading and learning strategies and has worked extensively with teachers to design instruction and assessment that promote literacy learning. Dr. Paris has published 12 books and written more than 150 book chapters and research articles. Dr. Paris twice received the Dean's Award for Outstanding Undergraduate Teaching, and in 1995 he received the University of Michigan Amoco Foundation Faculty Award for Distinguished Teaching. In 2007, he received the Albert J. Harris award from the International Reading Association.

Jennifer Prior, Ph.D., Assistant Professor, Northern Arizona University, 2626 East Pecos Road, Chandler, AZ 85225

Dr. Prior is an assistant professor of education at Northern Arizona University. Dr. Prior is currently responsible for the development of teacher education cohort programs in the Phoenix metropolitan area and teaches both undergraduate- and graduate-level classes in literacy and early childhood education. She is the author or co-author of several books, including *Environmental Print in the Classroom: Meaningful Connections for Learning to Read* (2004, International Reading Association) and *Family Involvement in Early Childhood Education: Research into Practice* (2007, Thomson Delmar Learning).

Donald J. Richgels, Ph.D., Presidential Research Professor, Department of Literacy Education, Northern Illinois University, DeKalb, IL 60115

Dr. Richgels is a professor of literacy education at Northern Illinois University, where he teaches courses in language development, language arts, and reading. His current research interests are preschool and kindergarten classroom practice and the relationship between spoken language acquisition and literacy development.

Roseann Rinear, M.A., Ed.D., Lecturer, San Diego State University, Child Development and Family Studies; Director, Preschool Source Consulting, 3235 Pleasant View Lane, Jamul, CA 91935

Dr. Rinear has been in the field of early childhood education for 32 years. Dr. Rinear's experiences are wide and varied and include 5 years as an elementary school teacher, 5 years as owner/operator of a private preschool, 10 years as a divisional director of 40 preschools, 3 years as a coordinator of specialists in a Head Start program, 15 years as professor of early childhood education, and 10 years as an early childhood trainer/consultant.

William H. Teale, Ed.D., Professor, University of Illinois–Chicago, 1040 West Harrison (MC 147), College of Education, Chicago, IL 60607

Dr. Teale is a professor of education at the University of Illinois–Chicago. Author of over 100 publications, his work has focused on early literacy learning, the intersection of technology and literacy education, and children's and young adult literature. *Emergent Literacy: Writing and Reading* (1986, Ablex Publishing), a book Dr. Teale co-edited with Elizabeth Sulzby, has become a standard reference in the field of early literacy. Dr. Teale has served as consultant to school districts and public libraries, Children's Television Workshop, Head Start, Reach Out and Read, and numerous other organizations. He is a former editor of *Language Arts* and was inducted into the Reading Hall of Fame in 2003.

Georgina Valverde, M.F.A., Artist/Educator, 3313 West Belden, First Floor, Chicago, IL 60647

Georgina Valverde is a practicing artist and art educator. She has extensive experience developing and managing arts programs for bilingual/bicultural and ethnically diverse students. She has taught in a variety of settings, including Chicago public schools, the University of Illinois–Chicago, the Chicago Children's Museum, and the Museum of Contemporary Art in Chicago, where she was Manager of Education Outreach from 1998 to 2000. She currently works on a Early Reading First project at Northeastern Illinois University's Chicago Teachers' Center. Ms. Valverde has exhibited widely, most recently at the Richard E. Peeler Art Center of DePauw University, Indiana, in 2006; the Palm Beach Institute of Contemporary Art in 2004; the International Contemporary Art Fair in Mexico City in 2003; and the Museum of Contemporary Art, Chicago, in 2002.

Junko Yokota, Ph.D., Professor of Education, National-Louis University, 2840 North Sheridan Road, Evanston, IL 60201

Junko Yokota is a professor of education at National-Louis University in Evanston, Illinois and a director of the Center for Teaching Through Children's Books. A former classroom teacher and a school librarian, she focuses her research and writing in children's literature on multicultural and international literature. She has published articles and review columns in a wide variety of reading/

language arts and children's literature journals, including *Kaleidoscope: A Multicultural Booklist for Grades K–8* (2001, National Council of Teachers of English). Her co-authored textbook, *Children's Books in Children's Hands* (2001, Allyn & Bacon), is in its third edition. She has also served on the Caldecott and Newbery Award Committees, chaired the Batchelder Award Committee, and served as President of the United States Board on Books for Young People. Dr. Yokota is a recipient of the Virginia Hamilton Award for Contribution to Multicultural Literature. She has been elected to her second term on the IBBY Hans Christian Andersen Jury to select the winners of the highest international award for children's literature.

Foreword

In this delightful book, you will hear the voices of teachers and children as they interact and engage in literacy learning. It is as exciting a moment in the young lives of children as it is for their mentors. Eager to learn, and eager to teach, it is a time when young learners are just beginning to discover that the world is full of print, that print means something, and that the adults in their lives are there to encourage and guide them in learning about the mysteries of print.

These are the years when children learn about the details of literacy: how letters represent sounds, how sounds go together to make words, how words combine to form sentences, and how sentences add up to a meaningful whole. But those are just the details. Children will put these skills together one by one to solve the larger puzzle of discovering meaning. Of course, that is the point of reading: to make connections between the words on the page and what they mean— and by doing so to make deeper connections between the reader and the world.

Researchers have learned a great deal in the past few decades about how reading works, although they are still figuring out some of the details. That is because reading is something a skilled reader does swiftly, silently, and internally. Even when one tries to observe the process, it is almost impossible to completely understand how it works. For this reason, many people assumed for a long time that skilled reading was natural and that reading just emerged as a result of accumulating a little bit of knowledge here and there and over time. All you needed, then, was an appealing environment and lots of opportunities to engage in these activities.

But now we know that skilled readers look at almost every letter of every word and their brains attend to the sound as well as the appearance of what they read. Some people might think that we read with our eyes, but what is even more important is the language-processing abilities of our brains. Reading is a language skill, and it is the basis for becoming literate.

In learning to read, children will first assemble what they learn about letters to build their ability to read words, then put this knowledge of words together to figure out how to comprehend sentences and text as a whole. Knowledge will be the goal, of course, but it cannot exist without the smooth assembly of its tiniest parts.

And it is the teacher who makes this critical connection of helping children assemble all of the parts together. But children would never have the patience to do all of that hard work if they did not know that it was going to add up to something worth having. That is why the most successful reading instruction teaches children not only the individual skills they will need, but also the larger context—the many ways that reading will make a difference in their lives.

In well-designed programs, children will become immersed in the world of print and will be given many enticing reasons to "join the club" of readers, from the sheer fun of reading to the value of acquiring new knowledge. They will also receive step-by-step instruction in each skill so that they can put all of this useful information together in meaningful ways. Once that happens for children, all of the steps will become automatic, fluent, and almost invisible.

Gathered in this book are the ideas of educators and researchers who have been able to capture examples of the ways in which literacy knowledge develops through the preschool years and in the early years of school. Each author provides critical ideas, never leaving the classrooms in which these activities occur. Each has a somewhat different message about how we can construct an environment that is helpful for learning and develop effective strategies for teaching young children. All of these ideas will help teachers improve their practices.

These approaches to literacy are helpful to both caregivers and parents. While sharing the excitement of working with children and watching them puzzle over the peculiarities of the codes we use for reading and writing, it becomes evident that even little children can do wonderful things with print. They can work out the complexities of the language they speak and apply equally ingenious approaches to their work with print. But to do these things well, children will need teachers' support and instruction to help put these skills together.

This is the critical message behind this book: Teaching matters. And when teachers demonstrate, model, share, and finally let go, we will watch all children soar and succeed in early literacy.

Susan B. Neuman
Professor, Ed.D.
University of Michigan
School of Education
610 East University
Ann Arbor, MI 48109

Acknowledgments

The idea for this book was born from conversations with preschool teachers, soon-to-be preschool teachers, and administrators who constantly ask me, "How can we use all of this 'scientifically based reading research and theory' to transform our classrooms into exemplary models of literacy instruction? What does all of this look like when teachers are using it?" Many of these present and future teachers and administrators attend professional development sessions and read extensively on the subject but still want clearer examples of how theory looks in real practice. I wish to acknowledge these questioners who spurred on the idea for this book.

I wish to acknowledge the authors of these chapters, well-known experts in the field who worked hard to begin their chapters with clear examples of practice before expounding on theory so that teachers and others could easily see how they link.

I also wish to acknowledge the wonderful editors at Brookes: Astrid Zuckerman, Johanna Cantler, and Marie Abate, who make working on a book with them a pleasure, and Heather Shrestha, Editorial Director, who is always so supportive of any project I bring her way.

Finally I wish to acknowledge my mother: my first teacher, whose wisdom over the years has made me a better person, and my HBMP, whose constant love and support helps me aspire to be all I can be.

Introduction

With the changing climate in early childhood literacy and the pressure on young children to develop formal literacy skills at younger and younger ages, it has become increasingly important that prekindergarten teachers receive current and theoretically based professional development in this area. While this professional development most often takes place in person, there are other ways for this development to occur. One way is through reading books that focus not only on theory, but also on how this theory looks in practice. This book achieves that goal.

The authors of the chapters in this book are nationally recognized in their fields and have, on numerous occasions, been called upon to provide professional development to teachers around the country and the world. The topics chosen by these authors are both timely and important and offer the reader a realistic window on current early literacy theory translated into successful practice.

Each chapter provides the reader with concrete examples of how early literacy research and theory supports excellent instruction. The primary goal of preschool teachers in regard to early literacy instruction is to assist children in developing the skills they need to become successful readers. This book can help guide their teaching and the setup of their classroom literacy environments.

In addition, this book can act as a resource for college professors looking for a text that will demonstrate to future teachers of young children what early literacy theory looks like in instructional contexts and how to apply this theory to their own teaching. The chapters provide a broad picture of a variety of early literacy issues that are of the utmost importance in today's preschool classrooms, and these topics can easily be used to promote lively discussion in teacher education settings.

In Chapter 1, "Creating a Literacy-Rich Preschool Classroom Environment to Enhance Literacy Instruction," Lesley Mandel Morrow focuses on how a well-constructed literacy environment can positively affect young children's skill development. The author states that the arrangement of space, choice of materials, and the aesthetic quality created in the room are essential ingredients for successful learning in preschool. She provides excellent examples of how to coordinate the curriculum and classroom environment so the most effective literacy instruction can occur.

In Chapter 2, "Exploring Intentional Instructional Uses of Environmental Print in Preschool and Primary Grades," Billie J. Enz, Jennifer Prior, Maureen R. Gerard, and Myae Han provide excellent information about using environmental print to enhance literacy instruction. The authors focus on phonemic awareness, letter recognition, and phonetic skills, and they explore creative and inexpensive ways teachers can build on children's interest in environmental print. The authors then explain how children's interest in environmental print relates to future reading skills.

The Chapter 3 authors, Alison H. Paris and Scott Paris, explore the very important topic of developing and assessing comprehension skills in their chapter, "Narrative Bridges to Comprehension." The authors assert that children's ability to construct and comprehend meaning from text is built on a foundation of language and literacy experiences in early childhood. They particularly discuss narrative thinking as a bridge from listening to reading, from experience to text, and from play to literacy.

Chapter 4, "Practice to Theory: Invented Spelling," by Donald J. Richgels, explains the role of young children's invented spelling in their literacy skill development and emphasizes why reading and writing should happen together. He describes five principles for supporting invented spelling in preschool and primary classrooms and explores the important connections between invented spelling and phonemic awareness.

Chapter 5, "Storybook Reading as a Standardized Measurement of Early Literacy Skill Development: The Early Literacy Skills Assessment," by Andrea DeBruin-Parecki, details current early literacy assessments and explains the need for more standardized, comprehensive, authentic, and accurate evaluations in the field. The Early Literacy Skills Assessment is presented as an example of this type of assessment.

Linda M. Espinosa addresses the very timely topic of English language learners' (ELLs') literacy instruction in Chapter 6, "Early Literacy for English Language Learners." She explains what we know about language and literacy development in young ELL children and what preschool teachers can do to promote literacy learning for all children. Also delineated are which early language and literacy skills are essential for later reading and writing and the most effective methods for teaching them to ELL children.

In Chapter 7, "Making Vital Home–School Connections: Utilizing Parent Stories as a 'Lifeline' for Developing Successful Early Literacy Experiences," Patricia A. Edwards and Gwendolyn Thompson McMillon tackle the very important issue of parent involvement in their children's early literacy experiences and instruction. They contend that home literacy environments and interaction patterns between parents and their children serve as contexts for children to learn strategies for literacy development.

Practical ways to address the communication problem experienced by many teachers and parents are discussed.

In Chapter 8, "The Book Matters: Evaluating and Selecting What to Read Aloud to Young Children," William H. Teale, Junko Yokota, and Miriam Martinez consider the importance of book selection on children's early literacy skill development. The authors provide guidelines for preschool teachers to consider in evaluating and selecting books for classroom read-alouds with young children.

Teale, Yokota, and Martinez claim that if teachers understand how to select effective read-aloud books, then they will be able to enhance the effects of one of the most important instructional activities in the early childhood classrooms.

In Chapter 9, "Early Reading First and Its Role in Defining High-Quality Professional Development," Lea M. McGee discusses Early Reading First. The author describes Early Reading First in general terms and then specifically focuses on the fact that grantees are required to provide intensive and ongoing professional development that includes mentoring and coaching of teachers in their own classrooms. She provides examples of effective professional development by discussing the progress made in the Early Reading First programs she actively guided and mentored. Her chapter also acts as an introduction to the two chapters that follow: case studies about professional development in Early Reading First programs written by program directors and their associates.

In the first case study chapter, "Developing an Early Literacy Professional Development Program," Roseann Rinear, a former director of an Early Reading First grant, outlines how to go about creating a professional development program that will assist teachers in a variety of early literacy contexts to become more effective in their instruction for children of diverse skill levels and cultural backgrounds. She emphasizes how important it is that all child development organizations have plans for training and provide tools for ongoing evaluations to ensure that the training is having a positive impact on instruction and student learning.

In the second case study chapter, "Creative Contexts for Literacy: A Reggio Emilia Approach Using Art and Documentation," authors Cynthia P. Gehrie, Elizabeth Landerholm, and Georgina Valverde describe a small-group workshop that was developed to assist teachers in an Early Reading First program to expand children's vocabulary and oral language. They depended on two principles to make this workshop successful: 1) Group process brings forward multiple perspectives, and 2) group process offers a context to compile words, practice vocabulary building, and participate in oral language expression.

While each of these chapters addresses different areas, they all blend together to provide the reader with a comprehensive view of how children develop early literacy skills, and how teachers can best assist them in this endeavor. Teachers who have deep knowledge of literacy skill development and an understanding of how to use this knowledge to best inspire young children to learn will be the ones who promote future academic success for those in their classrooms. To help equip these teachers and future teachers with the tools they need for this to happen, we offer this book.

Creating a Literacy-Rich Preschool Classroom Environment to Enhance Literacy Instruction

LESLEY MANDEL MORROW

The physical environment of a classroom, including the arrangement of space, choice of materials, and the aesthetic quality created in the room, are essential ingredients for successful learning in preschool. The literacy-rich classroom is filled with meaningful language experiences and materials that encourage exploration (Morrow, 2005). Preparing a classroom's physical environment is often overlooked in instructional planning. Teachers tend to concentrate on lesson planning and forget to give similar consideration to spatial arrangements in which teaching and learning occur. It is crucial that the curriculum and environment are coordinated so the most effective literacy instruction is created.

Neuman and Roskos (1997) described in vivid detail the necessary and critical connection between classroom literacy environments and human interactions related to literacy acquisition in the classroom. They asserted that classroom environments rich in written-language experiences provide opportunities for young children to become involved in literacy-related events. It is not only the environment, however, but also the human interactions in classrooms that determine in what way, how much, how long, or how often children engage in using literacy-related tools in classrooms for a variety of purposes (Neuman & Roskos, 1992). From a Vygotskian perspective, children use available literacy tools, such as furnishings, books, paper, and writing tools, in everyday problem-solving situations while interacting with peers, teachers, or other available cognitive mentors (Vygotsky, 1978). As children interact socially with a literacy-rich environment and with significant others, they begin to internalize the literacy processes and practices they observe.

Neuman and Roskos (1997) continued by explaining that "children's learning about literacy is integrally tied with practical action, resulting from their need to control, manipulate, and function in their environment" (p. 10). Consequently, the context of the language arts classroom is viewed as inseparable from the child's activity and his or her interactions with others in the classroom environment. Neuman and Roskos (1997) concluded that classroom learning contexts should support literacy learning by providing opportunities for two kinds of literacy learning: 1) situated learning in authentic contexts with real problems to solve using literacy tools, and 2) structured contexts for teaching children factual and conceptual knowledge about literacy.

Similar to many other behavioral settings, early childhood and elementary language arts classroom environments have been shown to elicit stable, predictable human behaviors (Neuman & Roskos, 1992, 1997). Stable and predictable human behaviors within language arts classroom settings are composed of three interlocking elements: 1) humans behaving, that is, teachers and students, 2) the presence and organization of inanimate physical objects, and 3) ongoing routines (Cambourne, 2001).

From this sociocultural perspective, young children derive their earliest understandings about oral and written language through engagement and interactions with others in print-rich and interaction-rich language arts classrooms. In order to better understand the environment–learning connection in language arts classrooms, I have chosen to organize our subsequent discussion of the effect of behavior settings in language arts classrooms using Cambourne's three interlocking elements, as previously stated.

It is important to recognize that the physical environment has a substantial effect on children's learning and development. Holmes and Cunningham (1995) found that very young preschool-age children, ages 3–4 years, evidenced a keen awareness of their classroom environments. These researchers found that children could, by looking at classroom photographs, identify appropriate activities for spaces in the classroom as well as draw their classrooms representing these activity spaces. In another study, Kershner and Pointon (2000) asked 70 children, ages 5 and 6, questions using the *Individualized Classroom Environmental Questionnaire*, so the children could express their views about their classroom environments as places for working and learning. The children expressed strong views about grouping schemes, seating arrangements, wall displays, general tidiness, noise levels, and choices to work alone or in collaboration with others, to name a few.

In the course of my career, I have observed or taught in preschool classrooms. In this chapter, I describe a composite of the best preschool classrooms that were observed over a 20-year period. As I speak of the teachers, keep in mind that the stories are based on a collective profile of several teachers who were identified as exemplary. By synthesizing findings from these expert teachers, I am able to present a description of an exemplary literacy-rich preschool classroom environment (Pressley, Rankin, & Yokoi, 1996).

THE PHYSICAL ENVIRONMENT IN
EXEMPLARY PRESCHOOL CLASSROOMS

Exemplary preschool classrooms are arranged so that they are student friendly. Materials are stored for easy access both visually and physically. The teachers find that a variety of materials enable them to meet the different abilities and interests of their students. One of the classrooms I visited was in the basement of an old inner-city school and was by no means picturesque; however, the ingenuity of the teacher made the environment quaint, warm, and inviting. The classroom had adequate space for 18 children, good lighting, and was kept clean.

In the classrooms I observed, the children's tables were arranged close together so that four to five students could sit together to encourage social interaction. The rooms had provisions for whole-group instruction with students sitting at their tables or on a rug in the literacy center. In the area for whole-group meetings, there was a chalkboard and/or white board, a pocket chart, and an easel with experience chart paper. Teachers had rocking chairs that they used when doing whole-class minilessons or when reading stories to the children.

All of the classrooms had morning meeting areas that included functional print such as a calendar, weather chart, helper chart, and rules. Signs communicated information, such as *Quiet please* and *Please put materials away after using them*. Environmental print, with their logos from the real world such as traffic signs, familiar clothing, and food chains, were important to display as well. All print had some type of picture or logo to help children understand what was written. The teachers used notice boards to communicate with the children through writing. In addition, there were word walls. The children's names were the most prominent words on the word walls as well as words dealing with current themes being discussed, such as plants or animals in the forest. Other materials in the room represented the units being studied, including children's literature, books made by the class, artwork, and so forth. An alphabet chart was on the wall at eye level for the children to see.

In addition to whole-class instruction, the teachers I observed arranged their rooms for small-group and one-on-one teaching. There was a table, in the shape of a half moon, situated in one side of the room. At this table, the teacher met with small groups and individual children, based on need, for explicit literacy instruction. The teacher had all of the materials she used for skill instruction available in this area. This included a pocket chart, an experience chart, individual writing slates, and magnetic boards with magnetic letters for dealing with knowledge about print and writing. There were also theme-related books and folders used to assess and record student accomplishments and needs. Corrugated cardboard bins, labeled with the children's names, were also used to store individual work. These materials were packaged in resealable baggies.

LEARNING CENTERS

To accommodate small-group independent work, teachers created learning centers. Each learning center was labeled according to content areas, such as dramatic play, music, art, social studies, science, and math. The centers were used to integrate literacy learning into content areas by featuring reading and writing activities. For example, in the block area there were pencils and paper to make signs for buildings created; in the dramatic play area there were paper and pencils for making shopping lists for the supermarket. The teachers believed that literacy activities had more meaning when integrated into content areas; therefore, it was common to find paper and pencils in the block and dramatic play area, and books in the art and music centers. The teachers used themes such as the family, the community, or the seasons for developing new vocabulary, new ideas, and purposes for reading and writing. Each of the centers had general materials that were typical of the content they represented and also had special materials added that were linked to the current thematic topics of study and literacy materials as well. The following centers were found in these teachers' classrooms:

Dramatic Play Center

This center included dolls, dress-up clothing, a telephone, stuffed animals, a mirror, food cartons, plates, silverware, newspapers, magazines, books, a telephone book, cookbooks, notepads, and a kitchen setting with a table and chair. The area had a broom, a dustpan, a refrigerator, storage shelves, and a theme that changed with the theme studied. For example, I often found restaurants from different multicultural backgrounds in the dramatic play area. One month it might be a Chinese restaurant with a menu, recipes, a cash register, play money, and fake checks. The next month it might change to be an Italian restaurant with a new appropriate menu. One day I recorded a conversation between two children, Darlene and Jamal, as they were pretending to be a mom and dad going to the supermarket.

Darlene: Now let's make a list for the supermarket. I have the pencil and paper. What do we need?

Jamal: We need more Sugar Pops cereal. We are all out of it.

Darlene: That's not so good for your teeth, and we will get fat from all of that sugar. We have to find another cereal.

Jamal: I know. We can get some cereal bars. They taste good, and my mommy said they are good for you. They have protein and other good stuff.

This conversation went on for quite a while with discussions about calories, fat content, protein, carbohydrates, sugar, and so forth. The children were studying good nutrition, and what they were learning was being assimilated into their play because the materials in the environment along with some modeling and scaffolding by teachers encouraged this productive activity.

Music Center

This area included a piano, a guitar, or other real instruments, as well as rhythm instruments such as bells, triangles, rhythm sticks, and cymbals. The teachers I observed made an effort to feature musical items from different countries, such as maracas from Mexico and a Caribbean steel drum. There were compact disc and tape players with music that linked to a particular theme, such as songs about the different seasons, when studying that topic. The teacher selected "Rain, Rain, Go Away" and "If All the Raindrops Were Lemon Drops and Gum Drops," when studying spring, because this was the rainy season in the area where these children lived. The children learned new vocabulary from the songs and selected some for their word wall. They drew rain pictures and had the teacher label them as they wished, or they wrote their own labels, and the rain pictures became a class book.

Art Center

This center included easels and multiple types of paper in different sizes. There were colored pencils; markers; watercolors; collage materials such as pipe cleaners, foil, paper, wool, and string; and fabrics for all types of creative artwork. Depending on the theme, different materials were added. In one classroom I observed, playdough was added when the class studied zoo animals, and the children chose an animal they wished to create. There were books that illustrated animals available for the children to look at to help with their designs as well as labels so the children could give their animal a name and write the type of animals they had made.

Social Studies Center

This center was particularly important for themes such as studying different cultures, families, friends, and communities. These themes focused students on getting along with others, recognizing and appreciating differences and likenesses in friends and family, developing respect for self and others, and developing a community of learners. Appropriate books accompanied these ideas such as one called *Your Fair Share*, which is an information book about how to share (Jordan, 2004). Some general social studies materials included maps, globes, flags from various countries, community figures, traffic signs, current events, and artifacts from other countries. When studying Mexico, José's father came in to read the *The Three Pigs* (Brenner, 1972) in Spanish and then the teacher read it in English.

The children talked about some words that sounded the same in both languages. And Juan's mom made tortillas for the class to eat for a snack.

Science Center

The science center was used to present a theme with accompanying materials to allow children to explore that theme. Other equipment included an aquarium, a terrarium, a thermometer, a compass, a prism, shells, rock collections, a stethoscope, a kaleidoscope, and a microscope. Also in this preschool environment, there was a theme studied with materials to explore about "The Five Senses" and "Good Nutrition and Good Health Habits."

Ms. Casey's preschool students, from one of the classes I observed, designed a veterinarian's office as part of a science theme on pets. The dramatic play area was designed as a waiting room with chairs; a table filled with magazines, books, and pamphlets about pet care; posters about pets; office hour notices; a *No smoking* sign; and a sign advising visitors to *Check in with the nurse when arriving.* A nurse's desk contained patient forms on clipboards, a telephone, an address and telephone book, appointment cards, a calendar, and a computer for recording appointments and patient records. Offices contained patient folders, prescription pads, white coats, masks, gloves, cotton swabs, a toy doctor's kit, and stuffed animals to serve as patients.

Ms. Casey guided the students in the use of the various materials in the veterinarian's office, for example, by reminding the children to read to pets in waiting areas, fill out forms with prescriptions or appointment times, or fill out forms with information about an animal's condition and treatment. In addition to giving directions, Ms. Casey also modeled behaviors by participating in play with the children when the materials were first introduced.

The following vignette relates the type of behavior that was witnessed in this setting—a setting that provides a literacy-rich environment with books and writing materials, models reading and writing by teachers that children can observe and emulate, provides the opportunity to practice literacy in real-life situations that have meaning and function, and allows children to collaborate and perform reading and writing with peers. While observing this classroom, I saw children using oral language they had not used before, such as pretending to read materials and write words they had never heard before.

Jessica was waiting to see the doctor. She told her stuffed animal dog, Sam, not to worry, that the doctor wouldn't hurt him. She asked Jenny, who was waiting with her stuffed animal cat, Muffin, what the kitten's problem was. The girls agonized over the ailments of their pets. After a while, they stopped talking and Jessica picked up a book from the table and pretended to read *Are You My Mother?* (Eastman, 1960) to her pet dog, Sam. Jessica showed Sam the pictures as she read.

Jovanna ran into the doctor's office shouting, "My dog got runned over by a car." The doctor bandaged the dog's leg, then the two children decided that the incident must be reported to the police. Before calling the police, they got out the telephone book and turned to a map to find the spot where the dog had been hit. Then they called the police on the toy phone to report the incident.

Preston, who was acting as the doctor, examined Christopher's stuffed teddy bear and wrote out a report in the patient's folder. He read his scribble writing aloud and said, "This teddy bear's blood pressure is 29 points. He should take 62 pills an hour until he is better and keep warm and go to bed." As he read, Preston showed Christopher what he had written so Christopher would understand what to do. Preston asked his nurse to type the notes into the computer. The children's play contributed to literacy instruction as they engaged in reading and writing for a real purpose. It helped them to both learn skills and practice skills.

Math Center

The children could find an abacus, various types of currency, scales, rulers, measuring cups, clocks with movable parts, a stopwatch, a calendar, a cash register, a calculator, a number line, a height chart, an hourglass, different types of manipulative numbers (e.g., felt, wood, magnetic), fraction puzzles, and geometric shapes in their math center. The units studied in this preschool program may have included activities emphasizing measuring in "Growing Like Me" and recording numbers of members in "My Family and My Community." For the "Growing Like Me" unit, the teacher placed a tape measure on the wall for measuring how tall the children were. Their heights were checked every 3 months. The children often discussed how tall they were as compared to others, and how much they had grown.

There are, of course, books and paper to add to this area to enhance the children's knowledge about a theme. The books can add to their knowledge of mathematical concepts to enrich the ideas discussed.

Block Center

In the block center I found many different sizes, shapes, and textures of blocks, figures of people, animals, toy cars, trucks, and items related to themes being studied, such as tractors for the "Building" unit. Books about the themes were useful for constructing theme-related structures. There were paper and pencils to make signs to label constructions the children created. When James and Josh were told that center time was over, they hadn't finished their building yet. Josh got a piece of paper and asked the teacher to write *Do not touch, under construction* so they could finish their building later, and no one would take it down.

Literacy Center

The literacy center should be one of the focal points in a preschool classroom. It should give the message that literacy is so important that a special spot is made to provide space for writing, reading, oral language, listening, comprehension, and word-study materials, as well as time to use this space.

In this area, there was a rocking chair and rug because many of the activities in this center took place on the floor and it was where the teacher had group meetings, lessons, and storytime. There were pillows and stuffed animals to add an element of softness.

Books were stored in open-faced shelving to display titles about themes being studied. These books were changed with the themes and to feature special selections. Books were also stored in plastic baskets that were labeled by genre, such as books about animals, seasons, poetry, families, and so forth. Pictures accompanied the labels.

Well-stocked preschool classroom libraries have between five and eight book selections per child at about 3–4 different levels of difficulty. The books included in the center were picture storybooks, poetry books, informational books, magazines, biographies, cookbooks, joke books, folk tales, fairy tales, and so forth. Children enjoy books with real information as well as narrative stories; therefore, there should be equal amounts of both fiction and nonfiction. Books can be acquired over time by purchasing them at flea markets, using points gained from book club sales, using donations from parents, and using allotted classroom budgets. The teachers rotated their books regularly to maintain the children's interest in them, and the children could check books out of the classroom to read at home. Literacy manipulatives such as puppets, taped stories with headsets, felt boards with story characters, and electronic stories were included in the literacy center to engage the children through different modalities dealing with books. The story manipulatives helped the children learn to retell stories, and they worked as excellent comprehension strategy and assessment tools. The literacy center also had a shelf of manipulative materials that offered practice in concepts about print. These materials, which included matching games, rhyming games, and magnetic, wood, and felt letters, helped the children learn the alphabet, phonemic awareness, and some sound–symbol relationships.

Author's Spot

A portion of the literacy center called the "Author's Spot" was set aside and included a table, chairs, and writing materials such as colored markers, crayons, pencils, chalk, a stapler, a hole punch, a chalkboard, and a white board. There were various types and sizes of paper such as newsprint, mural paper, lined paper, and colored paper. The children were provided with journals and were supervised to ensure appropriate use. There were index cards used for recording the children's

"Very Own Words" that were stored in index boxes. Folders, one for each child, were used to collect writing samples. Classrooms averaged two computers that were in good working order with excellent software for writing and reading activities. Some quality software for young children included Preschool Parade (Nordic Software), Elmo's Reading Preschool & Kindergarten (Creative Wonders), and I Spy Junior Puppet Playhouse (Scholastic).

Teachers prepared blank books for the children to write in that related to themes being studied. For example, there were different books shaped like animals when studying animals or books shaped like snowmen, flowers, and so forth to represent different seasons for that topic of study. There was a place for the children to display their written work, a mailbox, stationery, envelopes, and stamps for the children to write notes to each other and to pen pals.

Observations of the children in preschool literacy centers during center time revealed the following discussions and activities:

Natalie, Shakiera, and Dharmesh were snuggled in a large refrigerator box that had been painted to make it more attractive. Furnished with stuffed animals to make it look cozier, the box provided a "private spot" for reading.

Isabela and Veronica used the felt board and story characters for *The Three Bears* (Galdone, 1975), and took turns retelling the story while looking at the pages of the book and putting the figures up on the felt board at the appropriate times. When they came to repetitive phrases in the story, such as "Who's been sitting in my chair?" they said these phrases together.

James, Natalie, Brian, and Kim were listening on headsets to a compact disc of the story *Horton Hatches the Egg* (Seuss, 1940). Each child had a copy of the book and chanted along with the narrator every time they came to the phrase, "I meant what I said and I said what I meant, an elephant's faithful 100%."

Matthew and Gabriel were at the author's table looking at snake books, drawing pictures, and copying words from the book as they discussed the characteristics of the snakes such as, "This one is green and has a pointing tongue. This one has sharp teeth, and they look so big."

Tashiba had multiple copies of a story the teacher had read several times to the class. She handed out the copies to the other children and kept one for herself. She made a circle of chairs in which the group then sat as she pretended to be the teacher. She pretended to read to the others. She asked the children questions about the story when she was done reading.

When teachers were interviewed about what value they felt the literacy center had, they commented that children can choose activities they want to do, books they are interested in, to work alone or with others, or to use the manipulatives.

Teachers also said the children learned to work together, cooperate with each other, be independent, and make decisions. Children gained a better understanding about reading as they learned to practice holding the book right side up, turning the pages from left to right, learning the difference between the print and the pictures, beginning to read some words, and developing an appreciation for different book genres because they were accessible.

Student interviews revealed that they felt that reading was fun, that they could read and write with friends, that friends helped them during center reading time, that they liked the manipulatives, that there were many choices of books, and that they enjoyed having the teacher in the literacy center reading with them.

CLASSROOM REVIEW

Everything in the exemplary preschool classroom has a function, a purpose, and a place for it to be stored. The teacher models new materials, their purposes, how they are used, and where they belong. Early in the school year there are only a few items in the centers so the children can learn to use them properly. The teacher adds to them slowly as different themes and skills are studied.

The classrooms observed used philosophies and practices regarding classroom materials and the organization of space from current and historical perspectives about learning. In addition, teachers established clear rules, routines, and expectations for behavior. The children and their teachers decided upon the rules, practiced them early in the school year, and were consistent in adhering to them on a day-to-day basis (Weinstein & Mignano, 1996). The teacher communicated the rules and expectations in a supportive manner, and showed respect for students at all times.

Historically, theorists and philosophers emphasized the importance of the physical environment in early learning and literacy development. Pestalozzi (Rusk & Scotland, 1979) and Froebel (1974) described the preparation of manipulative materials that would foster literacy development in real-life environments. Montessori (1965) advocated a carefully prepared classroom environment to promote independent learning and recommended that each kind of material in the environment have a specific learning objective. She prepared her classroom with materials that were accessible for children.

Research has shown ways in which the physical design of the classroom affects the children's behavior (Loughlin & Martin, 1987; Morrow, 1990; Rivlin & Weinstein, 1984). Rooms partitioned into smaller spaces, such as centers, have facilitated verbal interaction amongst peers and have enhanced cooperative and associative learning. When rooms are carefully designed for specific types of instruction, such as a table for meeting with a small group of children, there is more productivity and greater use of language than in rooms where no attention is given to setting (Moore, 1986).

Literacy-rich environments stimulate activities that enhance literacy skill development (Morrow, 2005; Neuman & Roskos, 1992). Story props, such as puppets or a felt board with story characters, improve story production and comprehension, including recall of details and the ability to interpret text

(Morrow, 2002). Researchers have found that children like cozy corners with pillows and rugs to retreat to when things get hectic, and opportunities for privacy are important for children who are distractible and for those who have difficulty relating to peers (Weinstein & Mignano, 1996). Young children work best in rooms with variation; that is, rooms that have warm and cool colors, some open areas and cozy spots, as well as hard and soft surfaces (Olds, 1987).

The nature and quality of the literacy environment plays a central role in literacy learning and the acquisition of literacy behaviors and attitudes. Chall, Jacobs, and Baldwin (1990) observed that "No one will debate the idea that a rich literacy environment is helpful for achievement in literacy" (p. 162).

Barker (1978) is well known for his pioneering work in the field of ecological psychology. One major tenet of this field states that environment is linked to human behavior in lawful and predictable ways—meaning that what happens in an environment can be explained using theoretically derived principles grounded in the collection and analysis of empirical data. For several decades, Barker (1978) studied the connection between the environment and human behavior by focusing attention on a unit of study known as the behavior setting. A behavior setting is essentially defined as a location in which children come together to engage in predominantly predictable behaviors. As a consequence of this definition, Barker (1978) examined the significance of the environment in a variety of behavioral settings such as offices, shops, classrooms, stadiums, museums, grocery stores, and so forth and found that each of these environments elicited stable, predictable sets of human behaviors.

Barker's (1978) study of human behaviors yielded three generalizations that have influenced the study of human behavior and ecology: 1) human behavior changes from setting to setting to meet the requirements of each setting, 2) the behavior of people in each setting is more similar than different, and 3) each person's behavior tends to be consistent over time in the same or similar setting.

Research over the last 2 decades has provided plentiful and pertinent information about the design and implementation of print-rich classroom environments (Neuman & Roskos, 1992, 1997; Taylor, Blum, & Logsdon, 1986). Despite the widespread acceptance and awareness among teachers and children and the abundance of research information available, the findings of current research indicate that implementation of print-rich classroom environments is lagging behind what is known and available (Neuman & Roskos, 2002). Teacher educators, teachers, and school administrators need to understand at a deeper intellectual level how to assess the design of classroom literacy environments if they are to enlarge their understanding of what a print-rich classroom environment includes.

Until 1981, when Weinstein reported a synthesis of research on the physical environment of schools and classrooms, little attention had been paid to how or if elements within the physical environment influenced children's opportunities to engage in learning. Recent research has provided significant insights into how the language arts classroom environment influences children's opportunities to actively engage in literacy learning.

CONCLUSION

The classroom environment described throughout this chapter is designed to contain the characteristics described in research that have proven to be important influences on effective classroom instruction and management. With the support of appropriate materials and a well-designed classroom environment, instruction will flourish in preschool classrooms. Make the environment as important as the curriculum, and the two support each other during instruction.

REFERENCES

Barker, R.G. (1978). Stream of individual behavior. In R. Barker & Associates (Eds.), *Habitats, environments, and human behavior* (pp. 3–16). San Francisco: Jossey-Bass.

Cambourne, B. (2001). What do I do with the rest of the class?: The nature of teaching–learning activities. *Language Arts, 79*(2), 124–135.

Chall, J.S., Jacobs, V.A., & Baldwin, L.W. (1990). *The reading crisis: Why poor children fall behind.* Cambridge, MA: Harvard University Press.

Froebel, F. (1974). *The education of man.* Clifton, NJ: August A. Kelly.

Holmes, R., & Cunningham, B. (1995). Young children's knowledge of their classrooms: Names, activities, and purposes of learning centers. *Education and Treatment of Children, 18*(4), 433–443.

Kershner, R., & Pointon, P. (2000). Children's views of the primary classroom as an environment for working and learning. *Research in Education, 64,* 64–78.

Loughlin, C.E., & Martin, M.D. (1987). *Supporting literacy: Developing effective learning environments.* New York: Teachers College Press.

Montessori, M. (1965). *Spontaneous activity in education.* New York: Schocken Books.

Moore, G. (1986). Effects of the spatial definition of behavior settings on children's behavior: A quasi-experimental field study. *Journal of Environmental Psychology, 6,* 205–231.

Morrow, L.M. (1990). Preparing the classroom environment to promote literacy during play. *Early Childhood Research Quarterly, 5,* 537–554.

Morrow, L.M. (2002). *The literacy center: Contexts for reading and writing* (2nd ed.). York, ME: Stenhouse Publishers.

Morrow, L.M. (2005). *Literacy development in the early years: Helping children read and write* (5th ed.). Boston: Allyn and Bacon.

Neuman, S.B., & Roskos, K. (1992). Literacy objects as cultural tools: Effects on children's literacy behaviors in play. *Reading Research Quarterly, 27*(3), 203–225.

Neuman, S.B., & Roskos, K. (1997). Literacy knowledge in practice: Contexts of participation for young writers and readers. *Reading Research Quarterly, 32*(1), 10–33.

Olds, A.R. (1987). Designing settings for infants and toddlers. In C.S. Weinstein & T.G. David (Eds.), *Spaces for children: The built environment and child development* (pp. 117–138). New York: Plenum Press.

Pressley, M., Rankin, J., & Yokoi, L. (1996). A survey of the instructional practices of outstanding primary-level literacy teachers. *Elementary School Journal, 96,* 363–384.

Rivlin, L., & Weinstein, C.S. (1984). Educational issues, school settings, and environmental psychology. *Journal of Environmental Psychology, 4,* 347–364.

Rusk, R., & Scotland, J. (1979). *Doctrines of the great educators.* New York: St. Martin's Press.

Taylor, N.E., Blum, I.H., & Logsdon, D.M. (1986). The development of written language awareness: Environmental aspects and program characteristics. *Reading Research Quarterly, 21*(2), 132–149.

Vygotsky, L.S. (1978). *Mind in society.* Cambridge, MA: Harvard University Press.

Weinstein, C.S. (1981). Classroom design as an external condition for learning. *Educational Technology, 21,* 12–19.

Weinstein, C.S., & Mignano, A.J., Jr. (1996). *Elementary classroom management.* New York: McGraw-Hill, Inc.

CHILDREN'S LITERATURE REFERENCES

Brenner, B. (1972). *The three pigs.* New York: Random House.

Eastman, P.D. (1960). *Are you my mother?* New York: Random House.

Galdone, P. (1975). *The three bears.* Boston: Houghton Mifflin,

Jordon, D.M. (2004). *Your fair share.* Chicago: Heinman Library.

Seuss, Dr. (1940). *Horton hatches the egg.* New York: Random House.

2

Exploring Intentional Instructional Uses of Environmental Print in Preschool and Primary Grades

BILLE J. ENZ, JENNIFER PRIOR, MAUREEN R. GERARD, AND MYAE HAN

"I can read this," says nearly 4-year-old Ember, as she holds up a colorful paper plate. "It says 'Pokémon.' I got it at a birthday party."

Ms. Begay responds, "Yes, Ember, it says 'Pokémon.'"

Ms. Begay is always amazed at her preschoolers' abilities to recognize the print in their environment. To capitalize on their prior knowledge and to help them learn to hear initial sounds and recognize letters of the alphabet, Ms. Begay has created an environmental print (EP) alphabet chart.

Several other children have brought coupons, empty boxes, and cartons. After the children gather for morning greetings, they immediately go to the cut-n-paste table. They cut their EP logos to get ready for alpha time. During the 20-minute daily alpha time, the children and their teacher focus their attention on letters and sounds. Ms. Begay has placed alphabet-chart paper around the room.

When Ms. Begay completes taking attendance and going over the calendar, she turns her attention to the alphabet charts. She asks the children who has alphabet items to share. About 10 children raise their hands. There are about 15 logos today. Ms. Begay asks Ember to share her plate, and she asks Ember what it says. As Ember shows the class her Pokémon plate, Ms. Begay says "Pppp-pokemon." As she pronounces the word, she hyper-articulates the initial sound. She asks the children to say it with her.

EP is everywhere, including signs for fast food chains, names of popular children's characters, and street signs. Many people assume children learn to read when they

15

begin school, but most educators know that literacy development begins long before children reach school age. In fact, observational studies have demonstrated that children as young as 2 years old are aware of and can read print in their environment (Anderson & Markle, 1985; McGee & Richgels, 1996). And, as most parents can tell you, when a child recognizes a favorite toy or special treat, the object of their affections usually goes directly into the parent's shopping cart. Clearly, marketing experts know that young children read as they deliberately organize store shelves and checkout displays and place child-appealing products at cart height and at the small child's eye level.

In this chapter, we will explore many creative and inexpensive ways preschool and primary teachers may build upon children's natural knowledge of and often intense interest in EP to begin to build the basics of reading, including the following:

1. Phonemic awareness—the ability to hear the discrete sounds of language, called phonemes, and the ability to manipulate these sounds.

2. Letter recognition—the consistent ability to recognize and correctly label alphabet symbols.

3. Phonetic skills—the ability to correctly connect the letter symbols and sounds.

The vignettes throughout this chapter offer a glimpse into classrooms in which teachers are intentionally using EP as both the material and method to help children learn basic reading skills. The teachers' deliberate use of EP helps to connect children's prior knowledge to new reading concepts. In addition, all of these examples reflect Yopp's (1992) and National Reading Panel (2000) recommendations for teaching young children early reading skills:

• Keep a sense of playfulness and fun; avoid drill and rote memorization.

• Use group settings that encourage interaction among children.

• Encourage children's curiosity about language and print.

• Foster children's experimentation with language and print.

As we review Ms. Begay's intentional use of the EP alphabet chart, we can see that she is both teaching and reinforcing the children's knowledge of print and the initial sounds the words make. This strategy also utilizes the students' current interest in and prior knowledge of the print in their home and neighborhood community.

To extend the word recognition and letter-symbol activity, Ms. Begay next builds a phonemic awareness component into her lesson by playing a game. Phonemic awareness activities help children to isolate and hear the individual sounds, called phonemes, of their language. The game Ms. Begay uses is similar to

"Hot-Cold," in which the students use the volume of their voices to indicate that a student is close to or far from a hidden object. Ms. Begay takes the Pokémon plate off the *P* alphabet chart and sends one little boy, Martin, out to the hallway. When Martin is in the hallway, Ms. Begay hides the plate behind the large wooden clock in the front of the room; the other children watch carefully so they will know how to guide Martin. As she brings Martin into the classroom, Ms. Begay tells him that he is hunting for the Pokémon plate. She asks the children what sound clue they will give Martin to help find the plate. His classmates begin to quietly chant "ppp" as their reply. As Martin moves toward the front of the room, the other preschoolers begin to increase the volume "ppp." Taking his cues from the volume of the chants, Martin turns left. Suddenly, the volume drops to a whisper, so he knows he has gone astray. Turning around, he spots the target. As he quickly moves to pick up the Pokémon plate, the children yell "ppp." Ms. Begay asks the children why they are shouting "ppp." She calls on Jackson who responds, "Pokémon starts with the letter *P* and *P* says 'ppp'!"

In this example, Ms. Begay uses the EP item Pokémon to help the children isolate the sound of the letter *P*. She also adds another element in her instruction by reinforcing the alphabet letter *P*. Notice how the game approach keeps this activity exciting and fun for the children.

Early reading is an interwoven web of experiences, one part of which is children's early exposure to print in their world. Supplementing and enriching the curriculum with activities using familiar print provides an "auditory and visual anchor to remember letter, symbol, and sound" (Christie, Enz, Gerard, Han, & Prior, 2003a). By including EP activities in the classroom, primary teachers can provide opportunities for children to connect the print knowledge constructed at home to literacy lessons they are learning in school. Such experiences with familiar print assist children with word recognition, build confidence, and encourage word ownership.

The adult is the key element to effectiveness in using EP to teach beginning reading skills. Some research suggests that the recognition of EP does not transfer to conventional reading (Masonheimer, Drum, & Ehri, 1984; Ylisto, 1967), whereas other research (Christie et al., 2003a; Christie, Enz, Gerard, Han, & Prior, 2003b; Gerard & Prior, 2004; Prior & Gerard, 2004) suggests that when an adult draws attention to the letters and sounds in EP words, the children are more likely to transfer this knowledge to decontextualized print—text without color and graphics.

Once again, EP, in large part, includes brand names. It's print that is familiar to kids that they see on product packaging, signs, and in ads. For example, the word *pizza* is not EP. Even if a picture of pizza is beside it, it is not the way it appears in the environment. The point of using EP is using it as it appears in a child's surroundings. The next vignette demonstrates how Mrs. Garcia uses the children's knowledge of local fast-food restaurants to focus on alphabet letters and sounds.

Mrs. Garcia and her preschoolers are singing the Pizza Hut Song:

"Pizza Hut, Pizza Hut,
Kentucky Fried Chicken and Pizza Hut
McDonald's, McDonald's,
Kentucky Fried Chicken and Pizza Hut"

The children read the laminated songbook as Mrs. Garcia turns the pages. The children love singing and recognizing the colorful logos. Today, after the children sing the song several times, Mrs. Garcia directs their attention to the alphabet letters. She asks the children if they can find the letter *P*. Then she asks Araceli to circle every letter *P* she can find. Araceli uses a transparency pen to circle all of the *P*s. She commends Araceli on her efforts. Then Mrs. Garcia asks the children what sound the letter *P* makes. She smiles as 20 little sets of lips form pucker-pouts to make the /pppp/ sound.

Mrs. Garcia continues for a few minutes more asking the children to find the following letters: *H, K, F, C, M,* and *D*. As the children circle the letters and isolate the letter sounds, she reinforces their efforts.

Next, Mrs. Garcia shows the children the miniature Pizza Hut songbook that uses only the black and white logos. She asks the children if they would like to make their own little songbook. The children listen as Mrs. Garcia gives them the directions. As she circulates in the class, she notices that the children easily recognize the black and white logos. This immediate recognition means the children are already focusing on the shapes of the letters to reveal the meaning of the word.

As children read EP, they are influenced not only by graphic cues—color, specialized font, specific image—but also by social, contextual, grammatical, and language cues (Harste, Burke, & Woodward, 1982). Children respond to graphics, color, and context in which print is embedded. Children search for graphic cues in the squiggles and lines of print. As Prior and Gerard (2004) explained:

> The capital letter *K* in the Kmart sign and in the Circle K store sign are similar, red uppercase letters, yet children know the two separate logos because of the surrounding graphic and context clues that come before and after the big red letter *K*. Young children search for semantic cues by looking for what makes sense in the image and color context in order to read the Kmart logo. The blue background of the Kmart logo is quite different from the red circle background of the Circle K logo. Syntactic clues are internalized as grammar rules and word order emerges from logo reading. Burger King cannot correctly be read as King Burger. All of the linguistic cueing systems—graphophonics, semantics, and syntax—work together powerfully in the young child's reading of environmental print. (p. 6)

Initially, young children tend to the entire context of EP rather than just the print (Masonheimer et al., 1984). As they grow older, children become able to recognize increasingly decontextualized forms of print. Research has revealed a general developmental progression of EP recognition: an actual three-dimensional object, a two-dimensional color picture of complete logo, a stylized "word art" text from logo, and text in generic font (Cloer, Aldridge, & Dean, 1981; Kuby, Aldridge, & Snyder, 1994). Our research (Christie et al., 2003a; Christie et al., 2003b; Gerard & Prior, 2004; Prior & Gerard, 2004) suggests that teachers can help this progression from full-color, logo-graphic to more decontextualized print by explicitly drawing children's attention to the letters within the word. The following vignette demonstrates how Ms. Jordan, a kindergarten teacher, guides the lesson.

Sitting around a horseshoe table, Ms. Jordan and five kindergarteners begin to match logos to decontextualized print. At the table, Ms. Jordan holds up a Trix logo. She asks the children to look at their five cards to see which of their print cards match. Each child had a set of logos in the final decontextualized form. Ms. Jordon facilitates this activity by asking the following questions:

1. "How do you know that one says 'Trix'?"

2. "Do any of the others begin with the same letter?"

3. "Is the second letter r?"

4. "Are there any other letters in that word that you know?"

5. "What letter sounds do you hear?"

The activity lasts between 5 and 6 minutes, and then Ms. Jordon invites another group to play with her. She can simplify the difficulty level of the game by using logos that start with different initial letters. However, Ms. Jordon has found that the children really begin to pay close attention to the subsequent letters in the word if she has all the logos begin with the same initial letter. This activity is so successful that she has developed an entire alphabet deck of logos and print (see Figure 2.1 for an example).

Once a teacher has begun to use EP as an instructional approach, he or she can easily build on previous lessons. Introducing consonant blends and digraphs becomes a simple task of reviewing the EP alphabet chart. The following vignette provides an example.

Mr. Terry expands upon the use of the EP alphabet chart when he introduces digraphs and blends to his first-grade students. He begins by reviewing the alphabet charts in the classroom with his students. He focuses their attention on the letter C card and asks the students to see if all the items on the card make

Logo	Print
STOP	STOP
EXIT	EXIT
DANGER KEEP AWAY	DANGER
SPEED LIMIT 50	SPEED LIMIT
(restroom symbol)	RESTROOM

Figure 2.1. Logo–print match.

the same /K/ sound. As the children read the logos, they quickly realize that Chucky Cheese, Cheerios, Cheer, and Cheetos make a very unique sound: /ch/. Mr. Terry then asks them to see if these words have some letters in common. The children immediately see the *CH* digraph. Mr. Terry tells the students that the /ch/ is so special that it needs its own alphabet card. The following day, the students ceremoniously remove the *CH* words from the *C* card and pin them to the *CH* card. Two children, Charlie and Charlene, also ask if they can put their name tags on the *CH* card. Another child has brought in an empty cherry cough drop package. The students place the *CH* card directly below the *C* card. Figure 2.2 provides an example of a *C* alphabet chart without the logos. The teacher will be responsible for placing images of the logos on the chart for the students to identify.

Coke	Cheetos
Campbell's soup	Cheerios
Crunch (Nestle)	Chex

Figure 2.2. The *C* alphabet chart.

As the vignette with Mr. Terry illustrates, children, with the explicit and specific instruction from a knowledgeable teacher, are quickly able to build their skill in phonemic awareness and letter recognition. The easy accessibility of the EP enables the children to connect old information and expand to new concepts, in this case the *CH* digraph. Using these highly motivating and visually appealing materials creates a meaningful foundation for learning about the alphabetic principle. In addition, we have found that when teachers use EP as an instructional tool to teach letters and sounds, the print in the child's community serves as a constant reinforcement of the reading skills they are learning in school.

Another way preschool and primary teachers can use EP is to build sight-word vocabulary and comprehension. The following vignette demonstrates how Mrs. Rhodes, a first-grade teacher, created a rebus story chart with a series of blanks. The intent of her lesson was to build fluency, sight-word recognition, and comprehension.

Mrs. Rhodes noticed her first-grade students were beginning to use context clues to help them read. To encourage this process, she created several simple stories (see Figure 2.3 for an example). She asked the children to listen to the story very carefully. Next, she asked them to read the story again with her. She asked them about the type of words that should go into each spot. The children considered the EP logos that Mrs. Rhodes provided. They tried different versions of the story until they finally agreed upon the best version.

Once upon a time, _____ went to _____.

When she got to _____, she decided she wanted to eat _____.

After she ate _____, she saw her friend _____.

They started to play with _____. They had fun!

Insert a toy or cartoon character.	Insert a toy or cartoon character.
Insert a restaurant logo.	Insert a food logo.
Insert a restaurant logo.	Insert a toy logo.

Figure 2.3.   Build an environmental print story.

Mrs. Rhodes found that the children in her class became extremely confident in their ability to read these ministories. She deliberately tried to include a number of high-frequency words such as *once, went, when, the,* and *she*. She found that this simple and inexpensive activity has also become a popular center activity, and the children have begun to mix and match new logos in the blanks to create a number of funny stories. The children often share their new stories with the whole class, and Mrs. Rhodes has noticed how much more fluent the children have become at reading these stories.

Because EP is most effective when it is familiar to children, it is important for primary teachers to determine which words the students in the classroom know and understand. Teachers can begin by looking at print in the immediate neighborhood. What are the names of common grocery stores, convenience markets, and fast-food restaurants? Ask the children what they watch on television. To determine which game and product logos your students recognize, bring some to school and ask them which ones they know. Invite parents to send in empty containers of snacks, cereals, and other familiar items. Teachers can also go to the local grocery store and toy stores to see what draws the children's attention. It is vital that the print used for these activities be familiar to the children in order to assist them in making meaningful connections.

In this chapter, we suggest that EP can be used to meet early core literacy knowledge and skills identified by National Reading Panel (NRP) (2000), such as phonological awareness, alphabet knowledge, and letter–sound relationships (International Reading Association/NAEYC, 1998; Snow, Burns, & Griffin, 1998). With increasing attention on early reading and writing proficiency, using the print that children have in their own cultural and social experience is necessary to meet developmentally appropriate practice. The NRP has generated new expectations for early literacy and reading curriculum approaches from the Evidence-Based Reading Research (EBRR). It has also influenced language and literacy standards in many states. One of the valuable contributions of the EBRR movement is that it has identified the core knowledge and skills young children must develop to become successful readers. These skills are the foundation of early literacy and are known as predictors of academic success in elementary grades. We believe, and our studies and others indicate, that with the intentional and explicit assistance of an adult, EP activities can help children to develop these early literacy foundations. EP can be a bridge to create a meaningful foundation for learning about early literacy skills and knowledge with constant reinforcement because children encounter them in daily life with multiple exposures. Signs, logos, and other print are most certainly a part of our everyday print-rich environments and a growing body of research about the instructional use of EP in classroom can now be found. Like researchers Kuby et al. (1994), we have also made the following conclusions:

- Children benefit from instruction with EP by teachers who have been coached to incorporate it into the curriculum.

- Kindergarten children benefit most from activities with print that is familiar. It is important to transition children from experiences with logos to the decontextualized manuscript form of the word(s) in the logo.

- Children who bring EP items to school find creative ways to incorporate the print into their activities.

Using EP is a powerful way to connect children's home literacy to the new literacy activities they are learning at school. Teachers need not be afraid of what children already know from being members in our already commercial culture.

Instead, teachers can actually embrace children's interests and prior knowledge to speed letter and sound recognition. All it takes is inviting the children to share what they already know and having some creativity on the teacher's part to have a solid, culturally sensitive and inexpensive learning opportunity.

REFERENCES

Anderson, G., & Markle, A. (1985). Cheerios, McDonald's, and Snickers: Bringing environmental print into the classroom. *Reading Education in Texas*, 30–35.

Christie, J.F., Enz, B.J., Gerard, M., Han, M., & Prior, J. (2003a). *Examining the instructional uses of environmental print.* Paper presented at the International Reading Association annual convention, Orlando, CA.

Christie, J.F., Enz, B.J., Gerard, M., Han, M., & Prior, J. (2003b). *Examining environmental print as a learning tool for diverse classrooms.* Paper presented at the National Reading Conference, Scottsdale, AZ.

Cloer, T., Aldridge, J., & Dean, R. (1981). Examining different levels of print awareness. *Journal of Language Experience, 4*(1), 25–33.

Gerard, M., & Prior, J. (2004). *Environmental print in the diverse classroom.* Paper presented at the California Association for the Education of Young Children annual conference, San Diego, CA.

Harste, J., Burke, C., & Woodward, V. (1982). Children's language and world: Initial encounters with print. In J.A. Langer & M.T. Smith-Burke (Eds.), *Reader meets author/bridging the gap: A psycholinguistic and sociolinguistic perspective* (pp. 105–131). Newark, DE: International Reading Association.

International Reading Association/NAEYC. (1998). Learning to read and write: Developmentally appropriate practices for young children. *Young Children, 53*(4), 30–46.

Kuby, P., Aldridge, J., & Snyder, S. (1994). Developmental progression of environmental print recognition in kindergarten children. *Reading Psychology: International Quarterly, 15*, 1–9.

Masonheimer, P., Drum, P., & Ehri, L. (1984). Does environmental print identification lead children into word reading? *Journal of Reading Behavior, 1*, 257–271.

McGee, L., & Richgels, D. (1996). *Literacy's beginnings: Supporting young readers and writers* (2nd ed.). Boston: Allyn & Bacon.

National Reading Panel. (2000). *Teaching children to read: An evidence-based assessment of the scientific research literature on reading and its implications for reading instruction* (NIH Publication No. 00–4769). Washington, DC: U.S. Government Printing Office.

Prior, J., & Gerard, M.R. (2004). *Environmental print in the classroom: Meaningful connections for learning to read.* Newark, DE: International Reading Association.

Snow, C., Burns, M., & Griffin, P. (1998). *Preventing reading difficulties in young children.* Washington, DC: National Academies Press.

Ylisto, I. (1967). *An empirical investigation of early reading responses of young children.* Unpublished doctoral dissertation, University of Michigan, Ann Arbor.

Yopp, H.K. (1992). Developing phonemic awareness in young children. *The Reading Teacher, 45*(9), 696–703.

Narrative Bridges to Comprehension

ALISON H. PARIS AND SCOTT PARIS

Katie is 3 years old and lives with her grandmother Nana and several other family members. She attends daycare in the mornings, but Nana wants to make sure that Katie is learning new things, so she has "Book Time" every afternoon. Katie can choose a book from 4–6 books that Nana puts on the sofa, and they sit side-by-side to read. Sometimes they have "Book Time" after supper and sometimes they make hot chocolate, but it is always a special, quiet time for just the two of them. Katie is often fidgety, so Nana lets her hold the book and turn the pages. Sometimes Katie wants to look at the pictures, and sometimes she talks about them or makes up a story. Nana joins in by asking questions, asking for clarifications, or asking for more information as Katie talks about the text or pictures. Nana knows that Katie pays more attention when Katie turns the pages and tells stories, so she gives the 3-year-old opportunities to explore books in her own way. However, Nana also knows Katie is learning about the topics, words, and how to read each time they share a book.

Sometimes Katie and Nana look at just the pictures in the books as they take turns making up stories. Sometimes they read picture books with no words and talk about the artwork and the pictures. Alphabet books are fun because they look at each animal and object and see how the name begins with the specific letter. Katie learns many new words by naming pictures in these kinds of books. Some picture books tell stories so Nana and Katie make up new episodes for the characters. The book is a springboard for make-believe games that stimulate Katie's imagination and make them both laugh.

Nana teaches Katie in subtle ways. For example, when they read a Dr. Seuss book together, Nana points out the rhyming words and sometimes asks Katie to make up a rhyming word. When they read *Are You My Mother?* (Eastman, 1960), Nana asks Katie to point to the word *mother* so she recognizes it on each page.

Sometimes Nana asks Katie to point to a specific letter, or she shows the differences between upper- and lowercase letters in the book. She teaches Katie to read from left to right and from the top to the bottom of the page. She even points out punctuation marks so Katie can see the differences between letters, punctuation marks, and other symbols. Nana also talks about the pictures so Katie can see how the pictures are related to the text. New vocabulary words, such as *dainty, tiny,* and *purple,* are described in the pictures. Nana also pauses to talk about story events and asks Katie to make predictions, inferences about character motives, and connections between characters' reactions and her own experiences. Of course Nana makes "Book Time" fun for Katie, so she talks about the text with her and does not overwhelm Katie with questions or teaching. Indeed, a hidden benefit of "Book Time" is that Katie looks forward to reading new books and talking with Nana as they explore them together. Motivation to read books begins long before children can decode the words.

COMPREHENSION IS A FOUNDATION FOR LITERACY

Reading comprehension is crucial for lifelong learning, yet most parents and educators do not tend to it until children are in elementary school. Indeed, the good or poor comprehension of many children remains undetected until they receive reading test scores in grades 3, 4, or 5. By then, the developmental trajectory of reading comprehension is firmly established and difficult to change (Cunningham & Stanovich, 1997). It is the basis of a gap in reading, learning, motivation, and achievement that widens the gulf between successful and unsuccessful students throughout their school years. The main point of this chapter is to show that a child's ability to construct and comprehend meaning from text is built on a foundation of language and literacy experiences in early childhood. Parents who immerse their children in environments with rich language, worlds of print, and opportunities to use literacy in pragmatic and instrumental ways provide bridges from home to school, from oral language to print, and from experiences to knowledge. Children without those bridges begin school behind their peers, struggle to read and comprehend, and risk not only lack of success in school but also isolation from the knowledge-based economy of the future (Farver, Xu, Eppe, & Lonigan, 2006; Van Steensel, 2006; Whitehurst & Lonigan, 1998). It is a dire prediction for children who eagerly begin kindergarten and a huge challenge to preschool educators who strive to overcome the odds.

Fortunately, research on young children's emerging literacy has identified many ways that teachers and parents can help children build comprehension skills both before and as they learn to read. The general maxim is to read early and often to young children, at least 30 minutes every day to 2- and 3-year-olds, but it is important to read with and not to children. Shared book reading provides opportunities for learning when it is dialogic, according to Whitehurst, Arnold, Epstein, and Angell (1994), because conversations about the text promote comprehension and memory of information. Although reading aloud to children, such as reading bedtime stories, can be filled with positive emotions for both the parent and child, there are additional benefits when children are actively involved. For example, one benefit is the opportunity to make personal connections to the text by relating the text to the child's experiences. A second benefit is the active construction of meaning as parents ask questions about what happened, why events occurred, or what will happen next. Adults can elicit children's answers to questions, periodic paraphrases, and recalls to ensure that the children are paying attention and understanding. Third, participation in book reading allows children to monitor their understanding and to add new elements to the text. This promotes the construction and integration of meaning as the story unfolds and as the conversation enriches their children's understanding (Kintsch, 1998). Fourth, parents can expose children to a wide world of facts and fantasies through texts that provide vehicles for teaching new vocabulary and knowledge (Whitehurst et al., 1988). Pictures of unfamiliar animals and objects can be labeled and described for learning. Each of these features reinforces the bridges between texts and experiences, and they facilitate comprehension and learning among preschoolers.

The kinds of text that children experience are also important. Children need a variety of genres and topics to provide interest and novelty, but the preponderance of narrative texts for young children is not accidental. Stories in early childhood provide a powerful bridge for comprehension among preschoolers, whether from familiar to new words, from speech to print, or from predictable to unpredictable events. In particular, goal-based narratives that are common in fairy tales, adventures, and personal experiences allow young children to learn about the structure and elements of stories that they hear and create. Goal-based narratives have predictable structures with settings, characters, plots, and outcomes that are evident in media and daily life. For example, a young child might tell a narrative story about a shopping trip in which he wanted to buy a toy. The story might have a specific setting, characters, and outcome based on his personal desire and whether it was satisfied or not. Narrative comprehension occurs with familiar pictures, video, and text, whereas narrative production, or story generation, usually occurs in recounts of personal experiences and sociodramatic play. Understanding and telling stories enriches children's vocabulary, knowledge, and inferential skills, all good foundations for literacy learning. The following vignette illustrates how these processes can be facilitated at preschool.

Ms. Tee's Preschool Play

Ms. Tee decided that her 4-year-old students could put on a play for their parents. There were eight children in the 4-year-old group who were divided from the 3-year-olds for part of the morning. The children were comfortable with the staff and familiar with the routines at the Jack and Jill Learning Center, and Ms. Tee wanted to coordinate her language arts activities with other center-based activities at the preschool. She began on Monday by showing her 4-year-olds a big book of *The Three Little Pigs* (Seibert, 2002). She asked if anyone knew the story about the three little pigs. Marcus said he knew it was about a wolf that tried to eat the little pigs. Jeremy said the wolf was mean, and other children chimed in about the story. After a brief discussion, Ms. Tee began reading the big book and moved her finger under the words as she read. She pointed to some words, such as *pig*, so the children could recognize repeated words, and she pointed to some pictures, such as the house made of straw, as she explained what straw is. She paused in the story when the wolf had driven the first two pigs out of their homes, and she asked the children some questions: "How did they feel?" "What do you think the wolf will do?" "What can the three little pigs do to protect themselves?"

She listened patiently as the children talked about the story and what they thought would happen. When she finished reading the story, she told the children that they should go to the drawing center and draw a picture of the part of the story they liked best. On Tuesday, Ms. Tee asked the children to help her retell the story, and she asked them to first tell the things that happened in the beginning, then the middle, and then the end of the story. She connected the retellings to art by asking the children to finish their drawings so she could hang them on the wall. On Wednesday, Ms. Tee asked the children if they would like to put on a play about the three little pigs for their parents. They decided to call their play "The Six Little Pigs" and have two wolves so that everyone would get a part in the play.

On Thursday and Friday, Ms. Tee used the pictures in the big book as prompts for the children to rehearse the story. They also made and decorated three houses from cardboard boxes and drew their own face masks of pigs and wolves. They spent the next 3 weeks rehearsing the story, finishing the props for the play, and putting on a dress rehearsal for the rest of the preschool students and staff. Ms. Tee played the role of narrator to cue the children to move and speak. During the rehearsals, Ms. Tee allowed each child to speak and play a role, and she made sure that the children's dialogues were consistent with the story and characters. After just 4 weeks, the children performed "The Six Little Pigs" for their parents; it was in front of a standing-room-only crowd.

The play was a success, and the children learned a great deal about stories. They learned about characters, settings, motives, sequence, and outcomes. They learned to listen and understand stories, to use pictures as prompts, to infer characters' emotions, and to play the roles of characters and use appropriate dialogue. They also had fun drawing, decorating, and performing.

The key to success was Ms. Tee, who knew how to connect listening to stories with instruction about vocabulary and comprehension and with art and play. Effective preschool teachers embed comprehension instruction in language arts activities that are meaningful and fun for children. Shared book reading, games, listening centers, artwork, and storytelling can occur daily, and they provide opportunities to teach children how to understand and create narratives, a powerful genre that can be shown in pictures, video, or text. Ms. Tee illustrated how comprehension can be promoted among 3- and 4-year-olds. Next we describe why it is important for teachers and parents to engage young children with stories.

COMPREHENDING AND NARRATIVE THINKING

Comprehension includes all aspects of understanding, and it is impossible to consider learning and knowledge without comprehension. The inclusiveness of the construct makes it difficult to define, but we can identify cognitive processes involved in comprehending. Whether viewing or listening to someone reading print, comprehension includes interpretation of the literal meaning of the physical or symbolic event and may include additional analyses of evaluation, inference, and synthesis. It is the additional analyses that "go beyond the given information" (Bruner, 1974) that permit deeper understanding. This is consistent with the everyday use of the term to signify that comprehension results in literal interpretations, but also includes constructive aspects of meaning-making processes—personalized interpretations—that connect the event to a broader range of experiences and knowledge. Comprehension while viewing, listening, and speaking includes the same kinds of meaning-making processes as comprehension while reading text, so it provides a bridge to reading and writing. Thus, preschoolers' attempts to interpret and make sense of events, objects, media, games, pictures, and books are forerunners to the comprehension processes they will use to make sense of texts they read.

Bruner (1986) suggests that there are two fundamental modes of thinking: paradigmatic and narrative. Paradigmatic thinking is factual, scientific, and logical; it argues about the truth or reality of claims based on propositions and rules. Narrative thinking, in contrast, is based on personal actions and intentions; it places characters in time and contexts that are familiar and meaningful. Bruner (1986) suggests that narrative thinking includes a landscape of action—the outer reality of agents and intentions—and a landscape of consciousness—the inner reality of thoughts and feelings— and it is the integration of action and consciousness that brings narratives to life. Narratives are important because they embody personal and cultural stories, and through stories, people are able to understand themselves and others (Ferrari & Mahalingam, 1998). Adults use stories to tell children about history, nature, culture, and their own experiences, so meaning-making processes through narratives is important for learning and language as well as a bridge to literacy.

COGNITIVE DEMANDS OF UNDERSTANDING

Successful interactions with narrative text require cognitive skills to understand both the action elements of stories—landscape of action—and the internal elements of stories—landscape of consciousness. Understanding the landscape of action depends on story schema knowledge as well as knowledge of the causal organization of the action sequences. For example, in *Little Red Riding Hood* (Grimm, Grimm, & Hyman, 1982), understanding the landscape of action requires knowledge that the story of the little girl, the wolf, and the grandmother (characters), takes place in the woods (setting), in which the little girl wants to bring cake to her grandmother but encounters a wolf and tells him where her grandmother lives (goal and initiating event). This causes the wolf to arrive at the grandmother's house first, after which he threatens to eat the grandmother and the little girl (problem), but finally a huntsman saves them both (outcome resolution). Because the landscape of consciousness is comprised of information about thoughts, emotions, goals, and intentions, comprehension and production of this type of information requires the ability to understand and think about characters' perceptions of reality (e.g., that the wolf had his own not-so-benign motive for suggesting that Little Red Riding Hood take her time to look at all the flowers). Necessary cognitive demands to understand these mental events include the need for advanced social cognitive skills, such as an awareness of mental states in self as well as in others, an understanding that the mental states of story characters are representations of representations, and the ability to represent distinctive mental beliefs and feelings of numerous characters (Astington, 1990; Yussen & Ozcan, 1996).

Successful interactions with narratives also require constructive meaning-making processes. First, information must be integrated. The inner world of the landscape of consciousness (e.g., the wolf's intentions to arrive at the grandmother's first) must be integrated with the outer reality of the landscape of action (e.g., Little Red Riding Hood's excitement over the beautiful flowers that she was gathering) in order to create an emergent whole (Bruner, 1986; Snow & Ninio, 1986). Bruner (1986) stated that individuals, when interacting with stories, seek "precisely how plight, character, and consciousness are integrated" (p. 21). Secondly, constructing meaning from narrative texts is also about personalized interpretations, about "a reader making a strange text his own" (Bruner, 1986, p. 35). In order for individuals to understand that it is their responsibility to interpret text, they must acquire a metadiscourse concept called the text/interpretation (or say/mean) distinction (Olson, 1990). For example, children must understand that the wolf pretends to be nice, but he is really mean. As children assimilate the text to their own experiences and language, they need to understand ambiguity, figurative language, and character's intentions to know the meaning of the words and events. Third, narrative text requires inference-making in order to construct meaning, especially given that narratives often leave it up to the individual to infer the internal responses and intentions that underlie external actions. Often, readers must infer causal connections in order to explain the actions of characters and the relations between event episodes (Newcomer, Barenbaum, & Nodine, 1988). For example, in *Little Red Riding Hood*, inferences must be made about why the little girl did not recognize grandmother's extra large ears, hands, and mouth. Inferences must also be made about lessons to be learned such as to keep one's promises and to avoid talking to strangers.

ORIGINS OF NARRATIVE IN EARLY CHILDHOOD

Comprehending and creating narratives reflects several developmental accomplishments that can be facilitated in many contexts of young children's lives (e.g., shared book experiences with adults, personal storytelling, children's play), even prior to formal schooling or formal literacy instruction. We describe some of these accomplishments that serve as bridges to narrative thinking for young children's reading and writing.

Story Structure

Research indicates that children discern the narrative structure or grammar of stories, called story schemas. Story schemas include knowledge about main elements of stories (e.g., characters, settings, problems, outcomes) as well as concepts about the temporal and causal sequencing of events in stories (Mandler & Johnson, 1977, Stein & Trabasso, 1982). In addition to the types of events and rules about their order, story schemas include information about the relations between events, the difference between minor and major events, knowledge about characters' prototypical behavior, and story language patterns (Jenson, 1985). Children as young as 3 and 4 years of age can construct primitive stories with some of the structural elements, although they have a broad concept of story and often produce stories with incoherent action sequences that exclude characters' goals. Story structure knowledge increases significantly between the ages of 3 and 5 (Botvin & Sutton-Smith, 1977; Trabasso & Nickels, 1992). By age 5, children can produce stories with settings, main characters, and consequences, and they begin to include the intentions and goals that impel characters' action. Story grammar thus provides evidence that young children develop an understanding of the action landscape of narrative, but it does not account for how children develop an understanding of the internal landscape of stories.

Theory of Mind

Theory of mind research is concerned with how children develop an understanding of the mind, mental processes, beliefs, states, and experiences of self and others. In general, research has found that a crucial change occurs between the ages of 2 and 4 (Astington, 1993; Gopnik & Slaughter, 1991; Perner, 1991; Shatz, Wellman, & Silber, 1983). By the time children reach age 4, they develop an awareness of mental states in themselves and others. Children's developing theory of mind provides insight into the development of narrative thinking skills (Astington, 1990). In addition to events and actions in the external world (the landscape of action), narratives transmit knowledge about participants' perceptions of reality—beliefs, hopes, intentions, fears, goals, and values (the landscape of consciousness). Consequently, narrative thinking, particularly understanding the landscape of consciousness, depends at least in part on developing a theory of mind. Adequate narrative functioning relies on children's abilities to think about and understand characters' thoughts and feelings as well as their actions, requiring competence at representing distinctive beliefs and feelings of the various characters (Yussen & Ozcan, 1996).

Because the transition point in terms of theory of mind development occurs at age 4, it has been suggested that prior to age 4, children cannot synchronize both landscapes of narrative. Research showing that 2- and 3-year-olds do not relate actions to internal states (Trabasso & Nickels, 1992) may be attributed to their limited understanding of representational processes (Yussen & Ozcan, 1996). According to Astington (1990), "Four-year-old children [but not 2-year-old children] can comprehend the landscape of consciousness as the story character's mental representation of the actual situation that is depicted in the story on the landscape of action" (p. 158). Although shifts in the relationship between storytelling/understanding and theory of mind have not been examined directly, it seems logical to apply theory of mind explanations to children's development of narrative thinking and particularly to how they make sense of the landscape of consciousness. That children develop a theory of mind by age 4 suggests that they can begin to develop complex narrative skills prior to formal schooling.

Language

Language is the most salient and universal evidence of the development of narrative thinking. At a very young age, children learn to understand and use narrative language to respond to others' demands, requests, needs, and emotional reactions. In addition, children learn to use narrative language in order to communicate accounts of daily events and experiences. Four types of discourse show evidence of preschoolers' narrative thinking: recounts, accounts, event casts, and stories (Heath, 1986). Recounts are generally provided in response to a question, for example, when the parent asks the child to tell about a shopping trip. Accounts represent new interpretations of information, in which children may put their imagination into the narrative in order to provide a tale of an event that the adult likely has not experienced. Event casts are running narratives on events that are currently in the attention of both teller and listener, and stories involve an animate being that moves through a series of events with goal-directed actions. Children's narrative language develops when they are afforded regular and quality opportunities for sustained conversation using any of these four types of discourse.

Young children become increasingly skilled at understanding and producing narrative language. For example, they develop more decontextualized language,

language that is like the language of stories (Dickinson & Snow, 1987; Dickinson & Tabors, 1991; Sulzby, 1985); they learn what should be included in the memory of an event, become better at recalling events, and learn how to organize and relate the events in order to recreate the experience that is being recalled (Peterson & McCabe, 1994); and they improve their abilities to construct new stories (Heath, 1986). Young children increasingly engage in personal storytelling, creating accounts of daily happenings such as observing holidays, taking family excursions, having birthday parties, going shopping, and taking trips to the zoo, and experiences of physical harm such as nosebleeds or illness. By the age of 2 or 3, children have become "avid narrators of their own experience" (Wiley, Rose, Burger, & Miller, 1998, p. 834). Children also increase their ability to tell fantasy narratives. Initially, their oral fantasy stories are fragmented (ages 3–4), but they progress to simple narrative structures (ages 4–5), and later become complex with coherent action sequences (age 7) (Botvin & Sutton-Smith, 1977).

Children's Play

Narrative thinking is also evident in children's thematic and symbolic play in preschool (Heath, 1982). Symbolic play is an opportunity to develop narrative competence because it involves fictionalized or imaginary characters that encounter and resolve problems, has events that unfold temporally and causally, and requires information about setting, characters' actions, motives, and problem resolution (Pellegrini, 1985). Take, for example, child role play in symbolic play. As the children enact roles, they coordinate characters' knowledge, actions, motives, and goals in order to create a particular storyline, hence practicing narrative production and comprehension skills. Repetitious enactment of similar roles and events helps children become increasingly aware of appropriate action sequences and role actions (Pellegrini, 1985).

Children also use decontextualized behavior when engaging in symbolic play (Fein, 1981). Decontextualized behavior generally has children framing an everyday activity in a make-believe context, abstracting the activity from everyday routines and constructing narrative-like scripts using temporal and causal event structures. For instance, a child may pretend to eat dinner with his family when it is not dinnertime. In addition, as children's play becomes more decontextualized, they increasingly use more abstract object substitutions. Initially, children's play props depend on the immediate presence of an object. By 4 years of age, however, the majority of children utilize play themes that are less related to the physically present play objects that they use to represent the themes (Pellegrini, 1985). The object transformations that children learn to make during symbolic play are a characteristic feature of narrative thought. In order to tell and understand stories, children must be able to construct representations of objects that are not tangible.

Friendship dyads are another play context that promote the socialization of narrative thought. Pellegrini and colleagues (Pellegrini, 1985; Pellegrini, Galda,

Bartini, & Charak, 1998) found that friends, as opposed to nonfriend dyads, elicited more conflict/resolution cycles, reflected more on emotions, and generated more literate language. The trust and mutuality that characterizes friendship supports greater reciprocity and willingness to resolve disagreements, hence fostering qualities of narrative thinking, such as role taking and imagining future consequences.

Pictorial Narratives

Narratives can also be created through pictures. Bornens (1990) stated that for a picture sequence to be called a narrative, the action must be "represented in the pictures according to the rules of a figurative narrative" (p. 193). Although the processes required to understand picture narratives have not been as specified as those needed to understand text, "pictorial narratives" require narrative thinking skills similar to text-based narratives, including integration, inferential skills, and knowledge about main story elements. Young children's experiences with pictorial narratives help to promote increasingly sophisticated narrative skills. Cartoons and children's storybooks are among the most popular forms of picture-based narratives. The cognitive demands of picture narratives are particularly important given that children's earliest experiences with reading are often with picture storybooks. Picture books elicit awareness of narrative structure, inspiring thinking about narrative elements such as settings, characters, events, actions, motives, consequences, plots, and themes (Jenson, 1985; Snow & Ninio, 1986). They also require the ability to recognize the same character throughout different pictorial representations as well as to understand sequential and temporal organization (Bornens, 1990). Furthermore, understanding picture narratives requires that pictorial events be related to each other and integrated in order to understand the emergent whole (Bornens, 1990; Snow & Ninio, 1986).

Paris and Paris (2003) created and administered the narrative comprehension task to children in grades K–2 and found that kindergarten and first-grade children were able to make inferences and predictions as well as integrate pictorial information across pages to create coherent understandings. This study, and an earlier study by van Kraayenoord and Paris (1996), showed that comprehension of wordless picture books at 5–6 years of age predicts reading comprehension skills 1–2 years later. Findings also revealed a developmental progression across grades in narrative meaning-making skills. Van den Broek et al. (2005) assessed 4-year-olds' recall of television narratives and found that greater recall was associated with recall of elements with more causal connections. This suggests that even preschool-age children form mental representations of narratives that contain the main elements, thus preserving the causal structure of the story. It is clear that children in preschool and kindergarten begin to develop narrative thinking skills with picture books and media that they will use later while reading and writing.

Parental Book Reading Practices

Parental joint book reading practices prior to formal schooling are perhaps the most direct bridge between narrative as a general cognitive skill that is socialized early in life and narrative as a reading skill used for making sense of written stories. Because the primary basis for children's beginning reading materials are narrative books, when young children interact with storybooks they are necessarily confronted with the cognitive demands of the narrative. Consequently, parent–child book reading practices become meaning-making opportunities that foster the development of narrative thinking skills that are necessary for reading. During shared book reading experiences, children acquire a sense of story as they listen to and learn about the structural elements of stories. For example, they learn that all stories have beginnings, characters, settings, problems, sequenced events, resolutions, and endings (Jenson, 1985; Morrow, 1990).

Additionally, joint book reading enhances children's ability to understand and produce decontextualized, story-like language as well as their ability to integrate information into a coherent story (Snow & Ninio, 1986; Sulzby, 1985). In trying to make sense of stories in picture books, children learn that events on single pages are central but not sufficient elements in a narrative, and they begin to relate components of pictures to each other in order to create a complete story. Repeated storybook reading experiences with parents encourage children between the ages of 2 and 6 to interact with the pictures as if they were a single unit by using speech that builds a story across the pages, rather than viewing individual pages of books as if they were discrete units. In reading with their children, parents often interact with their children by asking questions and having discussions that help them negotiate meaning around books. They help children narrate, interpret, predict, associate, elaborate, and relate story events to their own life (Morrow, 1990). They ask how, what, when, and why questions that help to elicit a full understanding of event sequences, motives, and consequences. Hence, repeated shared reading episodes facilitate the development of narrative thinking.

The nature of the interaction style during joint book reading experiences also contributes to differences in the socialization of narrative thinking. For example, Dickinson and Smith (1994) found that interaction patterns that allow for reflection on story and language had the greatest effect on children's understanding of story. Similarly, Snow and Ninio (1986) showed that the types of questions that probe for predictions and explanations elicit a better understanding of event sequences, motives, and consequences. Differences in children's provisions about spatial–temporal context information (e.g., when, where) in their personal experience narratives were related to the frequency of parental prompting for contextual information (Peterson & McCabe, 1994). Flood (1977) showed that differences in parental style, such as the preparatory questions that they ask before reading, affect how well children assess, evaluate, and integrate information.

Thus, although narrative can be socialized in the first few years of life through many everyday activities, many children begin formal schooling without the skills that are requisite to interact meaningfully with written narrative forms that are dominant in beginning reading materials.

CONCLUSION

Comprehension of text builds on skills that children acquire long before they begin formal schooling and long before they can decode print. Understanding the physical, social, and mental worlds around them are major accomplishments of early childhood that provide a foundation for literacy and reading comprehension. We have discussed narrative thinking as an example of the cognitive skills that help children comprehend themselves and others in landscapes of action and consciousness. Narrative thinking provides a bridge from listening to reading, from experience to text, and from play to literacy. Parents and teachers who help children understand and tell stories can help build children's language, vocabulary, inferential thinking, and knowledge, which are all important aspects of comprehension that will pave the way to literacy.

REFERENCES

Astington, J.W. (1990). Narrative and the child's theory of mind. In B.K. Britton & A.D. Pellegrini (Eds.), *Narrative thought and narrative language* (pp.151–171). Hillsdale, NJ: Lawrence Erlbaum Associates.

Astington, J.W. (1993). *The child's discovery of the mind.* Cambridge, MA: Harvard University Press.

Bornens, M. (1990). Problems brought about by "reading" a sequence of pictures. *Journal of Experimental Psychology, 49,* 189–226.

Botvin, G.J., & Sutton-Smith, B. (1977). The development of structural complexity in children's fantasy narratives. *Developmental Psychology, 13*(4), 377–388.

Bruner, J. (1974). *Beyond the information given.* London: George Allen & Unwin Ltd.

Bruner, J. (1986). *Actual minds, possible worlds.* Cambridge, MA: Harvard University Press.

Cunningham, A., & Stanovich, K. (1997). Early reading acquisition and its relation to reading experience and ability 10 years later. *Developmental Psychology, 33*(6), 934–945.

Dickinson, D.K., & Smith, M.W. (1994). Long-term effects of preschool teachers' book readings on low-income children's vocabulary and story comprehension. *Reading Research Quarterly, 29*(2), 105–121.

Dickinson, D.K., & Snow, C.E. (1987). Interrelationships among prereading and oral language skills in kindergartners from two social classes. *Early Childhood Research Quarterly, 2,* 1–26.

Dickinson, D.K., & Tabors, P. (1991). Early literacy: Linkages between home, school, and literacy achievement at age 5. *Journal of Research in Childhood Education, 6,* 30–46.

Eastman, P.D. (1960). *Are you my mother?* New York: Random House.

Farver, J.A., Xu, Y., Eppe, S., & Lonigan, C. (2006). Home environments and young Latino children's school readiness. *Early Childhood Research Quarterly, 21*(2), 196–212.

Fein, G. (1981). Pretend play in childhood: An integrative review. *Child Development, 52,* 1095–1118.

Ferrari, M., & Mahalingam, R. (1998). Personal cognitive development and its implications for teaching and learning. *Educational Psychologist, 33*(1), 35–44.

Flood, J.E. (1977). Parental styles in reading episodes with young children. *The Reading Teacher, 30,* 864–867.

Gopnik, A., & Slaughter, V. (1991). Young children's understanding of changes in their mental states. *Child Development, 62,* 98–110.

Grimm, J., Grimm, W., & Hyman, T. (1982). *Little red riding hood.* New York: Holiday House.

Heath, S.B. (1982). What no bedtime story means: Narrative skills at home and school. *Language in Society, 11,* 49–76.

Heath, S.B. (1986). Separating "things of the imagination" from life: Learning to read and write. In W.H. Teale & E. Sulzby (Eds.), *Emergent literacy: Writing and reading* (pp. 156–171). Norwood, NJ: Ablex Publishing Corporation.

Jenson, M.A. (1985). Story awareness: A critical skill for early reading. *Young Children, 41*(1), 362–365.

Kintsch, W. (1998). *Comprehension: A paradigm for cognition.* New York: Cambridge University Press.

Mandler, J.M., & Johnson, N.S. (1977). Remembrance of things passed: Story structure and recall. *Cognitive Psychology, 9,* 11–151.

Morrow, L.M. (1990). Assessing children's understanding of story through their construction and reconstruction of narrative. In L.M. Morrow & J.K. Smith (Eds.), *Assessment for instruction in early literacy* (pp. 110–134). Englewood Cliffs, NJ: Prentice Hall.

Newcomer, P.L., Barenbaum, E.M., & Nodine, B.F. (1988). Comparison of the story production of LD, normal-achieving, and low-achieving children under two modes of production. *Learning Disability Quarterly, 11,* 82–96.

Olson, D.R. (1990). Thinking about narrative. In B.K. Britton & A.D. Pellegrini (Eds.), *Narrative thought and narrative language* (pp. 99–111). Hillsdale, NJ: Lawrence Erlbaum Associates.

Paris, A.H., & Paris, S.G. (2003). Assessing narrative comprehension in young children. *Reading Research Quarterly, 38*(1), 36–76.

Pellegrini, A.D. (1985). The relations between symbolic play and literate behavior: A review and critique of the empirical literature. *Review of Educational Research, 55*(1), 107–121.

Pellegrini, A.D., Galda, L., Bartini, M., & Charak, D. (1998). Oral language and literacy learning in context: The role of social relationships. *Merrill-Palmer Quarterly, 44*(1), 38–54.

Perner, J. (1991). *Understanding the representational mind.* Cambridge, MA: MIT Press/Bradford Books.

Peterson, C., & McCabe, A. (1994). A social interactionist account of developing decontextualized narrative skill. *Developmental Psychology, 30*(6), 937–948.

Seibert, P. (2002). *The three little pigs.* Columbus, OH: Mcgraw-Hill.

Shatz, M., Wellman, H.M., & Silber, S. (1983). The acquisition of mental verbs: A systematic investigation of the first reference to mental state. *Cognition, 14,* 301–321.

Snow, C.E., & Ninio, A. (1986). The contracts of literacy: What children learn from learning to read books. In W.H. Teale & E. Sulzby (Eds.), *Emergent literacy: Writing and reading* (pp. 116–138). Norwood, NJ: Ablex Publishing Corporation.

Stein, N.L., & Trabasso, T. (1982). What's in a story? In R. Glaser (Ed.), *Advances in instructional psychology* (pp. 213–267). Hillsdale, NJ: Lawrence Erlbaum Associates.

Sulzby, E. (1985). Children's emergent reading of favorite storybooks: A developmental study. *Reading Research Quarterly, 20*(4), 458–481.

Trabasso, T., & Nickels, M. (1992). The development of goal plans of action in the narration of a picture story. *Discourse Processes, 15,* 249–275.

van den Broek, P., Kendeou, P., Kremer, K., Lynch, J., Butler, J., White, M.J., et al. (2005). Assessment of comprehension abilities in young children. In S.G. Paris & S.A. Stahl (Eds.), *Children's reading comprehension and assessment* (pp. 107–130). Mahwah, NJ: Lawrence Erlbaum Associates.

van Kraayenoord, C., & Paris, S. (1996). Story construction from a picture book: An assessment activity for young learners. *Early Childhood Research Quarterly, 11,* 41–61.

Van Steensel, R. (2006). Relations between socio-cultural factors, the home literacy environment, and children's literacy development in the first years of primary education. *Journal of Research in Reading, 29*(4), 367–382.

Whitehurst, G.J., Arnold, D.S., Epstein, J.N., & Angell, A.L. (1994). A picture book reading intervention in day care and home for children from low-income families. *Developmental Psychology, 30*(5), 679–689.

Whitehurst, G.J., Falco, F.L., Lonigan, C.J., Fischel, J.E., DeBaryshe, B.D., Valdez-Menchaca, M.C., et al. (1988). Accelerating language development through picture book reading. *Developmental Psychology, 24*(4), 552–559.

Whitehurst, G.J., & Lonigan, C.J. (1998). Child development and emergent literacy. *Child Development, 69*(3), 848–872.

Wiley, A.R., Rose, A.J., Burger, L.K., & Miller, P.J. (1998). Constructing autonomous selves through narrative practices: A comparative study of working-class and middle-class families. *Child Development, 69*(3), 833–847.

Yussen, S., & Ozcan, N.M. (1996). The development of knowledge about narratives. *Issues in Education, 2*(1), 1–68.

Practice to Theory

Invented Spelling

DONALD J. RICHGELS

Invented spelling is beginning writers' ability to write words by attending to their sound units (phonemes) and associating letters with them in a systematic, though nonconventional, way. For example, beginning writers may spell *chain* as HAN because of the *C-H* sound in the name of the letter *H* ("ai<u>tch</u>"), the "ay" or long *A* sound that is the name of the letter *A*, and the *N* sound in the name of the letter *N* ("<u>en</u>"). Adults can support even very young children's exploration of sound–letter correspondences in written language by engaging them in talk about letters and sounds and words in the context of the children's experience of text, when reading a book, a storefront sign, or a food or toy logo, or when composing a label, a note, a letter, or a story.

SOUNDING OUT AND SOUNDING IN

The most important aspects of teaching spelling are directing a child's attention to print in comfortable, meaningful contexts; determining what letter names the child knows; and then talking in a matter-of-fact way about a fundamental fact of written language—that letters do not appear randomly and that the way a word sounds in speech has something to do with the way it looks in print. (Note that I just wrote "something to do with" and not "everything to do with." Sound–letter correspondences are not so regular as to eliminate the roles of other cuing systems.) Of course, this fact is fundamental to both reading and writing. Just as "sounding out" can play a role in word identification, so is "sounding in" a part of writing a word. Children put the sounds into their writing of words by choosing letters that have those sounds. And so adults' supportive talk will be similar in both reading and writing contexts, that is, whether a child is trying to make sense of someone else's writing or to make writing that someone else can make sense of. In fact, good invented spelling instruction is good word reading instruction, and vice versa.

39

SUPPORTIVE TEACHER TALK

Good supportive teacher talk sounds remarkably similar across such varied tasks as children's reading a conventionally spelled word, their following the teacher's modeling of word writing, or their writing of their own words. Consider the following three examples in an exemplary kindergarten:

Froggy and Freezing

On March 1, one of the kindergartners had brought a frog to school, and the teacher, Mrs. Poremba, guided her students' reading of the word *Frog*.

"Her frog's name is Froggy," said Mrs. Poremba. "And she spells *Froggy* like this." On a hand-held erasable board, Mrs. Poremba first wrote only the root word: *Frog*.

"*F*," said a kindergartner.

"*Frog*!" read another.

"Frrrr," said still another.

"There's that *F-R* again," said Mrs. Poremba, "the way we see it in a good friend's name."

Several kindergartners said a classmate's name: "Freddy."

"Freddy," repeated Mrs. Poremba. "And we also see the *F-R* in one of the days—"

"Friday," said several kindergartners together.

"—of the week. Well, *Froggy* starts with that same sound. Do you hear it? Frrrr."

"Frrr," repeated a kindergartner.

"Freddy and Froggy," said another.

Mrs. Poremba then added *gy* to make *Froggy*.

The kindergartners had personal sign-in sheets on clipboards for opening-of-the-day activities. One of them wrote *Frog* on her sheet and four others wrote *Froggy*. Later that morning, another kindergartner revealed what she had learned specifically about *F-R* and, in general, about sounding in. Kaitlynn volunteered to record her classmates' suggestions for weather words for the day. The words were *freezing cold*.

"She's writing it in kindergarten writing," observed a kindergartner.

And indeed, Kaitlynn invented a spelling on her own, by sounding in, that is, by attending to sounds and using her knowledge of sound–letter relations to represent those sounds in—put them into—her spelling.

As she wrote, Kaitlynn said, "Fuh. Rrrreee. Freezzzz-ing, cooooold. Freeeee." Kaitlynn had said "coooooold," but her classmate Deborah correctly noted that Kaitlynn was not yet writing *cold*.

"Freeee," continued Kaitlynn. "Freezing."

Her written product was *Firezzn,* with a backwards *n.* Then she wrote *colD* quickly and without sounding in. She knew that word from memory; it had been a frequent weather word over the winter.

Thus Kaitlynn demonstrated flexibility in her writing. She attended to sounds in a word (*freezing*) whose conventional spelling she did not know, and she spelled from memory a word (*cold*) whose conventional spelling was familiar from frequent exposures. When children know more than one way to spell, they are likely to write more often and to produce longer pieces than when they know only one way.

Turn Off the Lights

Ten days later, Mrs. Poremba talked about how to spell *turn* as she modeled making a sign: *Turn off the lights.*

"I want them to know to turn off the lights," she said. "That will save energy. I'm going to write: *Turn, off, the lights.* And I'm going to use my kindergarten spelling for this. I'm going to start with the word *t-turn.*"

"*T,*" said Zack.

"I hear *T* in the beginning too, Zack," confirmed Mrs. Poremba.

"Rrrrr," said a kindergartner.

"Turrrrrrn," said Mrs. Poremba.

"*R,*" said a kindergartner.

"I hear an *R.* Turnnnnnn."

"*N!*" *N!*" said two kindergartners.

"There's an *N* on the end," confirmed Mrs. Poremba.

After more talk and collaboration with her students, Mrs. Poremba's sign was *Trn off the lits.*

With her talk, Mrs. Poremba modeled the importance of message; her writing served her stated purpose ("I want them to know to turn off the lights"). She also capitalized on the opportunity to include explicit teacher talk about the process of sounding in. Her students' unprompted joining in that process demonstrates the effectiveness of her teacher talk.

A New Chick

In May, during a unit about chickens, several chicks hatched in an incubator in Mrs. Poremba's classroom. Zack wanted to write in his journal *A new chick came out of the egg.* With Mrs. Poremba's help, Zack's entry was *a no ck/km ot V/the egg.* This is how she helped with *came:*

Mrs. Poremba read what Zack had written so far: "A new, a new chick—" and asked, "What do you want—"

"Came," said Zack.

"*Came.* Okay. *Came.* What do you think *came* starts with?"

"*K.*" Zack wrote *k.*

"A *K.* Good for you. *Cammmmme. Cammmmme. Cammmmme.* Do you know that *mmmmm* sound? How do you write that?"

"*M.*" Zack wrote *m.*

"*M.* That's right, like in *Meagan.* Okay."

COMMONALITIES

In all three of these episodes, writing and reading occurred together. In all three episodes, writing and reading happened in meaningful contexts: a kindergartner's bringing a frog to school, the class's conservation unit, and the in-class hatching of chicks. The episodes included frequent naming of letters and elongated pronunciation of specific speech sounds, or phonemes. In all three episodes, Mrs. Poremba oriented the kindergartners to word parts, by first dealing with the root *Frog* in *Froggy* and by using such terms as *starts with, in the beginning,* and *on the end.* In two of the episodes, she used familiar words (*Friday, Freddy,* and *Meagan*) as reinforcers.

EXPERIMENTAL READING WITH INVENTED SPELLING

Mrs. Poremba's support for her kindergartners' word reading and invented spelling is consistent with the Experimental Reading with Invented Spelling (ERIS) method that I have described in previous work (Richgels, 1987). I emphasize using appropriate teacher talk, including making explicit the purposes for learning letter names and sounds, and providing plentiful opportunities for reading and writing:

> When teaching a list of *D* words, you may be used to saying things like, "Who can tell me a word that begins with *D?*" or "Who knows what sound *D* makes?" [However,] [s]tudents also need to hear, "You may want to write the word *digger*—what are some letters you would need?". . . .You can plan for and look for opportunities . . . [for] writing talk. When you display a poster or children's pictures . . . ask, "What letter should I write for this picture of a dinosaur?" or you might talk with a child about the picture s/he is drawing of an airplane and say, "You can *write* about your picture—what letter(s) do you need?" (p. 525)

ERIS also includes teacher talk about letters and sounds during the writing of language experience texts and during the reading of children's own compositions:

> "Look! I used the letter *D* when I wrote *duck*—it's a good thing I learned that *D* stands for the sound /d/, like at the beginning of *duck*. . . . Look at Eddie's picture of a digger. He wrote DGR–/d/–/g/–/r/–digger" by it." (p. 527)

Finally, modeling in ERIS can take the form of the teacher's use of invented spellings in his or her own compositions, as Mrs. Poremba did in *Trn off the lits* and as I suggested in *We cn us hs dggr at the sand table,* where the teacher models sounding in for the first five words (*We can use his digger*) and uses words that are familiar from classroom labels for the last two words *(sand table)* (Richgels, 1987, p. 528).

On March 1, Mrs. Poremba modeled story writing about dinosaurs. To write *A brontosaurus came to school,* she found *brontosaurus* in a book and copied it. She modeled an invented spelling of *came:*

"I've got the *brontosaurus* part," she said.

Then Mrs. Poremba and Kaitlynn said together, "*Came to school—*"

"*Kuh-kuh-kuh-K!*" said Kaitlynn.

"*K,* okay," said Mrs. Poremba. "*Cammmmmme.*"

"*M!*" said several kindergartners.

Mrs. Poremba read her *km:* "*Came.*" (See this complete episode and others from Mrs. Poremba's kindergarten in Richgels, 2003.)

Later that day, below a drawing of museum goers viewing a Tyrannosaurs Rex skeleton, kindergartner Tara wrote *PePL/ Kam to a museym/ and soa bonNS. The/ KiNG DiNaSor boNS.*

PRINCIPLES FOR SUPPORTING INVENTED SPELLING

These examples and the research reviewed later in this chapter suggest five principles of support for young children's invented spelling:

1. *Reading and writing should happen together.* Effective teachers support children's learning about sound–letter correspondences by showing connections between "sounding out" in word reading and "sounding in" in word writing. Teachers and students read together what they have written and write as extensions of what they read, with teachers often using the same kinds of supportive talk for both activities.

2. *Invented spelling, as with all literacy activities, should occur in meaningful contexts, in which written language serves real purposes in the everyday home and classroom lives of children.* Contextualized experiences usually involve whole texts. The immediate focus may be on words and letters and sounds within those words, but those words are found, for example, in the text of a big book the class is reading, in a poem they are rereading with the goal of eventually doing a choral reading, or in a list of facts generated from a discussion of a social studies or science topic of study.

3. *Instruction about invented spelling should include much teacher modeling and matter-of-fact teacher talk about (i.e., noticing and commenting on) the processes of sounding out and sounding in.* Likewise, effective teachers create opportunities for children to talk about what they know about words and letters and sounds. This occurs when the teacher and students collaborate, as

Mrs. Poremba and her kindergartners did in all the examples above. It is the deliberate aim of an activity called "What Can You Show Us?" (Richgels, Poremba, & McGee, 1996), in which teachers invite students to say anything they want about a displayed text *before* the teacher comments about it or reads it. Often preschoolers or kindergartners will identify a letter or a familiar word or say something about the form of a text, such as a repeated word in a poem.

4. *Teachers, as well as children, can spell inventively.* Effective teachers include examples of invented spelling in their own writing for children and accompany the examples with talk about sounds and what motivates their choices of letters for those sounds. Many teachers feel more comfortable about spelling unconventionally when they also tell children that this is how preschoolers or kindergartners sometimes write and that eventually the children will learn grown-up ways (Mrs. Poremba and her students called invented spelling "kindergarten writing" or "kindergarten spelling").

5. *Reading and writing should occur frequently throughout the preschool or kindergarten day.* Effective teachers do a lot of reading and a lot of writing and create opportunities for their students to do the same. Big books, posters, signs, labels, charts, poems on chart paper, computer screens—all provide numerous opportunities to read to and with children, occasionally calling their attention to specific characteristics of print (how it looks and how its letters are not random, but have something to do with what is spoken when the print is read). Writing centers, yes, but also play centers, opening-of-the-day routines, games, and classroom management devices (for example, sign-up sheets to claim a turn at a particular center or sign-out sheets to record having participated in the center activity, and even to comment on the activity or to provide a self-evaluation) are contexts for meaningful, purposeful writing. We have seen, for example, weather word writing and personal sign-in sheet writing as part of Mrs. Poremba's opening of the day.

ASSESSMENT

Children's invented spellings provide evidence of their phonemic awareness. They must isolate sounds in a word, or phonemes, when deciding what letters would best represent those sounds in writing that word. Invented spellings are a record of children's understandings of how sound–letter correspondences work in written language. Thus, invented spelling provides ongoing assessment opportunities. Teachers can take advantage of these opportunities if they are themselves aware of phonemes and if they know a bit about how to tell more sophisticated (but still unconventional) spellings from less sophisticated ones.

As accomplished readers and writers, teachers have long ago stopped needing to be phonemically aware. For the most part, their word identification and writing processes are automatic. Unlike beginners, adults usually do not depend on sounding out and sounding in. In order to teach phonemic awareness or to support invented spelling, teachers must reacquire phonemic awareness. They must work at putting themselves in their students' shoes, in which conscious attention to phonemes is needed. Can they quickly, confidently, and accurately answer such questions as "How many phonemes are in the word *check*?" "What are those phonemes?" "What are some key words in which those same phonemes occur, especially if not spelled the same way as in *check*?" (The answers are 3; /ch/, /eh/, and /k/; *cheese*, *episode*, and *kit*.)

One obvious indication of greater sophistication in invented spelling is the number of phonemes represented. A child who spells *light* as L or T is not doing as much with his or her sounding in as a child who spells *light* as LT. Beginning and ending sounds are usually more noticeable, so also spelling middle sounds, as in *LIT* for *light* is even more advanced.

Other indications arise from what we know about invented spelling strategies. The process of invented spelling can be described as breaking words into individual sounds, or phonemes, searching known letters of the alphabet for those sounds in the letters' names, and using the found letters in the right sequence to represent the words. Sounds that exactly match a letter's name (e.g., /ay/ in *ate*) are easier to spell than sounds that are only part of a letter's name (e.g., /t/ in *ate*, where the "t sound" is only part of name of the letter T ["tee"]). Therefore, the letter–name strategy is likely to appear earlier in children's invented spelling development than the part-of-a-letter's-name strategy.

Sounds that are absent from the names of the letters of the alphabet present a special challenge. An example is /i/, sometimes called "the short I sound," as in *it*. No letter's name contains that sound. Children who have discovered the need to represent every sound in a word don't want to write just T for *it*. They want also to represent that short I sound. So they take advantage of similarities, where there are not identities, in articulation. They use a strategy of searching sounds in letter names for one that is at least very close to the target sound. Thus, a frequent invented spelling for the short I sound is the letter E (*it* is spelled *ET*), because when saying the name of the letter E ("ee"), one makes one's mouth and teeth and tongue do *almost* the same things as when saying the short I sound (say "eat" and "it" and notice your mouth-teeth-tongue arrangement at the start of each).

Finally, when assessing invented spellings, teachers should be aware not only that inventive spellers are systematic like conventional spellers are (the many previous examples show that invented spellings are not random), but also that inventive spellers are abstract like conventional spellers are. Being abstract means that even when they are quite sophisticated, they do not always represent all the sounds in a word. Conventional spelling is abstract when it ignores the *C-H* sound in words like *train* and *trouble* (it's there between the *T* sound and the *R* sound; linguists call this an *affrication*). Again and again, inventive spellers have been found to be abstract by ignoring the *T* sound and spelling the *C-H* and *R* sounds in words such as *train* and *trouble,* for example, spelling them HRAN and HRBL.

Thus, an inventive speller's spelling of *train* as HRAN does not mean the same thing about his or her level of spelling development as if he or she had spelled *light* as *LT.* The former is the same kind of abstracting as found in conventional spelling; the latter is omitting an important middle part or vowel part of the word *light.*

One of the advantages of children's writing a lot and of teachers' frequently collaborating with children's invented spelling is that teachers are able to notice the development of the strategies just described. Children will not always use their most sophisticated strategies. In some contexts and when writing for some purposes, other non-spelling-related linguistic and cognitive processes demand much of their attention and effort, and children will seem to regress to less sophisticated spelling strategies. Over time, however, if students have enough writing opportunities, teachers can note what strategies students at least sometimes use and whether they use more sophisticated strategies increasingly often. This constitutes an appreciation of children's invented spelling ability that is more subtle, but also more useful (because it can better inform decisions about when to give what kinds of future support to writers), than merely labeling students as being at one stage or another of invented spelling.

INVENTED SPELLING RESEARCH

These teaching suggestions are based on a long history of invented spelling research, beginning with Read's (1971) "discovery" of invented spelling. Read is a linguist who was interested in children's phonemic awareness. His discovery of invented spelling was a serendipitous byproduct of his encouraging literacy-naive preschoolers to spell as a research task that would demonstrate what they knew or did not know about phonemes. He found that his preschool subjects could consciously segment strings of phonemes in spoken words and decide which phonemes to represent with which letters.

Legitimizing Invented Spelling

Read legitimized his subjects' invented spellings by demonstrating that they share with conventional spellings the characteristics of systematicity and abstractness. His subjects' spellings were not random; they were, in fact, the product of decisions compelled by phonemic awareness. In discussing the abstract nature of his subjects' spellings—for example, their abstracting away from the affrication in *T-R* words—Read wrote that inventive spellers

> are spontaneously employing one of the basic devices of spelling systems. . . . The nature of this accomplishment is theoretically more important than the fact that they choose the wrong dimension, from the adult point of view. . . . The fact that children's spontaneous spelling is already systematically abstract suggests that it is chiefly the facts of English, rather than the principle of spelling, that they have yet to learn. (p. 16)

Read hinted at the instructional implications that others would soon elaborate:

> The educational importance of this [study's] conclusion seems clear enough, at least in general. We can no longer assume that a child must approach reading and writing as an untrained animal approaches a maze—with no discernible prior conception of its structure. . . . Drill and memorization of words with *tr*- . . . may help the child to learn such cases, but these techniques suggest that spelling is arbitrarily related to speech and can only be memorized. This suggestion is not true of either standard spelling or the child's own invention. . . . [A child who spells *tr*- as HR] needs to be told, in effect, that his phonological judgments are not wrong (though they may seem so to most adults) . . . he is using the right principle, even if in the wrong place. We cannot teach him this principle if we ourselves continue to believe that to learn to spell is to get in the "habit" of associating sounds with letters, or phonemes with graphemes. (pp. 32–34)

In other words, teachers ought to build on rather than attempt to replace invented spelling. That injunction has been the theme of much of what has been written for teachers about invented spelling in the decades since Read's (1971) study (e.g., Bear, 2000; Manning & Underbakke, 2005; Paul, 1976; Sipe, 2001; Temple, Nathan, & Burris, 1982).

Stages of Invented Spelling

I suggested earlier that labeling children as to their stage of invented spelling development is a limiting approach to invented spelling assessment. Although stage related invented spelling research dates to the late 1970s, most researchers agree that children's spelling development is not a tidy, stage-by-stage progression. Rather, their spelling seems to move back and forth among stages, depending on their purposes for writing and the other, non-spelling-related cognitive and processing demands of the immediate literacy task. Only in the long term do they tend away from the less sophisticated spellings associated with early stages and toward the more sophisticated spellings associated with later stages. With that caveat in mind, it is nonetheless instructive to look at some of the stage-defining research.

As a kindergarten teacher, Paul (1976) encouraged her students to label their pictures by asking them "to listen very carefully to the sounds they heard in the words they wanted, so they could figure out what letters they needed to write" (p. 196). Eventually many of her students applied that process to writing longer texts, including stories. She identified four stages: 1) spelling the first sound of each word or syllable, 2) spelling first and last phonemes of words or syllables, 3) representing short vowel sounds surrounded by consonants, and 4) spelling "closer to the standard forms" (p. 199). Evidence for approaching standard included spellings of digraphs (/sh/, /ch/, and /th/) and correct spellings of words that had become sight words in the children's reading. Paul offered these stages as potential guidelines that "other teachers might find helpful when looking at their own students' spelling" (p. 198).

Beers and Henderson (1977) described first graders' invented spellings. They identified a first stage characterized by reliance on letter names; a second stage associated with greater awareness of vowels, so that, for example, spellers attempt to represent a vowel sound in every syllable even when it is difficult to find a letter name that reproduces that sound; and a third stage marked by attention to other than phonetic data, as when spellers use silent letters. Gentry (1978) named these the *semiphonetic,* the *phonetic,* and the *transitional* stages of invented spelling. He emphasized the developmental nature of invented spelling by adding two other stages that are not invented spelling at all, one before and one after Beers and Henderson's three stages. The first he called the *deviant stage* (he later renamed it *precommunicative*). It is characterized by letter strings that are random and lacks the systematicity that is required of spelling, whether invented or conventional. Gentry's fifth and last stage is called the *correct stage*; it is marked by conventional spellings and so is not *invented* spelling. These five stages became canonical; others have cited, adapted, and applied them in their work with invented spelling over the last 30 years.

CONNECTIONS: PHONEMIC AWARENESS-TO-READING, INVENTED SPELLING-TO-PHONEMIC AWARENESS, AND WRITING-TO-READING

Read (1971) established the connection between invented spelling and phonemic awareness. In fact, as we have seen, he discovered invented spelling while looking for phonemic awareness in his preschool subjects. Much subsequent invented spelling research (e.g., Martins & Silva, 2006) has emphasized that connection and the related connections between phonemic awareness and reading and between writing and reading.

In her extensive review of research about early reading, Adams (1990) emphasized the relation between phonemic awareness and learning to read:

> Faced with an alphabetic script, the child's level of phonemic awareness on entering school may be the single most powerful determinant of the success she or he will experience in learning to read and of the likelihood that she or he will fail. (p. 304)

And she made explicit the connection to invented spelling:

> The evidence that invented spelling activity simultaneously develops phonemic awareness and promotes understanding of the alphabetic principle is extremely promising, especially in view of the difficulty with which children are found to acquire these insights through other methods of teaching. (p. 387)

Phonemic awareness is related to reading, and spelling is related to phonemic awareness. Thus the benefits of exploiting writing–reading connections are present very early.

In 1971, Chomsky asserted those benefits by turning what was then the conventional wisdom on its ear in an article aptly titled "Write First, Read Later." According to Chomsky, writing first inevitably leads to reading; reading first does not necessarily lead to writing. She wrote:

> [W]hy do our reading programs as a matter of course expect children to deal with [word identification] first? The natural order is writing first, then reading what you have written. To expect the child to read, as a first step, what someone else has written is backwards, an artificial imposition that denies the child an active role in the whole process. Moreover it takes all the fun out of it. . . . Rather than a secret that only others are privy to, a ready-made impregnable code, [writing first] becomes for [the inventive speller] a means of expressing something in his head. This way the word is, in a very real sense, born of the creative effort of the reader. (pp. 296–297)

Many studies have explored the writing–reading connection's roots in invented spelling. Shanahan (1980) speculated that "allowing students to invent spelling patterns does not reduce spelling achievement . . . but it might stimulate word recognition development" (p. 364). Ferroli and Shanahan (1987) demonstrated a two-way relation. At the end of first grade, 50% of the variance in their subjects' invented spelling scores was explained by a combination of word reading performance and phonemic awareness. This is not surprising, considering that with progress from Gentry's (1978) phonetic third stage to his transitional fourth stage, spellers begin to employ nonphonetic, visual strategies, such as using silent letters and double consonants. It is likely that the acquisition of these strategies is at least partly the result of the increased experience of reading conventionally spelled texts that occurs in first grade.

In a series of experimental studies, Ehri and her colleagues found causal links between early spelling and reading (Ehri, 1987; Ehri, 1989; Ehri & Robbins, 1992; Ehri & Wilce, 1987; Scott & Ehri, 1990). For example, Ehri and Wilce (1987) trained alphabet-knowledgeable nonspellers to spell phonetically simplified words and word parts. These subjects then learned to read similar-sounding phonetically simplified words more easily than did control subjects. I had similar results with found inventive spellers (Richgels, 1995). Where Ehri and Wilce had taught nonspellers to spell, I used children who were not word readers but who already were inventing spellings in their kindergarten classrooms. I was then more successful teaching good inventive spellers to read phonetically simplified words than I was teaching poor inventive spellers to do so.

The connections described in this section are not limited to readers and writers of English. Silva and Martins (2003) trained Portuguese preschoolers in invented spelling, effecting their progress from what they characterized as pre-phonetic to early phonemic stages of invented spelling. Martins and Silva (2006) found that such invented spelling training resulted in greater gains in phonemic awareness for trainees than for controls.

CONCLUSION

The research reviewed here not only legitimizes invented spelling, but also validates the exemplary practices we saw in the first sections of this chapter. Read (1971) demonstrated the fundamental accomplishment of inventive spellers—that by being systematic and abstract in their writing, they are, in fact, spellers. The progress from invented to conventional is almost trivial—a mere adjustment—compared to that fundamental accomplishment. Read also established the connection between phonemic awareness and invented spelling. Because phonemic awareness is so closely tied to early reading success, the spelling–reading or writing–reading connection follows. It is not by chance that the effective teacher talk we heard from Mrs. Poremba is so similar in both reading and writing activities. The five principles described earlier for supporting invented spelling in preschool and primary classrooms can be summarized by the injunction to facilitate and exploit writing–reading connections, in the planning of activities and in the wording of teacher talk in the context of those activities.

REFERENCES

Adams, M.J. (1990). *Beginning to read: Thinking and learning about print.* Cambridge, MA: MIT.

Bear, D.R. (2000). *Words their way: Word study for phonics, vocabulary, and spelling instruction.* Upper Saddle, NJ: Merrill.

Beers, J.W., & Henderson, E.H. (1977). A study of developing orthographic concepts among first grade children. *Research in the Teaching of English, 11,* 133–148.

Chomsky, C. (1971). Write first, read later. *Childhood Education, 47,* 296–299.

Ehri, L.C. (1987). Learning to spell and read words. *Journal of Reading Behavior, 19,* 5–31.

Ehri, L.C. (1989). Movement into word reading and spelling: How spelling contributes to reading. In J.M. Mason (Ed.), *Reading and writing connections* (pp. 65–81). Boston: Allyn & Bacon.

Ehri, L.C., & Robbins, C. (1992). Beginners need some decoding skill to read words by analogy. *Reading Research Quarterly, 27,* 12–26.

Ehri, L.C., & Wilce, L.S. (1987). Does learning to spell help beginners learn to read words? *Reading Research Quarterly, 22,* 47–65.

Ferroli, L., & Shanahan, T. (1987). Kindergarten spelling: Explaining its relationship to first-grade reading. In J.E. Readence & R.S. Baldwin (Eds.), *Research in literacy: Merging perspectives, Thirty-sixth yearbook of the National Reading Conference* (pp. 93–99). Rochester, NY: National Reading Conference.

Gentry, J.R. (1978). Early spelling strategies. *Elementary School Journal, 79,* 88–92.

Manning, M., & Underbakke, C. (2005). Spelling development research necessitates replacement of weekly word list. *Childhood Education, 81,* 236.

Martins, M.A., & Silva, C. (2006). The impact of invented spelling on phonemic awareness. *Learning and Instruction, 16*, 41–56.

Paul, R. (1976). Invented spelling in kindergarten. *Young Children, 31*, 195–200.

Read, C. (1971). Preschool children's knowledge of English phonology. *Harvard Educational Review, 41*, 1–34.

Richgels, D.J. (1987). Experimental Reading with Invented Spelling (ERIS): A preschool and kindergarten method. *The Reading Teacher, 40*, 522–529.

Richgels, D.J. (1995). Invented spelling ability and printed word learning in kindergarten. *Reading Research Quarterly, 30*, 96–109.

Richgels, D.J. (2003). *Going to kindergarten: A year with an outstanding teacher*. Lanham, MD: Scarecrow Press.

Richgels, D.J., Poremba, K.J., & McGee, L.M. (1996). Kindergartners talk about print: Phonemic awareness in meaningful contexts. *The Reading Teacher, 49*, 632–642.

Scott, J.A., & Ehri, L.C. (1990). Sight word reading in prereaders: Use of logographic vs. alphabetic access routes. *Journal of Reading Behavior, 22*, 149–166.

Shanahan, T. (1980). The impact of writing instruction on learning to read. *Reading World, 19*, 357–368.

Silva, C., & Martins, M.A. (2003). Relations between children's invented spelling and the development of phonological awareness. *Educational Psychology, 23*, 3 16.

Sipe, L.R. (2001). Invention, convention, and intervention: Invented spelling and the teacher's role. *The Reading Teacher, 55*, 264–273

Temple, C.A., Nathan, R.G., & Burris, N.A. (1982). *The beginnings of writing*. Boston: Allyn & Bacon.

5

Storybook Reading as a Standardized Measurement of Early Literacy Skill Development

The Early Literacy Skills Assessment

ANDREA DEBRUIN-PARECKI

"Wow," said Squiggly. "Dante breathed fire,
Pilar talked to us, Elvis rhymed, and Violet leaped high!
You don't need the wishing stone. You've found what you
wished for by helping our friend Cappy! And look, everyone,
Cappy changed colors. You all grew up on this journey."

"What are some of the ways you help
your friends, Deshawn?" his teacher asked.

"Well, my friend Elise has abergies, and I always
bring her a Kleenex so she can blow her nose."

The preceding text is from an actual implementation of the Early Literacy Skills Assessment (ELSA), an authentic, standardized pre- and postassessment in the form of a children's storybook (DeBruin-Parecki, 2004, 2005). As the teacher read the story with the 4-year-old child, Deshawn, she came upon this comprehension question, a question that allows the child to connect his own experiences to those in the book. As you can see, Deshawn responded with an answer that indicated he understood the concept of helping friends. The ELSA is a unique instrument that provides multiple opportunities for children to express the early

53

literacy skills they have developed in ways that make sense to them. This type of assessment—an authentic assessment—puts children at ease and allows for more accuracy.

WHAT IS AUTHENTIC EARLY LITERACY ASSESSMENT?

Authentic early literacy assessment refers to evaluation that resembles reading and writing in the real world. The goal is to measure a variety of literacy skills in contexts that closely resemble actual situations in which those abilities are used. (Johnston & Costello, 2005; Valencia, Hiebert, & Afflerbach, 1994; Wiggins, 1993). This type of assessment engages children in a task that is personally meaningful, is grounded in a naturally occurring instructional activity, and is consistent with the goals, curriculum, and instructional practices of the classroom or program with which it is associated (McLaughlin & Vogt, 1997; Paris & Ayres, 1994). Authentic assessments look and feel like learning activities, not traditional tests. They examine a broad range of children's knowledge rather than one narrow area (Hart, 1994). They also do not rely on unrealistic or arbitrary time constraints, nor do they emphasize instant recall or depend on lucky guesses. Because this type of assessment takes place in a situation familiar to most young children, their attention is focused and they are motivated to participate. There are few such assessments in the area of early literacy.

Typically, authentic assessments in early literacy are not standardized diagnostic tests, although, like standardized tests, they are usually linked to standards, most often some form of state early literacy standards (Gronlund, 2006). They are more informal tests in which teacher discretion can play a bigger part. Many of these types of assessments are observational in nature in which a teacher completes a checklist while watching a child problem-solve or work on a task. They may also involve collections of work accumulated over time, such as portfolios (Dichtelmiller, Jablon, Marsden, & Meisels, 2001; McKenna & Stahl, 2003). The items in these portfolios may then be scored according to a prescribed system or may just be arranged in developmental progression to show growth. There are also teachers who take anecdotal notes on a regular basis and use these to inform instruction. These notes often appear in portfolios or are kept in children's folders. All of these methods are good examples of monitoring progress, an assessment that continues throughout the school year.

Authentic early literacy assessment is usually directly aligned with the early literacy curriculum being used in the classroom. Shepard, Kagan, and Wurtz found that "assessment and teaching are inseparable processes" (1998, p. 52). When an assessment is aligned with instruction, both students and teachers benefit (Valencia, 1997). Students are more likely to learn because the results of the assessment allow instruction to be focused specifically on skills that need improvement as well as concentrating on advancing skills. Assessment is more accurate because it is based on what students need to learn to move forward. Teachers can be more effective because assessment provides a guide for instruction and informs them of children's current knowledge of and progress on specific literacy skills development. They can modify and adjust their instruction, curriculum, and environment to address the skills their students need to improve and learn. In summary, for authentic assessment to be successful, teachers need to take the time to think about what children already understand, what they can accomplish, and what skills need further development (Ratliff & Winter, 2001/2002).

WHAT ARE STANDARDIZED TESTS?

Many people feel that using a typical standardized test is the best way to get accurate, reliable, and valid information about a student's current skill levels and his or her future progress in these skills. These tests generally ask questions out of the context of real-life activities, and rarely do they tap into critical-thinking skills. They are straightforward questions that all children are expected to answer in the same manner such as, "See all of the pictures on this page? I will say something, and then I want you to put your finger on the picture of what I said." All children are required to point to the one correct answer. They are not actively involved in constructing knowledge. In the case of this type of question, children may also be asked to identify pictures unfamiliar in their culture. For the test to be standardized, all children must be asked the same questions the same way under the same conditions (Ataya, 2007).

Standardized tests must demonstrate reliability and validity (Popham, 2005). To be reliable, a test must demonstrate stability of results. There are many types of reliability including test–retest reliability and alternative-forms reliability. Test–retest reliability is determined by giving the same test to the same students two different times with a short interval between the two tests. If the test is reliable, the students should score about the same on both tests. Alternative-form reliability is tested by using two different forms of the same test. If students score similarly on both tests, then this type of reliability is achieved (Ataya, 2007). Interrater reliability is the most common form, and it is vital because each assessor must assign similar scores when using the same instrument to evaluate the same young child under the same circumstances. If scores are nearly the same in these circumstances, then the test is reliable (DeBruin-Parecki, 2003). To be valid, a test measures what it is intended to measure and does so in a way that is justifiable. There are many kinds of validity, including content validity, meaning all concepts being tested are supported by research and are representative of the key aspects of the domain(s) it is measuring; concurrent validity, meaning that a child's scores on a new test are similar to those attained on an already valid instrument measuring the same content; and developmental validity, meaning the items being measured are developmentally suitable for the children being assessed. Connection to state early literacy standards, if available, are often used to assist in determining validity of a standardized measurement.

Standardized tests have many characteristics that allow them to be called *standardized*, but for our purposes it is most important to remember that a standardized test is administered, scored, and interpreted in a consistent manner whenever, wherever, and to whomever it is given. It is also important to know that standardized tests allow for the comparison of an individual child or group of children on a test to that of other children or groups of children who have similar characteristics. Standardized tests, however, can be biased, can cause young children undue stress, can provide inaccurate information due to testing methods, and can be used inappropriately to make important decisions about children's lives (Laing & Kamhi, 2003; Shepard et al., 1998; Wesson, 2001). They generally do not accomplish what assessments should always hold as a priority: providing teachers with a pathway to individualized instruction, modification of current curriculum and classroom environment to provide more focused learning opportunities, and a vision for needed professional development (Snow & Jones, 2001).

As programs that focus specifically on early literacy skill development, most notably the federal Early Reading First (ERF) initiative (ERF, 2007), began to appear across the country, there was a huge outcry for accurate, detailed, and statistically sound accountability. Many standardized early literacy tests came into play, some already in existence such as the Peabody Picture Vocabulary Test (PPVT) (Dunn & Dunn, 1997), and some new such as the GetitGotitGo! (2003). Each of these instruments and others that are similar in nature measured a slice of early literacy growth such as vocabulary development or rhyming, but none were comprehensive, and they did not measure skills from all four major areas of early literacy: comprehension, phonological awareness, alphabetic principle, and concepts about print (Snow, Burns, & Griffin, 1998). Most importantly, none were matched to naturally occurring literacy experiences of most children.

Most early literacy assessments used for determining funding and overall progress across large groups are not authentic assessments, but rather standardized surveys, screenings, or diagnostic tests. Survey evaluations, such as achievement tests, provide a broadly defined estimate of a child's overall achievement level in a given area. These tests are good for giving information about program effectiveness on a large scale, but not helpful in planning instruction. Screening tests are often used to identify in which areas children need more testing. Diagnostic tests can provide detailed information about a child's skills in a multitude of areas using a number of different tasks to determine these skills. What diagnostic tests can do is provide a level of information that may be useful in planning effective instruction (McKenna & Stahl, 2003).

All of these types of tests typically rely on traditional testing methods, such as having children point to answers on an isolated page with several choices. For example, in testing phonological awareness, a tester might point to a picture of a ball and say, "This is a ball. There are four pictures on this page, and one sounds the same as ball." The child would then listen as the tester reads the words and points to all the pictures. The child would be asked to point to and tell the tester the correct answer. This type of testing can be stressful for several reasons. Children may not understand the directions and what is required of them, what some of the pictures represent even after hearing the accompanying word, or the testing may take too long, causing the child to become restless. These, and other factors, can prevent the accurate evaluation of what the child knows.

EXAMPLES OF CURRENTLY USED STANDARDIZED TESTS

This section will include a discussion of the more traditional tests. These include the PPVT (Dunn & Dunn, 1997), the GetitGotitGo! (2003), the Woodcock Johnson III Letter and Word Identification Test (Woodcock, McGrew, & Mather, 2001), the Phonological Awareness Literacy Screening (The PALS) Prekindergarten (Pre-K) (Invernizzi, Sullivan, & Meier, 2001), and the Preschool Comprehensive Test of Phonological and Print Processing (Pre-CTOPP) (2002).

Peabody Picture Vocabulary Test

The PPVT (Dunn & Dunn, 1997) and the *Test de Vocabulario en Imagenes Peabody* (TVIP) (Dunn, Lugo, Padilla, & Dunn, 1986) both measure children's receptive (listening) vocabulary acquisition and serve as tests of children's English or Spanish verbal ability. The tests are not timed and are administered to children individually. Each student is shown a page with four pictures on it. The teacher then says a word or phrase, and the student points to the picture that represents what the teacher said. The test is leveled by age and begins at age 2 and ends at age 6. There has been criticism of the Spanish version of the test because some feel it is an inaccurate assessment of Spanish language ability due to the targeting of inappropriate features of the Spanish language (Kester & Peña, 2002).

GetitGotitGo! Test

The GetitGotitGo! (2003) test was designed for use with children ages 3–5. The test is individually administered and used to measure picture naming (expressive vocabulary), alliteration, and rhyming. Children are presented with a card that has a number of pictures on it, and, depending on the task, they are asked to point to and/or verbalize the correct answer. For example, an alliteration card will have a picture at the top and three pictures in a row beneath it, one of which starts with the same sound as the top picture. The child is asked to point to the picture that starts with the same beginning sound as the top picture. The score is determined by the number of pictures correctly identified.

Woodcock Johnson III Letter and Word Identification Test

The Woodcock Johnson III Letter and Word Identification Test (Woodcock, McGrew, & Mather, 2001) is just one subtest of the Woodcock Johnson III Test of Achievement. It is used with young children beginning at age 2. It is individually administered, and it measures uppercase and lowercase alphabet identification and word recognition. Although there are many other parts to the Woodcock Johnson III, this is one of the most commonly used. For example, when children are asked to identify letters, they are shown a page with several letters in a row. They are asked to point to the letter the examiner verbalizes. This test is also available in Spanish.

The Phonological Awareness Literacy Screening Prekindergarten Test

The PALS Pre-K (Invernizzi, Sullivan, & Meier, 2001) test is composed of six tasks: name writing, alphabet knowledge, beginning sound awareness, print and word awareness, rhyme awareness, and nursery rhyme awareness. It is designed to be used with 4-year-olds at the beginning and end of the school year. The alphabet knowledge task is widely adopted and is required to be used by all ERF grantees. Children are asked to name the 26 uppercase alphabet letters presented in random order, and if they know 16 or more, they then take the lowercase recognition test. If children know more than nine lowercase letters, they go on to produce sounds associated with letters and three consonant digraphs, such as /ch/. Children are asked to point to and/or verbalize their answers.

Preschool Comprehensive Test of Phonological and Print Processing

The Pre-CTOPP (2002) was designed to be used with children ages 3–5 years old. It provides assessment for three areas of phonological processing: phonological sensitivity (i.e., blending, elision, omission of initial sounds or one or more sounds—such as a vowel, a consonant, or a whole syllable—in a word or phrase), phonological memory (e.g., nonword repetition, word span tests), and phonological access (e.g., rapid object naming tests). Print knowledge is also assessed as is reading vocabulary (i.e., receptive listening, expressive speaking). This is a very long test, and many choose to just use specific parts. As an example of how this test works, the print awareness section under print concepts shows a child a page with four pictures on it. The administrator says to the child, "These are pictures of a book. Which one shows the title of the book?" Children are asked to point to their answer.

After reading about many of the most commonly used preschool early literacy assessments, it is apparent that the field of early literacy needs the following tools and assessments: 1) a comprehensive pre- and postassessment standardized tool that would look across all four major areas of early literacy skill development and easily map onto the majority of state early literacy standards, 2) an assessment that is more in tune with children's real experiences with literacy, 3) an authentic assessment that is accurate and statistically sound, and 4) a comprehensive assessment that works equally well for both English and Spanish speaking preschoolers. After studying all of these tools, and determining the need for such an instrument, the ELSA was created (DeBruin-Parecki, 2004, 2005).

WHAT IS THE EARLY LITERACY SKILLS ASSESSMENT?

The ELSA was designed to respond to the weaknesses of the instruments previously mentioned (DeBruin-Parecki, 2004, 2005). It is a unique instrument in the form of a children's storybook and is available in both English and Spanish. There are two versions of the ELSA: *Violet's Adventure/La Aventura de Violeta* and *Dante Grows Up/El Cambio en Dante*. The first book tells the story of a young unicorn far away from her mother who goes on a journey with new friends to find her. The second book is about a young dragon who wishes he could breathe fire like his mother, father, and big sister. He and his friends go on an adventure and discover they have developed the grown-up skills they desire.

The ELSA is a reliable and valid standardized authentic assessment originally designed for use with 3- to 6-year-olds (Cheadle, 2007). Though many have distinguished authentic assessments as ones that do not incorporate the use of standardized tests (Gronlund, 2006), the ELSA demonstrates that this is not necessarily true.

The ELSA is given twice each school year: at the start of the program, and again at the end. Written to link with scientifically based reading research, the ELSA takes up to 25 minutes to complete, is taken in one session, and measures skills in the areas of comprehension, phonological awareness, alphabetic principle, and concepts about print. These skills are emphasized in the federal No Child Left Behind Act of 2001 (PL 107-110), the National Reading Panel report (2000), and the summary of the National Early Literacy Panel's work (Strickland & Shanahan, 2004). Typically, children who develop competence in these areas before entering kindergarten experience more academic success than those who do not (Dickinson & Neuman, 2006; Neuman & Dickinson, 2001; Snow et al., 1998).

The ELSA is a unique assessment because it doesn't make children feel anxious or scared during testing. It takes place in a familiar and natural context to most children, and for others it becomes familiar once in the school environment. It measures knowledge in the context of a real-life literacy activity: interactive storybook reading. Even for children without much home experience with books, the ELSA tends to be successful because it is never given before all children have had the opportunity to read with an adult alone or in a small group. It gives children the opportunity to spend 20 minutes reading one-to-one with their teacher or a familiar other, an experience that is rare in a preschool classroom. This can assist in teacher–child bonding at the beginning of the year.

HOW DOES THE EARLY LITERACY SKILLS ASSESSMENT MEASURE SPECIFIC EARLY LITERACY SKILLS?

Comprehension

Comprehension is the process of deriving meaning. During interactive storybook reading, preschool children construct an understanding of story language and structure by connecting ideas from the story to prior knowledge, predicting what will happen next in the story, retelling story sequences, and linking new words to known concepts and experiences. (DeBruin-Parecki, 2007; McKeown & Beck, 2006; Paris & Paris, 2003).

No other comprehensive early literacy assessment has attempted to measure these skills. There are, however, vocabulary assessments, most commonly the PPVT/TVIP (Dunn & Dunn, 1997), that measure receptive language (i.e., learning to listen and understand). This test only measures this one skill, however, and not the skills previously mentioned. Individual differences in vocabulary can be used to explain a reliable portion of variance in young children's eventual success in reading comprehension (Hart and Risley, 1995; Senechal, Ouellette, & Rodney, 2006). But vocabulary development is not the only skill children need to master to learn to comprehend. Children also need other comprehension skills to be able to put their increased vocabulary to use. The ELSA measures these other important research-supported skills: prediction, retelling, and connecting to real-life experiences (Teale, 2003; Teale & Martinez, 1996).

When measuring comprehension, the ELSA uses the following definition: Comprehension is the process of deriving meaning from action, speech, and text by connecting what is being learned to what is already known. Prediction is defined as guessing what will happen next in a story based on picture cues or previous text. Retelling is defined as explaining, in sequence, what has happened so far in a story or summarizing the complete story sequentially. Connecting to real-life experiences is defined as relating plot, concepts, or characters in a book to real-life experiences. For example, on the title page of the assessment, a child is asked to answer the following question: "What do you think will happen in this story?" It was important for the author and artist of the assessment to work closely together to provide children with a detailed picture so the children are able to give more than just a description. If on the title page of *Dante Grows Up*, children just saw a dragon, then the majority of children would probably say, "It is about a dragon." By providing them with a more detailed picture, children can use their imagination and give more comprehensive answers like the following example taken from an actual testing situation: "The flying dragon and his friend are going to save the unicorn because he is in trouble. They are like superheroes." (See picture on the following page.)

Phonological Awareness

Phonological awareness is the general ability to attend to the sounds of language as distinct from its meaning, including rhyme awareness and sound similarities, and at the highest level, awareness of syllables or phonemes (Neuman, Copple, & Bredekamp, 2000; Snow et al., 1998). Through rhyme and word play, preschool children begin to hear and identify the smaller chunks of sounds that make up words, including rhymes, initial phonemes in alliterative phrases, and syllables in names. As Lonigan (2006) stated, "Children who are better at detecting and manipulating syllables, rhymes, or phonemes are quicker to learn to read" (p. 78).

The definition the ELSA uses for measuring phonological awareness is the general ability to recognize the sound structure of speech, to perceive sounds that make up words, and to pronounce words and parts of words. The phonological awareness skills measured by the ELSA are rhyming, segmentation, and phonemic awareness, specifically alliteration (same first letter sound). Rhyming is defined as pairing words with corresponding ending sounds. Segmenting is defined as orally dividing words into syllables, and phonemic awareness is defined as understanding that a spoken word consists of a series of individual sounds and attending to the sound structure of a word rather than the meaning. On pages 6 and 7 of the ELSA, children are asked about rhyming. The text in *Dante Grows Up* reads as follows:

"I know what I'll do," Squiggly decided. "I'll fly up over the rainbow to see Violet. Along the way I'll rest on the rhyming clouds."

Up, up he flew to the first rhyming cloud. Here he saw many things: a fluffy gray bunny, a bright blue bug, a striped tiger, and a star in a jar.

"Star, jar," he said. "They sound alike. They rhyme!"

After a short rest, he flew up to the next rhyming cloud. Help Squiggly rhyme on the other clouds so he can fly to see his friend Violet.

This text involves the child in the story and motivates participation. After reading the excerpt, the teacher goes to the bottom of the page and continues reading:

On the second cloud he saw a bear. What rhymes with *bear*?
  hair, trumpet, sheep, umbrella
  Bear rhymes with____. (See pictures on this page.)

Alphabetic Principle

The term *alphabetic principle* involves recognizing letters, connecting letter sounds to letters, and understanding that a word is a consistent sequential set of letters and sounds (Neuman et al., 2000). According to McKenna and Stahl

(2003), there are two reasons for children to learn letter names: 1) Fluent readers do not recognize words as whole units, but rather they do so by identifying component letters, and 2) teachers need some way to refer to letters during instruction. In addition, they state it is important for children to learn both uppercase and lowercase letters because both are commonly used in the print they see. Children also need to be able to connect letter sounds to letters. Research has shown that children develop this skill at a much slower rate than letter identification (Burgess & Lonigan, 1998). More supported instruction in this area might greatly help children in developing this skill (Burgess, 2006). To become readers, children also need to understand the concept of *word,* meaning that a specific word is always composed of the same letters in the same order. Word awareness begins when children see and learn to read words in print (Ehri, 1975).

Similar to the definition above, the definition the ELSA uses for measuring alphabetic principle consists of recognizing letters, connecting letter sounds to letters, and understanding that a word is a consistent, sequential set of letters and sounds. The alphabetic principle skills measured by the ELSA are alphabet letter recognition, letter–sound correspondence, and sense of word. Alphabet letter recognition is defined as recognizing and naming uppercase and lowercase alphabet letters on sight. Letter–sound correspondence is defined as identifying sounds associated with specific letters. Sense of word is defined as understanding that a word is a consistent set of letters and sounds. On pages 16 and 17 of the ELSA, children are asked to identify uppercase letters that are embedded in lily pads floating in a river. All 26 letters are available for the child to identify. The child does not have to select one from a group of four as is common on many identification tests. This will only tell the assessor which letter the child doesn't know and whether or not he or she knows another. It is not known what the child knows about the remaining letters on the page. Letters are also often in a chart and clustered close together, which often leads to a child getting confused and overwhelmed. The text in *Dante Grows Up* reads as follows:

After they crossed the colored stones, they came to the Alphabet River. Tied to a tree on the riverbank was a boat. A note on the boat said, "To get to the woods in this boat, name as many letters as you can along the way."

They climbed into the boat. Can you help them name the letters?

[Child's name], let's start by finding the first letter in your name. What is it called?

What other letters can you point to and name to help Dante and his friends get to the wishing stone?

Okay, let's go on. (See pictures on next page.)

Concepts About Print

The term *concepts about print* refers to children's knowledge of the functions of print and how print works (Strickland & Schickedanz, 2004). Over time, young

children engage with print around them and in books, and they learn some things about looking through a book in an orderly manner. It takes much more than this to learn, and this process takes time (Clay, 2002). Children need to learn how to handle books, what directional movement across print is, how letters are orientated, and that there is a sequence of letters, words, and ideas (Clay, 2002). In 1972, Marie Clay developed a concept about print assessment called *Sands* (Clay, 1972). This has been the basis of the majority of concepts about print evaluations.

The ELSA definition for measuring concepts about print includes how print is organized—on the page, on signs, on the screen—and how print is used for reading and writing. Simply put, this is how books work. The concepts about print skills measured by the ELSA are orientation, story beginning, direction of text, and book parts. Orientation is defined as knowing how to hold a book so it is ready to read. Story beginning is defined as identifying where in the text one begins to read. Direction of text is defined as understanding that text is read from left to right and top to bottom. Book parts are defined as identifying the front cover, back cover, and title page of a book. Children are asked questions about concepts about print as an integral part of the story. The beginning of *Dante Grows Up* evaluates children's knowledge of story beginning and direction of text:

Once upon a time, in a land above the clouds on Dragon Hill, there lived a young dragon named Dante. He was not a happy dragon because he couldn't breathe fire, and no one would teach him. He asked his father and mother, and even his big sister, Diana, but they just shook their heads. "You're not old enough yet," they said.

"Show me with your finger where I should start reading on this page."
"Thanks!"
"Show me with your finger which way I go on this page when I read."
"Show me with your finger where I go on this page after that." (See picture on this page.)

WHAT IS THE VALUE OF EARLY LITERACY SKILLS ASSESSMENT SCORES?

The ELSA is composed of 23 questions, some with multiple parts. The ELSA scores provide information on a number of levels. Like any standardized test, numerical scores for pre- and postcomparison are available. Category scores, as well as scores in related individual skill areas are provided, allowing for a more comprehensive picture of a child's developing literacy skills. Unlike a typical standardized early literacy assessment, the ELSA can directly inform instruction. Teachers who implement the ELSA are able to see the child putting his or her early literacy skills into practice providing a window on how these skills are developing and being used. The teacher can easily transfer this information into individualized instruction as well as integrated group lessons.

WHAT ABOUT AUTHENTIC EARLY LITERACY ASSESSMENT FOR SPANISH-SPEAKING CHILDREN?

"In essence, children utilize native language abilities as a tool to construct higher order thinking processes. Limiting their opportunities to learn in their first language will limit their cognitive growth and related academic achievement" (Garcia, 2005, p. 33). So it follows that assessing children in their first language would also be critical to understanding their cognitive growth. Often, young second-language children are mistakenly placed in special education services due to improper assessment. By assessing a child in his or her first language, a teacher has a better idea of the early literacy skills he or she has developed and can use this information to help him or her transfer these skills into English (Tabors, 1997). To test children in Spanish, however, the tool used has to be more than a direct translation. Differences in the features of the language must be taken into consideration (Kester & Peña, 2002). In addition, some skills, such as rhyming and phonological awareness skills, clearly don't directly translate.

Currently, there are few early literacy assessments in Spanish, and there are none that are comprehensive at the preschool level. Most common is the TVIP (Dunn et al., 1986), the Spanish version of the PPVT (Dunn & Dunn, 1997). This instrument measures a child's receptive vocabulary, or the words that a child can understand even if he or she doesn't use them. The Woodcock-Muñoz Language Survey—Revised (Woodcock, Muñoz-Sandoval, Ruef, & Alvardo, 2005) has been most commonly used in preschools for letter–word identification and dictation (e.g., measuring emergent writing skills).

The ELSA is geared toward providing a more comprehensive picture of a child's early literacy skills development in Spanish. Each of the areas assessed in English are also assessed in Spanish. The books *La Aventura de Violeta/El Cambio en Dante* are not direct translations of the English books. Rather, they have been changed to reflect language differences. Both Spanish versions have been shown to be reliable and valid across diverse Spanish-speaking populations from Mexico, Cuba, South and Central America, and Puerto Rico (Cheadle, 2007). As mentioned previously, the ELSA is unique because of its comprehension measure. Young Spanish speaking children's comprehension skills are rarely assessed. Promising results on the Spanish ELSA have demonstrated that young Spanish speaking children's comprehension skills grow at a greater rate than any of the other populations that have been tested.

WHAT DOES THE FUTURE LOOK LIKE FOR EARLY LITERACY ASSESSMENT?

The future for early literacy assessment appears grim in many cases, as decision makers continue to choose instruments that assess selected skills, in many cases, in a very short period of time. The emphasis appears to be more on ease of testing, rather than on useful results. If comprehensive and effective curriculum and assessment were more closely linked, it would be apparent that children are often not tested on everything they are learning, so the picture of the skill development is incomplete (DeBruin-Parecki, 2007). In order for teachers to plan effective early literacy skill instruction, they have to know what their students know across all key areas. Tests that focus on one or two skills can't provide them with enough information. In addition, if children aren't engaged in the testing process, results will be inaccurate. Using fewer comprehensive evaluations will better serve teachers and children, and if these tests are given in meaningful contexts in familiar situations to children and teachers, results are more likely to be precise.

Teachers have to disassociate from the notion that tests are a necessary evil and begin to see them as informative and useful. Then, perhaps they will invest more in the assessment process and what it has to offer them in terms of their future teaching. High stakes testing has teachers disillusioned in many cases. Often, strangers come into their classroom to test their children, and they see this process as unrelated to what they do in the classroom. Involving teachers directly in authentic assessments and providing the professional development they need to understand these tests and how to best use the results would seem prudent.

Instruments like the ELSA and future authentic early literacy assessments yet to be created will allow young children to be tested in a meaningful situation and offer teachers tremendous insight into a child's current early literacy skills and their development each year. This insight can only assist in improving overall teaching and individualizing instruction, two of the primary goals of effective assessment.

REFERENCES

Ataya, R.I. (2007). Policy and technical considerations for classroom assessment. In P. Jones, J.F. Farr, & R. Ataya (Eds.), *A pig don't get fatter the more you weigh it: Classroom assessments that work.* New York: Teachers College Press.

Burgess, S.R. (2006). The development of phonological sensitivity. In D.K. Dickinson & S.B. Neuman (Eds.), *Handbook of early literacy research* (Vol. 2, pp. 90–100). New York: Guilford Press.

Burgess, S.R., & Lonigan, C.J. (1998). Bidirectional relations of phonological sensitivity and prereading abilities: Evidence from a preschool sample. *Journal of Experimental Child Psychology, 70,* 117–141.

Cheadle, J. (2007). *The Early Literacy Skills Assessment psychometric report.* Ypsilanti, MI: High/Scope Press.

Clay, M.M. (1972). *Sand: The concepts about print test.* New Zealand: Heinemann.

Clay, M.M. (2002). *An observation survey of early literacy achievement.* New Zealand: Heinemann.

DeBruin-Parecki, A. (2003). Evaluating adult/child interactive reading skills. In A. DeBruin-Parecki & B. Krol-Sinclair (Eds.), *Family literacy: From theory to practice* (pp. 282–302). Newark, DE: International Reading Association.

DeBruin-Parecki, A. (2004). *The Early Literacy Skills Assessment:* Violet's adventure/La aventura de Violet. Ypsilanti, MI: High/Scope Educational Research Foundation.

DeBruin-Parecki, A. (2005). *The Early Literacy Skills Assessment: Dante grows up/El cambio en Dante.* Ypsilanti, MI: High/Scope Educational Research Foundation.

DeBruin-Parecki, A. (2007). *Let's read together: Improving literacy outcomes with the Adult–Child Interactive Reading Inventory.* Baltimore: Paul H. Brookes Publishing Co.

Dichtelmiller, M.L., Jablon, J.R., Marsden, D.B., & Meisels, S.J. (2001). *The work sampling system developmental guidelines* (4th ed.). Matwah, NJ: Pearson Early Learning.

Dickinson, D.K., & Neuman, S.B. (2006). *Handbook of early literacy research* (Vol. 2). New York: Guilford Press.

Dunn, L., Lugo, D.E., Padilla, E.R., & Dunn, L.M. (1986). *Test de Vocabulario en Imágenes Peabody.* Bloomington, MN: Pearson Assessments.

Dunn, L.M. & Dunn, L.M. (1997). *Peabody Picture Vocabulary Test-III.* Circle Pines, MN: American Guidance Service.

Early Reading First. (n.d.). Retrieved April 28, 2007, from http://www.ed.gov/programs/earlyreading/index.html

Ehri, L. (1975). Word consciousness in readers and prereaders. *Journal of Educational Psychology, 67,* 204–212.

Garcia, E.E. (2005). *Teaching and learning in two languages: Bilingualism and schooling in the United States.* New York: Teachers College Press.

Getitgotitgo! (2003). Retrieved April 28, 2007, from http://ggg.umn.edu/get/index.html

Gronlund, G. (2006). *Making early learning standards come alive: Connecting your practice and curriculum to state guidelines.* St Paul, MN: Redleaf Press.

Hart, B., & Risely, T. (1995). *Meaningful differences in the everyday experience of young American children.* Baltimore: Paul H. Brookes Publishing Co.

Hart, D. (1994). *Authentic assessment: A handbook for education.* Menlo Park, CA: Addison Wesley Publishing Co.

Invernizzi, M., Sullivan A., & Meier, J. (2001). *PALS Pre-K Phonological Awareness Literacy Screening.* Charlottesville, VA: University Printing.

Johnston, P. & Costello, P. (2005). Principles for literacy assessment. *Reading Research Quarterly, 40* (2), 256-67.

Kester, E.S., & Peña, E.D. (2002) *Limitations of current language testing practices for bilinguals.* College Park, MD: ERIC Clearinghouse on Assessment and Evaluation. (ERIC Document Reproduction Service No. ED470203)

Laing, S.P., & Kamhi, A. (2003). Alternative assessment of language and literacy in culturally and linguistically diverse populations. *Language, Speech, and Hearing Services in Schools, 34,* 44–55.

Lonigan, C. (2006). Conceptualizing phonological processing skills in prereaders. In D.K. Dickinson & S.B. Neuman (Eds.), *Handbook of early literacy research* (Vol. 2, pp. 77–89). New York: Guilford Press.

McKenna, M.C., & Stahl, S.A. (2003). *Assessment for reading instruction.* New York: Guilford Press.

McKeown, M.G., & Beck, I.L. (2006). Encouraging young children's language interactions with stories. In D.K. Dickinson & S.B. Neuman (Eds.), *Handbook of early literacy research* (Vol. 2, pp. 281–294). New York: Guilford Press.

McLaughlin, M., & Vogt, M. (1997). *Portfolios in teacher education.* Newark, DE: International Reading Association.

National Reading Panel. (2000). *Teaching children to read: An evidence-based assessment of the scientific research literature on reading and its implications for reading instruction.*

Washington, DC: National Institute of Child Health and Human Development, National Institutes of Health.

Neuman, S.B., Copple, C., & Bredekamp, S. (2000). *Learning to read and write: Developmentally appropriate practices for young children.* Washington, DC: NAEYC.

Neuman, S.B., & Dickinson, D.K. (2001). *Handbook of early literacy research.* New York: Guilford Press.

No Child Left Behind Act of 2001, PL 107-110, 115 Stat. 1425, 20 U.S.C. §§ 6301 *et seq.*

Paris, A.H., & Paris, S.G. (2003). Assessing narrative comprehension in young children. *Reading Research Quarterly, 38*(1), 36–76.

Paris, S.G., & Ayers, L.R. (1994*). Becoming reflective students and teachers with portfolios and authentic assessment.* Washington, DC: American Psychological Association.

Popham, W.J. (2005). *Classroom assessment: What teachers need to know* (4th ed.). Boston: Allyn & Bacon.

Preschool Comprehensive Test of Phonological and Print Processing. (2002). Retrieved April 28, 2007, from http://www.psy.fsu.edu/~lonigan/Pre-CTOPPP.html

Ratliff, N.J. (2001/2002, Winter). Using authentic assessment to document the emerging literacy skills of young children. *Childhood Education, 78*(2), 66–69.

Senechal, M., Ouellette, G., & Rodney, D. (2006). The misunderstood giant: On the predictive role of early vocabulary. In D.K. Dickinson & S.B. Neuman (Eds.), *Handbook of early literacy research* (Vol. 2, pp. 173–184). New York: Guilford Press.

Shepard, L., Kagan, S., & Wurtz, E. (1998). Goal 1 early childhood assessments resource group recommendations. *Young Children, 53* (3), 52–54.

Snow, C.E., Burns, S., & Griffin, P. (Eds.). (1998). *Preventing reading difficulties in young children.* Washington, DC: National Academies Press.

Snow, C.E., & Jones, J. (2001, April 25). Making a silk purse: How a national system of testing might work. *Education Week, 20*(32), 41, 60.

Strickland, D.S., & Schickedanz, J.A. (2004). *Learning about print in preschool: Working with letters, words, and beginning links with phonemic awareness.* Newark, DE: International Reading Association.

Strickland, D.S., & Shanahan, T. (2004). Laying the groundwork for literacy. *Educational Leadership, 61*(6), 74–77.

Tabors, P.O. (1997). *One child, two languages: A guide for preschool educators of children learning English as a second language.* Baltimore: Paul H. Brookes Publishing Co.

Teale, W.H. (2003). Reading aloud to young children as a classroom instructional activity: Insights from research and practice. In A. van Kleek, S.A. Stahl, & E.B. Bauer (Eds.), *On reading books to children* (pp. 114–139). Mahwah, NJ: Lawrence Erlbaum Associates.

Teale, W.H., & Martinez, M.G. (1996). Reading aloud to young children: Teachers' reading styles and kindergarteners' text comprehension. In C. Pontecorvo, M. Orsolini, B. Burge, & L.B. Resnick (Eds.), *Children's early text construction* (pp. 321–344). Mahwah, N.J: Lawrence Erlbaum Associates.

Valencia, S. (1997). *Understanding authentic classroom-based literacy assessment.* Boston: Houghton Mifflin Company.

Valencia, S.W., Hiebert, E.H., & Afflerbach, P.A. (Eds.). (1994). *Authentic reading assessment: Practices and possibilities.* Newark, DE: International Reading Association.

Wesson, K.A. (2001). The Volvo effect: Questioning standardized tests. *Young Children, 56*(2), 15–18.

Wiggins, G.P. (1993). *Assessing student performance: Exploring the purpose of limits of testing.* San Francisco: Jossey-Bass.

Woodcock, R.W., Muñoz-Sandoval, A.F., Ruef, M., & Alvarado, C.G. (2005). *Woodcock Language Proficiency Battery—Revised: Spanish Form.* Itasca, IL: Riverside Publishing.

Woodcock, R.W., McGrew, K.S., & Mather, N. (2001). *Woodcock-Johnson III Tests of Achievement.* Itasca, IL: Riverside Publishing.

Early Literacy for English Language Learners

Linda M. Espinosa

Lisa, Maria, Linda (4-year-old Latina girls), and Jade (African American girl of the same age) are playing in the dramatic play area of Ms. Sims' Title I prekindergarten (pre-K) classroom. The Latinas are speaking Spanish to each other and to Jade, even though she does not speak Spanish. The girls are chatting, smiling, and pointing to each other and to the cooking utensils as they create an imaginary scenario.

Linda says to the girls, "Que rico ese pan, verdad?" (The bread is good, isn't it?) as she holds out her piece of plastic pizza. All of the other girls nod and smile in agreement.

Jade responds, "I love pizza."

Ms. Sims notices the interaction and decides to take advantage of this opportunity. She sits in the center and says to the girls, "I am hungry. May I have some bread, please?"

Linda replies, "You want ese pan?" as she hands her plastic pizza to Ms. Sims.

Ms. Sims takes the piece of pizza and replies, "This is good. We call it *bread* in English and *pan* in Español."

Then Ms. Sims picks up other pieces of plastic food—meat, tomatoes, and eggs—and asks Maria to tell her the Spanish name. As Maria tells her the Spanish words, Ms. Sims writes the words down and repeats them to the group. She says, "Carne, tomate, huevos" as she holds each object up and carefully checks her pronunciation with the Latina girls.

The next day, Ms. Sims brings in materials to make menus and adds them to the dramatic play area. She labels all the items in both English and Spanish (color-coding each language) and then makes simple menus in English and Spanish. Throughout the day, children order food, write down orders, serve each other imaginary meals, and chat to each other about the tastes of each item (in both Spanish and English) (Castro, Gillanders, Buysse, & Machado-Casas, 2005).

In American society, literacy is essential for school success, civic participation, and economic stability. It has been defined as "a lifetime process of learning how to take meaning from text. This is a complex process that is always changing as each individual brings new experiences to interact with the text" (Williams, communication, September 2000). In fact, low levels of literacy have been associated with high unemployment, increased welfare dependency, and teenage parenting (Baydar, Brooks-Gunn, & Furstenberg, 1993). The negative consequences for not becoming fluent and literate in English appear early and are persistent across the life span.

One of the primary responsibilities of the American public school system is to teach all children to read fluently in English. The No Child Left Behind Act of 2001 (PL 107-110) requires that each school district assess all students' language and literacy progress annually from fourth through eighth grade (as well as each nonnative English speaker's English proficiency) and document progress toward full English fluency annually. During the last decade, much research has identified early childhood as a critical time for developing skills that lay the foundation for later reading and writing (Bowman, Donovan, & Burns, 2001; International Reading Association [IRA], 2005; Snow, Burns, & Griffin, 1998). We are also learning a great deal about the process of language and literacy development of young children who are English language learners (ELLs)—children whose home language is not English (Espinosa & Burns, 2003; Tabors, 1997; Tabors & Snow, 2001). The need to understand and promote effective teaching practices for young ELLs is urgent for two reasons: 1) There is an explosion of young children who live in homes in which English is not spoken (currently more than 20% of all kindergarten through 12th grade students), and the rate is expected to continue to increase (National Center for Education Statistics [NCES], 2003), and 2) children who have limited fluency in English when they enter school are at greater risk for reading difficulties (Regalado, Goldenberg, & Appel, 2001). An additional cause for concern is recent program evaluation data indicating that some of our early childhood programs may not be as effective for Spanish-speaking children as for English-speaking children. For example, the Head Start National Reporting System (NRS) has revealed that Spanish-speaking children enter and exit the preschool program significantly behind their English-speaking peers on all measures of language and literacy.

This chapter addresses what we know about language and literacy development in young ELLs and what preschool teachers can do to promote literacy learning for all children. What are the early language and literacy skills that are essential for later reading and writing and how can ELLs learn them?

EARLY LITERACY FOR ENGLISH SPEAKERS

Literacy includes listening, orating, reading, and writing and is a continuous learning process that begins during infancy. In the first 3 years of life, oral language development and listening skills play a central role in early literacy development.

Books and environmental print are salient contexts for language and listening. The ability to use symbols is gradually acquired during the first years of life, and at age 3, for example, most children in the United States recognize that golden arches represent McDonald's. Young children learn that certain types of marks (print) represent meanings. Children first think of print as a visual object, then move to the understanding of its symbolic form. Children grasp the notion that one object or event may stand for another well before they start really reading (Marzolf & DeLoache, 1994). Learning that the alphabet is a symbol system for sounds fits into this stream of development.

Much research has identified five interrelated areas that are important during the preschool years for future reading and writing (Snow et al., 1998):

- Alphabetic knowledge

- Phonological awareness

- Book and print concepts

- Vocabulary knowledge

- Discourse skills

These same strands of development are also important for ELLs in the process of learning to speak, read, and write in English. Some of these skills may have been learned in the child's home language and do not need to be relearned, just transferred to the English language system.

EARLY EDUCATION AND CHILDREN FROM DIVERSE BACKGROUNDS

Children from diverse cultural backgrounds can be distinguished by their ethnicity, social class, or language (Au, 1993). Ethnicity usually refers to one's national heritage, although people usually identify their ethnicity with a country of family origin. Social class refers to one's socioeconomic level as reflected in parents' occupations and family income. Children from diverse backgrounds may have a language other than English as their first language.

ELLs are also frequently described as linguistic minority students, or, more recently, as linguistically diverse students. Internationally, it is estimated that there are as many children who grow up learning two languages as one. The number of children enrolled in preschool and Head Start programs whose home language is not English has been steadily increasing over the past 2 decades. During the 2002–2003 program year, 27% of children enrolled in Head Start did not speak English as their home language. Of these, the vast majority were from Spanish-speaking homes, with 139 other language groups also reported.

Most researchers in language development have concluded that the process of learning a second language is similar in quality to learning the first language (Hakuta & Pease-Alvarez, 1992; McLaughlin, 1984, 1998; Tabors, 1997). Becoming a fluent language user, whether first or second, depends on many factors, some within the child and some in the environment. All children have individual differences in personality, motivation, personal experiences, and learning styles. In addition, their exposure to meaningful language, their opportunity to interact with other language users, and their ability to use play to facilitate language development all influence the rate at which a child will acquire a first or second language.

During the first years of life, virtually all typically developing children learn to communicate using language, whatever that language may be. This process begins in infancy and occurs within the context of personal connections and social interaction within the child's family. Preschool children must learn the distinguishing sounds, or phonology, of the language; the grammar and meaning of the language structure; and the pragmatics, or rules of when to use the language. Although this is a monumental task, most 5-year-olds have also mastered the culturally appropriate ways to use language, when and where to speak, under what conditions, and to whom. For example, in the Inuk culture young children are rarely asked to speak alone in front of adults, raise their hands to answer questions individually, or look an adult in the eye (Genesee, Paradis, & Crago, 2004). Throughout the world, all young children are highly motivated to learn to use language appropriately, to communicate, to establish social bonds, and to explore the meaning of their world. The vast majority of children accomplish this task prior to kindergarten.

Young children whose home language is not English must also learn a second language when they enter a preschool setting in which English is the dominant language. They are engaged in what is called the sequential acquisition of a second language, that is, after the basis for the first language has been established.

Learners of a second language already know what language is all about and how to use it to communicate in their immediate environment. Their new task is to learn the particular sounds, grammar, and meaning of the second language. It is important for early childhood professionals to understand that a young child who is learning English as a second language in the school setting is confronted with social, psychological, and cognitive challenges. All the personal and individual challenges that make the learning of a second language difficult are present, in addition to the complex relationships among the status and cultural value between the first and second language. These young learners of a second language can successfully become fluent in English and participate in the social and academic life of the classroom if they are supported in their overall language development and given opportunities to hear, understand, and use their new language (Genesee et al., 2004).

WILL TWO LANGUAGES HELP OR HURT YOUNG CHILDREN?

Research increasingly shows that most young children are capable of learning two languages and that bilingualism confers cognitive, cultural, and economic advantages (Bialystok, 2001; Genesee et al., 2004; Hakuta & Pease-Alvarez, 1992). Bilingualism has been associated with a greater awareness of and sensitivity to linguistic structure, an awareness that is transferred and generalized to certain early literacy and nonverbal skills (Bialystok, 2001). Prior research has shown that preschool-age children can successfully learn two languages and experience multiple cognitive benefits when English acquisition is not at the expense of home language maintenance and development (Bialystok, 2001; Espinosa & Burns, 2003; Rodriguez, Duran, Diaz, & Espinosa, 1995; Winsler, Diaz, Espinosa, & Rodriguez, 1999). In addition to supporting a child's home language, early childhood classrooms can intentionally promote the acquisition of English. When introducing children to English in an early childhood program, however, it is important to implement an *additive* model of English acquisition and not a *subtractive* model in which English is substituted for the home language (Garcia, 2003). When teachers and other school personnel communicate a respect and appreciation for the child's home language and the family continues to use the first language, the child will value and show positive outcomes in both languages.

Children who have the opportunity to speak two languages should be encouraged to maintain both so they can enjoy the linguistic and cultural benefits that accompany bilingual status and cultivate their home language as well as English. Maintaining the home language is essential, not just to the child's future academic and cognitive development, but also to the child's ability to establish a strong cultural identity, to develop and sustain strong ties with his or her immediate and extended families, and to thrive in a global, multilingual world (Garcia, 2003; Wong-Filmore, 1996).

HOW DO CHILDREN LEARN A SECOND LANGUAGE?

It is commonly assumed that preschool-age children can just "pick up" a second language without much effort or systematic teaching. Becoming proficient in a language, however, is a complex and demanding process that takes many years. As with any type of learning, children will vary enormously in the rate at which they learn a first and a second language. The speed of language acquisition is due to factors both within the child and in the child's learning environment. The child's personality, aptitude for languages, interest, and motivation interact with the quantity and quality of language inputs and opportunities for use to influence the rate and eventual fluency levels.

Simultaneous versus Sequential Second-Language Acquisition

Barry McLaughlin and his colleagues (1984, 1995) have made a distinction between children who learn a second language simultaneously or sequentially. When a child learns two languages simultaneously (i.e., before 3 years of age), the developmental pathway is similar to how monolingual children acquire language.

In fact, the majority of young children in the world successfully learn two languages (or more) in the first years of life. In the European Union, 70% of the residents speak more than one language, and 32% successfully speak more than two languages. There is some disagreement in U.S. research literature, however, over whether bilingualism results in a slower rate of vocabulary development than children learning a single language. As children are acquiring two languages and becoming bilingual, one language may dominate. That is normal. It is rare for emerging bilinguals to be equally balanced in the development of both languages (Genesee et al., 2004).

The language development of children who learn a second language after 3 years of age sequentially follows a different progression and is highly sensitive to characteristics of the child as well as the language learning environment. At this point, the basics of the child's first language have been learned. The child knows the structure of one language but now must learn the specific features, grammar, vocabulary, and syntax of a new language. According to Tabors and Snow (1994), sequential second-language acquisition follows a four stage developmental sequence:

1. *Home language use:* When a child has become competent in one language and is introduced to a setting in which everyone is speaking a different language (e.g., an ELL entering an English-dominant preschool classroom), the child will frequently continue to speak his home language even when others do not understand. This period can be short, lasting a few days, or in some cases the child will persist in trying to get others to understand him for months.

2. *Nonverbal period:* After a young child realizes that speaking his home language will not work, he enters a period in which he rarely speaks and will use nonverbal means to communicate. This is a period of active language learning for the child. He is busy learning the features, sounds, and words of the new language (receptive language), but not verbally using the new language to communicate. This is an extremely important stage of second-language learning that may be brief or last a long time. Any language assessments conducted during this stage of development may result in misleading information that underestimates the child's true language capacity.

3. *Telegraphic and formulaic speech:* The child is now ready to start using the new language and does so through telegraphic speech that involves the use of formulas. This is similar to a monolingual child who is learning simple words or phrases (content words) to express whole thoughts. For instance, a child might say, "Me down" to indicate he wants to go downstairs. Formulaic speech refers to unanalyzed chunks of words or sometimes even syllables strung together that are repetitions of what the child has heard. For example, Tabors (1997) reports that ELLs in the preschool she studied frequently used

the phrase, "Look it" to engage others in their play. This is a phrase the children had heard from others who helped to achieve their social goals, even though the children probably did not know the meaning of the two words and were only repeating familiar sounds that were functionally effective.

4. *Productive language:* Now the child is starting to go beyond telegraphic or formulaic utterances to create his or her own phrases and thoughts. Initially, the child may use very simple grammatical patterns such as "I wanna play," but over time he or she will gain control over the structure and vocabulary of the new language. Errors in language usage are common during this period as the child is experimenting with his or her new language and learning its rules and structure.

As with any developmental sequence, the stages are flexible and not mutually exclusive. McLaughlin and his colleagues (McLaughlin, Blanchard, & Osanai, 1995) preferred to describe the process as waves "moving in and out, generally moving in one direction, but receding, then moving forward again" (pp. 3–4).

Sequential bilingual children may have somewhat different patterns of development than monolinguals in certain aspects of language development in the short term. This may include vocabulary, early literacy skills, and interpersonal communication. Young ELLs frequently know fewer vocabulary words in both English and their home language than monolingual children. This may be due to the limited memory capacity of young children or limited exposure to a rich and varied vocabulary. If the child speaks one language in the home and is learning English at preschool, he may also know some words in one language and not the other. For instance, the child may have learned the English words *recess*, *chalk*, *line*, and so forth at school but never learned the corresponding words in Spanish because there was no need or opportunity to do so in the home. However, when the total number of words the child knows in both languages is considered together, most often it is comparable to the number and range of vocabulary words monolingual children know (Genesee et al., 2004).

Code-Switching/Language Mixing

It is important for early childhood educators to understand that code-switching (i.e., switching languages for portions of a sentence) and language mixing (inserting single items from one language into another) are normal aspects of second-language acquisition. This does not mean that the child is confused or cannot separate the languages. The main reason that children mix the two languages in one communication is because they lack sufficient vocabulary in one or both languages to fully express themselves. Research has shown that even proficient adult bilinguals mix their languages in order to convey special emphasis or to establish cultural identity (Garcia, 2003). In any case, code-switching or language mixing is a normal and natural part of second-language acquisition that should not concern parents and teachers. The goal must always be on enhancing communication, rather than on enforcing rigid rules about which language can be used at a given time or under certain circumstances.

Culture and Learning

Culture influences both how a child approaches learning and how the child is socialized into being a reader and writer. Whether a child approaches learning as a cooperative task, emphasizing group understanding and performance or individual achievement, is a function of early cultural learning. All cultural groups share attitudes and beliefs about the uses and values of literacy and have preferred literacy practices. For young children, language development and learning about one's own culture are closely linked. "Culture and linguistic identity provides a strong and important sense of self and family belonging, which in turn supports a wide range of learning capabilities, not the least of which is learning a second language" (Garcia, 1991, p. 2).

There is considerable variation among families in the ways in which they socialize their young children into language and literacy use. There is some evidence that particular cultural groups use distinctive methods in their approaches to early literacy. For instance, in most middle-class nonminority families, the mother assumes the major responsibility for socializing the children into literacy. Mothers typically talk frequently with their babies, share books, and ask questions that call for labels, clarifications, and descriptions of daily activities. They also expect young children to actively participate and construct their own stories (Faltis, 1993; McGee & Richgels, 1996). In contrast, African American families are more likely to share the early caregiving responsibilities among family members and close friends (Heath, 1983). In a carefully documented ethnographic study, Heath revealed that working-class African American families are more likely to socialize their young children to learn by allowing them to observe the adults' actions and conversation rather than by participating in language activities with the children. Thus, children from these backgrounds were less likely to respond appropriately when asked to answer school questions that were of an unfamiliar discourse style. For example, when a child from this home background was asked by a teacher what happened on a recent field trip, the child may just stare blankly at the teacher without responding because he knows the teacher went on the field trip and knows everything that happened. The child may not understand why the teacher is asking a question that she already knows the answer to, and he or she doesn't know what kind of a response the teacher expects. The typical middle-class discourse style of question-and-answer, which translates quite well to the school culture, may not be familiar to a child from a culturally diverse home background.

For young children from culturally and linguistically diverse groups, their early socialization experiences and the accompanying values acquired in their home and community environment frequently may not be those celebrated by the school setting or used as the basis for academic learning and socialization. These discrepancies between the literacy culture of the home and that of the school result in cultural discontinuity for the child and can lead to a feeling of vulnerability for the child (Garcia, 1993; McGee & Richgels, 1996). Children who experience cultural discontinuity between the home and school are more likely to have a negative perception of themselves as a learner, reader, writer, and speaker (Garcia, 1993). Many researchers and multicultural scholars have argued for learning and teaching contexts that are socioculturally and linguistically meaningful for all learners (Au, 1993; Diaz, Moll, & Mehan, 1986; Gee, 1990; Heath, 1986). Improving the continuity between home and school requires culturally responsive curriculum and pedagogy. Culturally responsive approaches include the students' histories, languages, early experiences, and values in the classroom activities and instruction that is "consistent with the students' own cultures and aimed at improving academic learning" (Au, 1993, p. 13). This approach to curriculum would require that teachers understand the communication styles, the cultural values, and the narratives that carry meaning for the children, and make sure they are represented in the literature and instructional strategies of the classroom.

LITERACY FOR ENGLISH LANGUAGE LEARNERS

Children who speak a language other than English in their homes have access (or lack of access) to language and literacy opportunities in their homes, in their communities, and in their preschools. They may be around adults who frequently read to them, have extended conversations with them, point out the features of the alphabet and how words are formed, or they may be growing up in environments with limited early literacy opportunities. It is important to consider how the various settings support acquisition of both the first and the second language, and literacy in both those languages, in predicting likely outcomes. The following is a brief listing of specific teaching strategies that synthesize previous research findings. These teaching strategies focus on strategies around home language development and English language acquisition in light of the importance of cultural sensitivity and the home literacy environment.

Home Language Support

Even when teachers do not speak the child's home language, there are many specific teaching practices they can implement to support primary language development and provide long-term help to build children's primary language literacy skills throughout the day in all kinds of learning situations.

First, the teachers and administrators must agree on the short- and long-term goals of the program. There must be a consensus on the value of supporting the child's home language and the specific type of program that will be provided. Without clarity of goals and agreement about the purposes of language instruction, it is very easy to become confused about teaching strategies and language of instruction when a young child is learning English as a second language. This is of the utmost importance. As has been documented by Oller and Eilers (2002), Páez (2004), and from my own recent training experiences, the current pressures for rapid English acquisition can lead to the tolerance for the loss of home language abilities. This is a serious consequence that can have long-term negative consequences for the child's academic, social, and cultural future. Much research has documented the cognitive, academic, and linguistic benefits of bilingualism when the child achieves advanced levels of language proficiency in both languages as well as the negative consequences when development in either language is discouraged. "Continuous, consistent, and rich exposure to both languages is important to full dual language development" (Genesee et al., 2004, p. 59).

Previous research suggests that the following practices can support the continued development of a home language while children are also acquiring English fluency (Au, 1993; Ballenger, 1999; Espinosa & Burns, 2003; Garcia, 1993; Purcell-Gates & Dahl, 1991; Tabors, 1997):

- Provide bilingual instructional support including paraprofessionals (e.g., instructional assistants, parent volunteers, older students) whenever possible.

- Incorporate children's home language into the daily classroom activities through song, poetry, dance, rhyme, and counting. Create materials in the children's home language to represent familiar stories, songs, or poems that will improve early primary language literacy.

- Have simple print material in the children's home language in learning centers, on labeled objects, and on writing utensils to further support early literacy abilities for non–English speakers. Each language can be printed on different colored paper to help children distinguish between them.

- Encourage parents and other family members to continue to use the home language during family activities and also encourage early literacy development in the primary language.

- If age-appropriate books and stories are available in the child's home language, loan them to parents with encouragement to engage in playful, interactive reading times that will contribute to the child's motivation to read.

- Learn and use words of the students' home language to communicate respect for the home language and culture. However, if you do not speak the child's home language, it is important to pronounce the words correctly.

- Include family members and other community representatives in the classroom to provide language models in the first language. They can tell or read stories, help with translation if they are bilingual, and teach the rest of the class new words.

Effective Classroom and Instructional Approaches

There are many classroom and instructional approaches that have proven effective for ELLs (Carey, 1997; Cazden, 1986; Garcia, 1993; Tabors, 1997). The following items are specific suggestions to support English acquisition for young children who are not native English speakers. These strategies are based on this research and can also promote children's bilingual development if combined with home language support.

- Embed all instruction in context cues that connect words to objects, visuals, and body movements. This is what Tabors (1997) calls "doubling the message." By connecting words with concrete objects and physical movements, teachers can increase the probability that children will understand their meaning.

- A consistent and predictable routine that frequently uses cooperative learning groups, small-group interactions, and regular opportunities for ELLs to converse informally with English speakers supports second-language learning.

- Small peer groups that give children opportunities to learn English in non-threatening, secure environments promote friendships among children who speak different languages.

- Allow children to practice following and giving instructions for basic literacy tasks such as turning pages during reading, using pictures to tell a story, telling a story in sequence, and noting the names of main characters in a story.

- Allow for voluntary participation instead of strictly enforced turn-taking or teacher-led lessons.

- Help young ELLs become a part of the social fabric of the classroom by systematically including a mix of first- and second-language children in organized small-group activities.

- Teach English-speaking children in the classroom to be language resources for second language learners and "act as a catalyst to language development" (Hirschler, 1991, p. 125).

- Have students dictate stories about special personal events.

- Repeat words and directions frequently and explicitly throughout the day, calling attention to their sounds and meanings.

- Modify language use so that it is comprehensible for young second language learners. Make it as simple, direct, and concrete as possible while systematically introducing new words that are unfamiliar.

- Speak at a standard speed with some pausing between phrases, use simple short sentences with clear referents, and use more gestures, movements, and facial expressions to help convey meaning (Carey, 1997).

SPECIFIC STRATEGIES FOR EARLY LITERACY DEVELOPMENT FOR ENGLISH LANGUAGE LEARNERS

In addition to providing explicit and systemic support for ELLs' home language, it is also important and possible to promote early literacy skills in English. The following recommendations will support both goals.

Alphabetic Knowledge

Young ELLs need to learn the English alphabet as they are learning to read and write in English. It is important to determine if the child's home language is based on an alphabetic symbol system and if the child has learned any letters or characters of the home language. If so, then the child already knows that a symbol (e.g., *b*) stands for a letter that has a name corresponding to the sound that is part of the language system, which is made up of many combinations of these sounds. In all preschool classrooms, teachers should engage in activities that focus on letter recognition. These can start with identifying the letters of a child's first name, include singing the alphabet song, and extend to emergent writing activities. These strategies are also important for ELLs in addition to having print in the child's home language and encouraging the child to read and write in the language that he or she is most familiar. Having representations of multiple alphabets or different writing systems (e.g., Chinese characters) helps all children learn the metalinguistic skills associated with bilingualism.

Phonlogical Awareness

Learning to identify the sounds that make up the words in a specific language and how those sounds relate to the letters of the alphabet are also important for ELLs. Some of the more effective activities for children who are in the early stages of acquiring English include using a lot of choral singing in small groups, frequently reading predictable books with attention to the sounds and letters of the vocabulary, and using rhyming books and songs. For ELLs who are reticent to participate, they may need extended periods to watch other children, imitate the sounds and words of the new language privately or in a small group, and have the opportunity to code-switch or make mistakes in a safe and supportive environment.

Book and Print Concepts

ELLs may already know how books work, how the print is read, and what a sentence looks like. These concepts can be learned in any language, and in most languages, the rules are consistent with English books. If books are available in the child's home language, it will be informative to have the child read the book to you to see how much he or she knows about general book reading and handling.

For ELLs, it is important to keep book-reading sessions short and preferably in small groups. Using all of the recommended strategies for making the text comprehensible, the preschool teacher can individualize lessons for ELLs who have varying levels of English fluency.

Vocabulary

Knowing a word in one language does not mean that you will know that word in English; this is one literacy skill that does not transfer from home languages to English. Learning age-appropriate vocabulary in English, therefore, is essential to future reading ability. The more words a child knows, the more conceptual understanding the child will have of the print content as well as specific word sounds and meanings when encountered in print. Teachers of ELLs will need to develop English vocabulary all day long, through introducing new words, explaining word meanings, attaching concrete objects to specific words, highlighting words as they occur, and pointing out how one concept (e.g., "dog") can be presented in different languages. I have found that it is important to be explicit about which language you are using so the children will be able to discriminate between the home language and English.

Discourse Skills

The ability to have extended conversations with multiple turn-taking is important for the development of in-depth conceptual knowledge and abstract learning. This decontextualized language is intrinsic to formal education and is challenging for ELLs. Teachers can tell stories with colorful pictures and include ELLs by asking simple questions. They can also engage them in one-on-one conversations about important events in their lives. Helping ELLs socialize with native English speakers is an effective strategy for promoting conversational English. The dramatic play area requires fairly sophisticated discourse skills and provides a wonderful backdrop for imaginative and decontextualized language development as well as social skills; however, for young children who know very little English, they may need to have more scripted play settings and adult facilitation before they are confident enough to join English-speaking play groups.

Conclusion

Spoken language and reading have much in common. Children's ability to efficiently recognize words using sound–letter correspondence is interconnected with phonological awareness, which in turn is dependent on knowledge of words. These skills are important to the young ELL as well as to the monolingual English-speaking child. Vocabulary, skills in comprehending and producing extended discourses, and knowledge about the world are acquired as parents, teachers, and peers interact with children by having interesting conversations, reading books, telling stories, singing songs, chanting rhymes, and playing, given that these activities take place in a language that the children understand. The most current research suggests that young ELLs are fully capable of learning these skills in more than one language and can capitalize on their linguistic resources by becoming proficient bilinguals. In order to become literate in English, young children do not need to lose their home language. In fact, we all benefit when more children become proficient in multiple languages.

REFERENCES

Au, K.H. (1993). *Literacy instruction in multicultural settings.* New York: Harcourt Brace Publishing.

Ballenger, C. (1999). *Teaching other people's children: Literacy and learning in a bilingual classroom.* New York: Teachers College Press.

Baydar, N., Brooks-Gunn, J., & Furstenberg, F.F. (1993). Early warning signs of functional illiteracy: Predictors in childhood and adolescence. *Child Development, 64*(3), 815–829.

Bialystok, E. (2001). *Bilingualism in development: Language, literacy & cognition.* Cambridge, UK: Cambridge University Press.

Bowman, B.T., Donovan, M.S., & Burns, M.S. (Eds.). (2001). *Eager to learn: Educating our preschoolers.* Washington, DC: National Research Council.

Carey, S. (1997). *Second language learners.* Los Angelcs: Stenhouse Publishers.

Castro, D., Gillanders, C., Buysse, V., & Machado-Casas, M. (2005*). Nuestros niños: Early language & literacy program.* Chapel Hill: The University of North Carolina, FPG Child Development Institute.

Cazden, C. (1986). English as a Second Language (ESL) teachers as language advocates for children. In P. Rigg & D.S. Enright (Eds.), *Children and ESL: Integrating perspectives* (pp. 9–21). Washington, DC: TESOL.

Diaz, S., Moll, L., & Mehan, H. (1986). Sociocultural resources in instruction: A context-specific approach. In Bilingual Education Office, California State Department of Education (Ed.), *Beyond language: Social and cultural factors in schooling language minority students* (pp. 197–230). Sacramento, CA: Author.

Espinosa, L., & Burns, S. (2003). Early literacy for young children and English language learners. In C. Howes (Ed.). *Teaching 4- to 8-year olds: Literacy, math, multiculturalism, and classroom community* (pp. 47–69). Baltimore: Paul H. Brookes Publishing Co.

Faltis, C. (1993). *Joinfostering: Adapting teaching strategies for the multilingual classroom.* New York: Macmillan.

Garcia, E.E. (1991). Caring for infants in a bilingual child care setting. *The Journal of Educational Issues of Language Minority Students, 9,* 1–10.

Garcia, E.E. (1993). The education of linguistically and culturally diverse children. In B. Spodek (Ed.), *Handbook of research on the education of young children* (pp. 372–384). New York: Macmillan.

Garcia, E.E. (2003). *Student cultural diversity: Understanding and meeting the challenge.* Boston: Houghton Mifflin.

Gee, J. (1990). *Sociolinguistics and literacies: Ideologies in discourses.* London: The Falmer Press.

Genesee, F., Paradis, J., & Crago, M. (2004). *Dual language development and disorders: A handbook on bilingualism & second language learning.* Baltimore: Paul H. Brookes Publishing Co.

Hakuta, K., & Pease-Alvarez, L. (1992). Enriching our views of bilingualism and bilingual education. *Educational Researcher, 21,* 4–6.

Heath, S. (1986). Sociocultural context of language development. In California State Department of Education (Ed.), *Beyond language: Social and cultural factors in schooling language minority students* (pp. 143–186). Los Angeles: California State University.

Heath, S.B. (1983). *Ways with words: Language, life, and work in communities and classrooms.* Cambridge University Press.

Hirschler, E. (1991). Preschool children's help to second language learners. *The Journal of Educational Issues of Language Minority Students, 14,* 227–239.

International Reading Association. (2005). *Position statement on literacy in early childhood education.* Newark, DE: Author.

McGee, L.M., & Richgels, D.J. (1996). *Literacy beginnings. Supporting young readers and writers.* Needham Heights, MA: Allyn & Bacon.

McLaughlin, B. (1984). *Second language acquisition in childhood: Preschool children (vol.1).* Hillsdale, NJ: Lawrence Erlbaum Associates.

McLaughlin, B. (1998). *Fostering the development of first and second language development in early childhood.* Sacramento, CA: California Department of Education, Early Childhood Division.

McLaughlin, B., Blanchard, A., & Osani, Y. (1995). *Assessing language development in bilingual preschool children.* Washington, DC: George Washington University.

Marzolf, D.P., & DeLoache, J.S. (1994). Transfer in young children's understanding of spatial representations. *Child Development, 65,* 1–15

National Center for Education Statistics (NCES), (2003). *Young children's access to computers in the home and at school in 1999 and 2000* (NCES 2003–036). Washington, DC: Author.

No Child Left Behind Act of 2001, PL 107-110, 115 Stat. 1425, 20 U.S.C. §§ 6301 *et seq.*

Oller, D.K., & R.E. Eilers (Eds.). (2002). *Language and literacy in bilingual children.* Tonawanda, NY: Multilingual Matters.

Páez, D. (2004). Culturally competent assessment of English language learners: Strategies for school personnel. *Helping children at home and school II: Handouts for families and educators.* Bethesda, MD: National Association of School Psychologists.

Purcell-Gates, V., & Dahl, K.L. (1991). Low SES children's success and failure at early literacy in skills-based classrooms. *Journal of Reading Behavior, 23,* 1–34.

Regalado, M., Goldenberg, C., & Appel, E. (2001). *Beginning reading and early literacy: Building community systems for young children.* Los Angeles: UCLA Center for Healthier Children.

Rodriguez, J.L., Duran, D., Diaz, R.M., & Espinosa, L. (1995). The impact of bilingual preschool education on the language development of Spanish speaking children. *Early Childhood Research Quarterly, 10,* 475–490.

Snow, C.E., Burns, M.S., & Griffin, P. (Eds.). (1998). *Preventing reading difficulties in young children.* Washington, DC: National Academies Press.

Tabors, P.O. (1997). *One child, two languages: A guide for preschool educators of children learning English as a second language.* Baltimore: Paul H. Brookes Publishing Co.

Tabors, P.O. (2002). How can teachers and parents help young bilingual children become (and stay) bilingual? *Head Start Bulletin, 78.*

Tabors, P.O., & Snow, C. (1994). English as a second language in preschools. In F. Genesee (Ed.). *Educating second language children: The whole child, the whole curriculum, the whole community* (pp. 103–125). New York: Cambridge University Press.

Tabors, P.O., & Snow, C.E. (2001). Young bilingual children and early literacy development. In S.B. Neuman & D.K. Dickinson (Eds.), *Handbook of Early Literacy Research.* New York: Guilford Press.

Winsler, A., Diaz, R.M., Espinosa, L., & Rodriguez, J. L. (1999). When learning a second language does not mean losing the first: Bilingual language development in low-income, Spanish-speaking children attending bilingual preschool. *Child Development, 70*(2), 349–362.

Wong-Filmore, L. (1996). What happens when languages are lost? An essay on language assimilation and cultural identity. In D. Slobin, J. Gerhardt, A. Kyratzis, & J. Guo (Eds.), *Social interaction, social context, and language: Essays in honor of Susan Ervin-Tripp* (pp. 435–446). Mahwah, NJ: Lawrence Erlbaum Associates.

Making Vital Home-School Connections

Utilizing Parent Stories as a "Lifeline" for Developing Successful Early Literacy Experiences

PATRICIA A. EDWARDS AND GWENDOLYN THOMPSON MCMILLON

Home literacy environments and interaction patterns between parents and their children serve as contexts in which children learn strategies for literacy development at home and in the classroom. The manner in which these children view and interpret such literacy events influences their social construction of literacy. In other words, parents are a child's first, and most important, teacher. Because of the major influence that parents have on their children's conceptions of literacy, it is imperative that teachers conscientiously make every effort to develop home–school connections.

As experienced literacy researchers, we realize that most teachers understand the importance of developing relationships with their students' parents. They attempt to utilize the "team concept" by including parents in various activities such as field trips, special class projects, and fundraising efforts. Teachers keep parents informed by sending newsletters, conducting curriculum nights, holding parent–student reading and writing workshops, and having parent–teacher conferences. Although many teachers are implementing numerous creative strategies to connect with parents, many parents still do not respond. Communication between school and home for some teachers and parents is little more than a brief wave when students are dropped off or picked up from school. Many teachers might wonder why the parents aren't responding to their requests, whether the parents care about their children's education, if they realize that their children are suffering and need help, what the parents are thinking, where the parents' priorities are, and if the parents have any values at all.

We wrote this chapter to share some discoveries from seminal research. These findings gave rise to develop a practical way to address the communication problem experienced by many teachers and parents. The chapter is divided into two parts. In the first part, specific strategies that will improve teacher–parent communication are discussed. In the second part of the chapter, there is a concrete example from a teacher in the field, which provides evidence from a case study that communication between teachers and parents can be improved, resulting in higher academic achievement and improved classroom behavior.

PATRICIA EDWARDS'S STORY: A TEACHER'S SIMPLE REQUEST, BUT A PARENT'S NIGHTMARE

"Read to your child" is probably the single most frequent request made from teachers and other educators. The importance of reading is advertised on television, in magazines, at conferences, and at school. Few would question the importance of reading aloud to children, but a number of researchers have questioned the feasibility of teachers requesting parents to read to their children when they, themselves, are unable to read. According to the National Center for Educational Statistics (2003), in 2003 the National Assessment of Adult Literacy (NAAL) reported that there were 30 million adult Americans (14% of the population) who could not perform the most basic, simple, and concrete literacy skills; an additional 63 million (29%) could only perform simple and everyday literacy activities. The simple request made by the teacher, "Read to your child," can be a nightmare to parents who cannot read themselves, and can invoke feelings of despair, inadequacy, frustration, and fear. More than 15 years ago in my work with parents at Donaldsonville Elementary School (Donaldsonville, Louisiana), I learned from personal experience how uncomfortable parents felt when teachers asked them to read to their children.

Angela, a 32-year-old African American mother with five children, ranging in age from 22 months to 16 years, shared with me that she became fearful and defensive when her child's teacher requested that she read to her child. The mother quietly admitted to me something that mirrors the reality of some parents:

> I'm embarrassed, scared, angry, and feel completely helpless because I can't read. I do care 'bout my children and I want them to do well in school. Why don't them teachers believe me when I say I want the best for my children? I know that my children ain't done well in kindergarten and first grade and had to repeat them grades. My older children are in the lowest sections, in Title 1, and are struggling in their subjects. My children are frustrated, and I am frustrated, too. I don't know how to help them, especially when the teacher wants me to read to them. These teachers think that reading to children is so easy and simple, but it's hard if you don't know how to read yourself. (Edwards, 1995a, p. 55)

I met with Angela and other kindergarten and first-grade students' parents to talk with them about a series of questions, which are listed here along with their responses:

Edwards: What does reading to your child mean?

Parent 1: I think it means helping your children sound out words.

Parent 2: Reading means opening the book and reading to the end, just try to get the job done. My problem is my children won't sit still.

Parent 3: Could it mean selecting fun books for your child?

Parent 4: I really don't know what teachers mean when they say, "Read to your child."

Edwards: Why do you think your child's teacher often requests that you read to your child?

Parent 1: Because it is good for them, I think.

Parent 2: That's something teachers tell me every year, but they don't tell me what they mean.

Parent 3: Maybe it is something that kindergarten and first-grade teachers just say to parents, I don't know. I get so tired of them saying the same thing every year. I don't even know what they mean, anyway.

Parent 4: Books can help our children learn to speak better.

Edwards: Do you understand what the teacher means when he or she asks you to read to your child?

Parent 1: No, I don't know what the teacher means.

Parent 2: No, I don't know the correct way to begin reading to my child.

Parent 3: I don't know what to do when I open the book. I mean I don't know what to do first, second, third, and so on.

Parent 4: I wish somebody would tell me what to do, because I am fed up with teachers saying, "Read to your child."

Edwards: What difficulties have you encountered when you have attempted to read to your child?

Parent 1: I guess my answer to this question is if you can't read or don't feel comfortable reading, you ain't gonna wanna read to your children.

Parent 2: I try to read, but I guess I am not doing it right. My child becomes bored and not interested in the book, so I quit trying to read.

Parent 3: I don't know what books to read to my child.

Parent 4: Because I don't read well, I don't make time in my schedule. I just pray that they will learn to read in school.

Edwards: Is storybook reading an important part of your daily interactions?

Parents: No, storybook reading is not an important part of my daily interac-
            tions with my child. (This comment was made unanimously by the
            parents.) (Edwards, 1995a, pp. 55–56)

Learning from the Conversation with Parents

Conversations with parents led me to conclude that they wanted their children to
succeed in school, but they did not have a plan for helping them succeed. Perhaps
one of the reasons storybook reading was not an important part of the parents'
daily interactions with their children was that many of them were unable to
assume the responsibility of being their child's first tutor in "unraveling the fascinating puzzle of written language" (Anderson, Hiebert, Scott, & Wilkinson, 1985,
p. 57). As a result, the "global statements teachers [made] to parents about book
reading interactions 'sail[ed] right over their heads,' making it difficult for parents
to translate into practice the much requested teacher directive, 'Read to your
child'" (Edwards, 1995b, p. 269).

Storybook reading meant, as one parent explained, "opening the book and
reading to the end, just to get the job done." Most of the parents appeared not to
know that they could stop before finishing the book. When parents were asked
what they would do if their children did not cooperate, they responded that they
would scold them and/or threaten to punish them, which was discouraged.

The parents were unsure about what to do once they "got into the book."
Directing children's attention to the story, asking questions, and permitting them
to explore the text were storybook-reading behaviors unknown to these parents.
Not surprisingly, the parents were unsure of how to involve their children in the
story. "Do I point to the pictures? Do I say the title of the book?" asked one
father. Other caregivers asked, "What do I do while holding the book?" I also discovered in my conversation with the parents that they did not know how to label
or describe the pictures or to connect items in a book to their child's life, which
implied that these parents could not provide the necessary scaffolding for their
children. The teachers had assumed that these parents had this knowledge.

Perhaps the most revealing insight gained from conversations with the parents was that many of these parents were not competent readers, which supports
France's and Meeks's (1987) contention:

> Parents who do not have basic literacy skills are greatly handicapped in meeting the
> challenge of creating a 'curriculum of the home' to prepare their children to succeed
> in school. Furthermore, they can't help their children build a foundation for liter-
> acy because they are unable to read to them. (p. 222)

Darling (1988) reiterated this point by stating that "Parents who lack basic
literacy skills cannot know the joy of reading a story to their children, and

these children cannot reap the documented educational benefits of being read to" (p. 2).

These comments regarding caregivers who lack basic literacy skills characterized the Donaldsonville Elementary School parents. Also, the comments made by Angela (the African American mother of five children) about storybook reading represented a majority of the parents' thoughts and concerns. The parents felt as Angela did—embarrassed, scared, angry, and helpless because they could not read.

In response, I decided to introduce these parents to book-reading techniques that could help them assist the teacher in building their children's background in reading instruction and correlating the reading program to goals and objectives of the kindergarten and first-grade reading curriculum (Edwards, 1992). Showing these parents how to share books with their children was not to justify a "transmission of school practices" model, in which the only solution, as Auerbach (1989) states, is for nonmainstream families to become acculturated. Instead, I informed the parents of the following:

> Ideally, schools should recognize and incorporate the different patterns and literacy events that characterize nonmainstream communities. For this to happen, however, we need considerably more research—documenting the different types of interaction patterns and literacy events common in nonmainstream communities—and more teacher training. (Edwards & Garcia, 1991, p. 183)

A New Way of Listening to Parents

An action research project with a group of first-grade teachers in Lansing, Michigan was implemented to understand the importance of conducting research on how teachers and parents could connect in ways other than through storybook reading. The teachers were asked to identify a pool of students who were having difficulty learning to read and write and who were at risk of failing the first grade. It is my belief that the first grade is a good place to start investigating how at-risk status is created, and how this impacts students' literacy development. Parents can offer vital insights that may help teachers understand their children's progress in school. When a parent takes a child to the doctor, the doctor is very dependent on the parent's history of the child's illness. Teachers, like doctors, are professionals who need information from parents in order to assist their children. Unfortunately, very few first-grade teachers have a history of a child's literacy development from the parent's point of view. According to Sara Lightfoot (1978),

> First grade is considered the critical period of family–school contact—when mothers are most distressed about releasing their child to the care of a distant person; when school is no longer a world of sand boxes and Play-Doh but a place for learning to read and write; where parents fear the external judgments made about the quality of their parenting during the first 5 years of the child's life; and when the

child experiences the inevitable trauma of moving from a relatively egocentric, nurturing home environment to the more evaluative, social experience of school. (p. 87)

Rita Roth (1984) reiterates Lightfoot's point:

> When children enter first grade, they begin an extended period of compulsory education intended as basic preparation for adult life. The central part of this preparation is the acquisition and application of literacy. Entering what children call 'real school' is perceived as a major event in the lives of children in our culture. It is that bittersweet transition from the world of young child into the world of student. Here the child is taught to read—a crucial step toward acquiring the knowledge our society sees as significant. The meanings children take from this early encounter with school knowledge help to shape their perceptions of themselves as learners, of school learning, and of what society considers valid knowledge. (p. 291)

Roth felt that one way to bridge the gap between home and school or between parents and teachers was to begin designing what Potter (1989) called a "participatory role" for parents. In order to provide a participatory role for parents, I began a year-long study of first-grade students' parents' literacy stories. Over the last 15 years, it appears that "stories are, at long last, coming into their own as a text—a database—for researchers, and I would add for teachers as well" (Edwards, Pleasants, & Franklin, 1999; Jensen, 1989, p. xvi). Vygotsky (1978) has argued for the value of stories.

> Telling stories is a meaning-making process. When people tell stories, they select details of their experience from their stream of consciousness. It is this process of selecting constitutive details of experience, reflecting on them, giving them order, and thereby making sense of them that makes telling stories a meaning-making experience. Every word that people use in telling their stories is a microcosm of their consciousness. (pp. 236–237)

Active listening is a powerful strategy used to understand the increasing challenges presented by students and parents. I call my approach to active listening "parent stories." I define parent stories as the narratives gained from open-ended conversations and/or interviews. In these interviews, parents respond to questions designed to elicit information about traditional and nontraditional early literacy activities and experiences that have happened in the home. Some examples of the questions used to collect parent stories are as follows:

- What do you and your child enjoy doing together?

- All children have potential. Did you notice that your child had some particular talent or "gift" early on? If so, what was it? What did your child do to make you think that he or she had this potential? Were there specific things you did as a parent to strengthen this talent?

- Is there something about your child that might not be obvious to the teacher but might positively or negatively affect his or her performance in school if the teacher knew? If so, what would that something be?

- What activities and/or hobbies do you participate in as an individual? With your spouse or friends? As a family?

- Can you describe something about your home learning environment that you would like the school to build upon because you feel that this something would enhance your child's learning potential at school?

By using stories as a way to express the nature of the home environment, parents can select anecdotes and personal observations from their own individual consciousness to give teachers access to complicated social, emotional, and educational issues that can help teachers unravel the mystery around their students' early literacy beginnings. Still further, many parents have vivid memories about the kinds of routines they performed with their children, specific interactions they had with their children, observations of their children's beginning learning efforts, ways in which their children learned simply by watching them, perceptions as to whether their occupation determined how they raised their children, descriptions of "teachable moments" they had with their children, and descriptions of things about their children that may not be obvious to the teacher but would help their children's performance if the teacher knew about them. In addition, many parents have scrapbooks, audiocassettes, videotapes, photographs, or other artifacts to share their children's literacy history.

Parent stories can provide teachers with the opportunity to gain a deeper understanding of the human side of families and children (e.g., why children behave as they do, children's ways of learning and communicating, problems parents have encountered and how these problems may have impacted their children's views about school and the schooling process). On a final note, I suggested that because teachers' evaluations of students are sometimes based on quick observations, they frequently fail to take into account the experiences that students have brought with them to school. Teachers are thus lacking vital information, which can help them better understand and teach their students (Gonzales, Moll, & Amanti, 2005). Parents can fill in some of the missing pieces by providing stories about their child's early learning experiences at home.

The Importance of Listening to Parent Stories

In her book, *Composing a Life*, Mary Catherine Bateson (1990) suggested that a commonly held assumption—that people's lives progress in single and unwavering lines toward specific goals—is rarely true for most people. She argued instead that we craft our lives, just as painters or poets or musicians craft their works of art, by bringing together various elements and experiences, shaping them to fit our visions, and forming them into a coherent whole. She believed that if teachers were to allow able parents to act like skilled novelists, parents would create stories, and it is through these stories that parents would be able to incorporate even seemingly unconnected "bits and pieces" about their children into a cohesive literacy life story. And, because the process of composing a life is ongoing and requires a "continual reimagining of the future and reinterpretation of the past to give meaning to the present" (Bateson, 1990, p. 29), parent stories are evolving. Metzger (1986) offered a similar analysis of why stories are a useful way for parents to share information with the teacher about their child:

> Stories go in circles. They don't go in straight lines. So it helps if you listen in circles because there are stories inside stories and stories between stories, and finding your way through them is as easy and hard as finding your way home. And part of the finding is the getting lost. If you're lost, you really start to look around and listen. (p. 104)

I feel that inviting parents to tell their stories will, in turn, invite and encourage teachers to really listen to parents in the way that Metzger has described. Inviting parents to tell their stories shifts the order of relationship between teachers and parents. Parents become the "more knowledgeable other" about their child, especially when it comes to interpreting and describing their child's home environment and the role they play in preparing their child for school. Through the telling of these stories, parents are recognized (whether they are literate or not) as experts in describing and interpreting methods and codes used in their home environment that may be invisible to teachers. This is especially important given the perspective that parents and school teachers are a child's first and second most important teachers—parents must have the opportunity to give teachers personal information that may help teachers to understand how children can learn best in their classroom.

GWENDOLYN THOMPSON McMILLON'S STORY: AN EXAMPLE FROM THE FIELD—"HERE'S HOW AND HERE'S WHY"

Concerned about home–school disconnections, I shared Edwards's idea of collecting parent stories with some teachers in the field. The following is one of those stories.

Mrs. Warren has been teaching first grade for 3 years at Cramer Elementary School, where 47% of the students receive free or reduced lunch. At Cramer Elementary, some of the students are lacking in some basic literacy skills. Some of the students have never been read to at home, but Mrs. Warren decided when she first started working that she was going to do everything in her power to help every one of her students become good readers and writers.

When Matt first entered Mrs. Warren's classroom this year, he immediately caught her eye. Matt was a well-dressed young man who, at first glance, appeared to be ready for school. He was behaved and quiet most of the time. Matt seemed to enjoy all of the read-alouds, but never volunteered to answer questions. Mrs. Warren gives all of her students assessments, including the Michigan Literacy Progress Profile, during the first week of school to determine their strengths and weaknesses before formal instruction begins. This year, many of her students scored at or above their grade level because most of them attended preschool and kindergarten at Cramer Elementary. By the time they reached first grade, they have already had 2 years of formal schooling. However, Matt did not attend Cramer's preschool or kindergarten. He had recently moved into the neighborhood.

Mrs. Warren used state standardized assessments to evaluate alphabet recognition, concepts of print, phonemic awareness, sight-word decoding, and sentence dictation. She noticed that Matt became frustrated after the first few minutes. He only knew six letters. He did not give correct answers to any of the questions in the other categories, and was unable to write anything during the sentence dictation. After the assessment, he looked at Mrs. Warren and said, "Will I learn how to read today? I want to learn how to read." Touched by his eagerness and willingness to learn, Mrs. Warren responded, "It takes a little while to learn to read, Matt, but I promise you will learn." That day during the read-aloud after lunch, Matt hurried to sit next to Mrs. Warren. He raised his hand to participate in the discussion even though he did not know the answers to the questions. Each time he gave an answer, Mrs. Warren would say, "Good try, Matt," or she would take his comment and use revoicing techniques to scaffold his response effort. She would simply add words to his statements for clarification purposes.

When Mrs. Warren gave homework, Matt usually did not get it done. She would ask him about his homework. He told her he didn't get a chance to do it. She asked him to have his mother call her. Matt would smile and say, "Okay, Mrs. Warren, I'll tell her." She would send notes home and there was never a response. Finally, Mrs. Warren decided to take the advice of the researcher conducting research in her school and make an appointment to collect a parent story. She left the time and date of the appointment on the answering machine because no one ever answered the telephone. She was pleasantly surprised to see Matt's father enter her classroom after school to meet with her.

Mrs. Warren explained that she wanted to audiotape their conversation rather than take notes while they were talking. Mr. Stanza agreed to be taped during the interview.

Here's Mr. Stanza's story:

I lost my wife 3 years ago, and we moved here to be closer to my family because I needed help with Matt. I read over the questions that you want me to answer for you today. Let me show you what I have. Here's a photo album of my family before my wife died. My wife read to him every day. Matt loved to read books over and over and over again. Shelley died when Matt was 2 years old, and every time we would try to read, I would fall apart. It was just easier to stop reading. The preschool and kindergarten teachers at Matt's old school did not focus on academics. Matt never had any homework or anything like that. I know that he's behind the kids around here because my mother told me that most teachers give homework. What can I do to help Matt? Is it too late for him? I have my mother and my sister to help him now, but I know he's my responsibility.

Mrs. Warren immediately went to work to develop an intensive plan to help Matt. She shared her parent story with several colleagues and asked them for help. Her goal was to bring Matt at least up to grade level by the end of the school year. She would focus on alphabet recognition, concepts of print, phonemic awareness, sight-word decoding, sentence dictation, storybook reading and response, and expository text comprehension strategies.

Because the initial assessments showed that her students were at different levels, Mrs. Warren knew that it would be necessary to implement differentiated instruction in her classroom. Many researchers have written on the importance of implementing instructional strategies that address the varied levels and learning styles of students (Banks et al., 2000; Irvine & Armento, 2001; Marzano, 2003; McKinley, 2003). Mrs. Warren's colleagues suggested that she continue organizing her literacy instruction around the Four Blocks Classroom (Cunningham, Hall, & Defee, 1998). The Four Blocks include guided reading, working with words, writing blocks, and self-selected reading. It would be necessary to scaffold Matt's learning in various ways, but it was also important that he be allowed to intermingle with the other students as much as possible.

Mrs. Warren sponsored a parent–student reading workshop night for all of her parents. She called Mr. Stanza to invite him personally. She also asked him to bring his mother and sister. The workshop was a complete success. Thirteen parents attended with their children, along with Mr. Stanza, his mother, his sister, and Matt. Mrs. Warren explained the importance of reading to children. She had everyone practice going through all of the different steps of adult–child interactive reading. She passed out a reminder sheet that listed important questions to ask children when reading, such as making sure they can point to the front cover, the back cover, and title page. Questions about making predictions and questions about illustrations were also included. Mrs. Warren emphasized the importance of facial expression, voice animation, and repeated readings. Parents were given an opportunity to practice with their children. Matt felt exceptionally special because he had "three" parents in attendance.

With his father, his grandmother, and his aunt reading to Matt at home, Mrs. Warren felt confident that concepts of print and storybook reading would be covered at home. In class, Mrs. Warren would occasionally ask questions related to the topics as a review for the other students and also as an authentic assessment for Matt. She observed him becoming more confident as he gave more correct answers.

When implementing guided reading, Mrs. Warren put Matt in a group with two other struggling readers. She taught them how to use graphic organizers to get their ideas on paper. Initially they were allowed to draw pictures that represented their ideas, but as time went by, they began writing words. Sometimes Mrs. Warren would use the guided reading time to conduct a read-aloud related to the topic and/or theme from an expository text. She was determined to help them become familiar with reading and writing about informational text.

Working with words began as a way to focus on alphabet recognition and phonemic awareness. Mrs. Warren used magnetic letters, letter die, flash cards, and other manipulatives to motivate Matt to learn the alphabet. While learning the alphabet, he also learned letter sounds using word sorts and picture sorts. Mrs. Warren sent a traveling book bag home every day with assignments related to alphabet recognition and phonemic awareness. After about 6 weeks of intense learning, Matt knew the alphabet and the letter sounds, and he began making words. He made his own personal word-wall glossary book and convinced his dad to play word-wall bingo almost every night. He learned most of the sight words in his personal word-wall glossary before Thanksgiving.

Although Matt focused on alphabet recognition and letter sounds, he was also required to write the letters as he learned them. When he moved to learning sight words, he was also required to write them. In addition to writing letters and sight words, Matt was encouraged to keep a journal. He wrote in his journal every day at home. Mr. Stanza was really beginning to see improvement in Matt's writing. Mrs. Warren also began dictating sentences to Matt during his writing block. She also had some of his friends in the class dictate sentences.

By the end of the first semester, Matt was almost reading at a first-grade level. His teacher, dad, grandmother, and aunt were very proud, but most importantly, Matt was proud of himself. For Christmas, Matt received a lot of presents, but his favorite presents were the books he received. During self-selected reading, Mrs. Warren noticed that Matt was beginning to choose books that were at higher reading levels.

Matt finished the first grade at a third-grade reading level. His story has a happy ending because his teacher, Mrs. Warren, reached out to his dad, who reached back in return. Together, they bridged the gap between home and school. Mr. Stanza's parent story was the lifeline necessary for Mrs. Warren to develop practical ways to help Matt have successful early literacy experiences at home and at school.

CONCLUSION

Not all parents and teachers hold answers to their children's literacy problems, but by combining the knowledge of both of these groups of people, we will have a more complete picture of children's home and school lives.

The story approach also empowers parents by giving them the chance to participate in their child's education in a personally meaningful way—one that respects the family's viewpoint. As parents and schools continue to wrestle with vast challenges—changing family demographics, time constraints, cultural divides, privacy issues, and, of course, economics—stories remain a nonthreatening and practical vehicle for collaboration.

REFERENCES

Anderson, R.C., Hiebert, E., Scott, J.A., & Wilkinson, I.A.G. (1985). *Becoming a nation of readers: The report of the commission of reading.* Washington, DC: The National Institute of Education.

Auerbach, E.R. (1989). Toward a social-contextual approach to family literacy. *Harvard Educational Review, 59,* 165–181.

Banks, J.A., Cookson, P., Gay, G., Hawley, W., Irvine, J.J., Nieto, S., et al. (2000). *Diversity within unity: Essential principles for teaching and learning in a multicultural society.* Seattle: University of Washington Center for Multicultural Education, College of Education.

Bateson, M.C. (1990). *Composing a life.* New York: Plume Books.

Cunningham, P.M., Hall, D.P., & Defee, M. (1998, May). Nonability grouped, multilevel instruction: eight years later. *Reading Teacher, 51*(8), 652.

Darling, S. (1988). *Family literacy education: Replacing the cycle of failure with the legacy of success.* Washington, DC: Office of Educational Research and Improvement. (ERIC Document Reproduction Service No. ED332749).

Edwards, P.A. (1992, Autumn). Involving parents in building reading instruction for African-American children. *Theory Into Practice, 31*(4), 350–359.

Edwards, P.A. (1995a). Combining parents' and teachers' thoughts about storybook reading at home and school. In L.M. Morrow (Ed.), *Family literacy: Multiple perspectives to enhance literacy development* (pp. 54–60). Newark, DE: International Reading Association.

Edwards, P.A. (1995b). Connecting African American families and youth to the school's reading program: Its meaning for school and community literacy. In V.L. Gadsden & D. Wagner (Eds.), *Literacy among African American youth: Issues in learning, teaching, and schooling* (pp. 263–281). Cresskill, NJ: Hampton Press.

Edwards, P.A., & Garcia, G.E. (1991). Parental involvement in mainstream schools. In M. Foster (Ed.), *Readings on equal education: Qualitative investigations into schools and schooling* (pp. 167–187). New York: AMA Press, Inc.

Edwards, P.A., Pleasants, H.M., & Franklin, S.H. (1999). *A path to follow: Learning to listen to parents.* Portsmouth, NH: Heinemann.

France, M.G., & Meeks, J.W. (1987). Parents who can't read: What the schools can do. *Journal of Reading, 31,* 222–227.

Gonzales, N., Moll, L.C., & Amanti, C. (2005). *Funds of knowledge: Theorizing practice in households, communities, and classrooms.* Mahwah, NJ: Lawrence Erlbaum Associates.

Irvine, J.J., & Armento, B.J. (2001). *Culturally responsive teaching: Lesson planning for elementary and middle grades.* New York: McGraw-Hill.

Jensen, J.M. (1989). Preface. In J.M. Jensen (Ed.), *Stories to grow on: Demonstrations of language learning in K–8 classrooms* (pp. xv–xx). Portsmouth, NH: Heinemann.

Lightfoot, S.L. (1978). *Worlds apart: Relationships between families and schools.* New York: Basic Books.

Marzano, R.J. (2003). *What works in schools: Translating research into action.* Alexandria, VA: Association for Supervision and Curriculum Development.

McKinley, J. (2003). Leveling the playing field and raising African American students' achievement in 29 urban schools. *New Horizons for Learning.* Retrieved August 27, 2007, from http://www.newhorizons.org/strategies/differentiated/mckinley.htm

Metzger, D. (1986). Circles of stories. *Parabola, IV* (4).

National Center for Educational Statistics. (2003). *Key concepts and features of the 2003 National Assessment of Adult Literacy.* Washington, DC: U.S. Department of Education, Institute of Education Sciences.

Roth, R. (1984). Schooling, literacy acquisition, and cultural transmission. *Journal of Education, 166*(3), 291–308.

Potter, G. (1989). Parent participation in the language arts program. *Language Arts, 66*(1), 21–28.

Vygotsky, L.S. (1978). *Mind in society: The development of higher psychological process.* Cambridge, MA: Harvard University Press.

The Book Matters

Evaluating and Selecting What to Read Aloud to Young Children

WILLIAM H. TEALE, JUNKO YOKOTA, AND MIRIAM MARTINEZ

On a sunny, late September morning at Learning Adventures, Ms. Tatum had finished reading aloud *That Pesky Rat* (Child, 2002) to her group of twelve 4-year-olds. "I just don't get it," she said. "That didn't go well at all. They didn't seem to get much out of it. Usually Derek and LaBron have a lot to say, and Heather doesn't have a problem paying attention like she did today." Ms. Tatum was right, the read-aloud did not go well. And it was certainly different from what had happened 2 weeks earlier when she and the same children spent a little more than 15 minutes reading and talking about *The Chick and the Duckling* (Ginsburg, 1972). During read-aloud, each of the children individually contributed something to the discussion at least once, and there were also numerous group responses. The children's contributions included predictions on three different occasions about what the chick would do next, comments about whether or not a chick could catch a butterfly, reactions to the chick's jumping in the water, and discussion of the issue of copying what other people do.

Subsequent observations of read-alouds in Ms. Tatum's classroom led to the conclusion that the main factor contributing to the comparative lack of instructional value in the read-aloud of *That Pesky Rat* was the book itself, rather than other potential factors like time of day, teacher reading style, or child-centered issues such as tiredness and illness. Simply put, *That Pesky Rat*, as wonderful a book as it is, is not well suited to be read aloud to a group of preschool children because its complicated format and design and the unusual use of print make the book something that children cannot readily follow in a group read-aloud experience.

Ms. Tatum is a good preschool teacher, and she is aware of the need for appropriate attention to literacy in a prekindergarten classroom. At any given time, she has a classroom library stocked with approximately 75 children's books.

Most of the books are titles that children's literature experts would recommend or at least recognize; there are not many mass-market books or books based on popular culture fads. Ms. Tatum reads to her children on a regular basis. But even with her high degree of awareness and her commitment to reading aloud as an instructional activity, it turned out that she did not regularly reflect on her read-aloud selections. Ms. Tatum tended to rely on books that she had used in the past, what the children occasionally brought in, and recommendations she got from colleagues or at the periodic Child Development Associate workshops she attended.

Teale (2003) discussed four features that affect the degree of "instructional power" read-alouds actually provide in the classroom: 1) how much to read aloud, 2) what to read aloud, 3) how to read aloud, and 4) the place of reading aloud in the curriculum. As we looked more closely into read-alouds in early childhood class-rooms, we came to realize that, of these four features, the topic of what to read aloud has received very little attention in research and in teacher preparation and/or professional development information. As a result, in this chapter we offer guidelines for preschool teachers to consider in evaluating and selecting books for classroom read-alouds with young children.

WHY THE BOOK MATTERS FOR CLASSROOM READ-ALOUDS

Reading aloud can significantly enhance young children's background knowledge, vocabulary, concepts about print, familiarity with different text structures, and even their phonological awareness, letter knowledge, and sight-word knowledge. It also serves as the foundation for developing a lifelong joy of reading. But the degree to which reading aloud succeeds in accomplishing any of these goals, we believe, begins with the books the teacher selects to read aloud.

Over the course of a year, most preschool teachers read aloud hundreds of books to their children. The quality and content of these books make an impact on children; therefore, book evaluation and selection is something to consider carefully. Two issues are especially central to choosing the books to be read aloud. First is the general question of what makes a book a good book for reading aloud to young children. Literary quality, book design features, and the curricular role the book plays all figure in the mix. Second is selecting books that, over the course of time, offer the children a range of topics and genres so that important content and individual interests can both be addressed.

FEATURES OF A GOOD BOOK FOR READING ALOUD

High Literary Quality

It is not easy to find an agreed upon definition of the term *quality literature*, but we like to think of a good book as one in which one (or more) of its elements "sparkle." That is, in a quality picture book, all of the elements are crafted successfully and at least one of them is distinctive and memorable.

Especially important to consider when looking for quality stories for preschoolers are the following literary elements (Temple, Martinez, & Yokota, 2006):

- *Plot:* The sequence of action that propels the story. Young children want to know how the problem in a story will be solved. In exciting stories such as *Harry and the Terrible Whatzit* (Gackenbach, 1977) or in humorous stories such as *The Wolf's Chicken Stew* (Kasza, 1987), children get caught up in predicting what characters will do. What is the terrible "whatzit"? Will the wolf really eat the chicken he is trying to fatten up? The plots of such stories build suspense and hold children's attention.

- *Setting:* The time and place in which the events of a story occur. Setting is established through a rich description of a place. Setting "sparkles" in a book such as Ezra Jack Keats' *The Snowy Day* (1962). The weather changes the landscape, and the text details all the ways in which Peter goes out into the snowy day to play. Setting is clearly the reason for the events of Peter's day, and when listeners close their eyes, they can just imagine what the snowy day must have looked like.

- *Character:* The people created by the words of the book. Preschoolers remember and relate to vivid characters, characters who come alive for them such as Big Anthony, who doesn't pay attention and suffers the consequence of his inattentiveness in *Strega Nona* (dePaola, 1975); Chrysanthemum (Henkes, 1991), who reacts to her classmates' teasing of her name; and Wemberly (Henkes, 2000), who constantly worries in ways that preschoolers can relate. When reading stories about Everett Anderson (Clifton, 1983, 1987, 1992, 2001) or poems about Danitra Brown (Grimes, 1994, 2002), young children may feel that they, too, are friends of Everett or Danitra because their characterizations are so vivid.

- *Theme:* The central idea that a story brings to a reader's consciousness. Even young children like to think about issues that matter in their lives, and many books hold the potential for engaging them in rich discussion. For instance, most preschoolers have a great deal to say about whether the hen in *The Little Red Hen* (Galdone, 1979a) was justified in not sharing the bread with her friends, and they also find the issues of honesty and doing the best they can that feature prominently as themes in *The Empty Pot* (Demi, 1990) something important to talk about.

- *Interesting language:* The authors' uses of attention-grabbing vocabulary and literary language, as well as fun rhythms and language patterns. Playing with language is a hallmark of preschool experiences, and text that includes interesting uses of language supports such experiences. A good example is

William Steig, whose appealing stories such as *Sylvester and the Magic Pebble* (1969) or *Doctor De Soto* (1982) feature a wide range of rich words that children enjoy using and learning. For just plain fun language, a story such as David McPhail's *Pigs Ahoy!* (1995), a predictable book such as *Who Took the Cookies from the Cookie Jar?* (Lass & Sturges, 2000), or a book such as *The Cow that Went Oink* (Most, 1990) that plays inventively with language, all involve young children in using and thinking about words and language patterns.

In addition, there are distinct criteria for examining expository books. Accuracy, clarity, interpretation, and visual presentation of information are important aspects to examine. When the book is narrative nonfiction, however (i.e., information presented through the format of a story), the elements to consider overlap, to some extent, with literary elements. Many informational books for preschoolers fall into this latter category.

- *Accuracy, clarity, and interpretation of information:* Young children are very interested in the people and the world around them. A book such as *Houses and Homes* (Morris, 1995) shows preschoolers how people all over the world live in different types of homes and makes the information come alive through realistic photographs and simple text that preschoolers can understand. As a bonus, a double-page spread at the end of the book provides additional information about each one of the houses and homes depicted in the photographs that the teacher may want to use in discussion with the children.

- *Visual presentation of information:* Charts, diagrams, graphs, and other forms of visually presented information should be clear, accurate, and easy to interpret. Similarly, illustrations must reflect a true representation of the information depicted. *Ducks Don't Get Wet* (Goldin, 1965/1989) is an example of a carefully crafted information book. This book contains paintings of a variety of ducks, each shown in remarkable detail. In addition, at the end of the book the author includes directions for an experiment children can conduct under the supervision of an adult. These directions are accompanied by easy-to-follow drawings that guide young children through each step of the experiment. *Jelly Beans for Sale* (McMillan, 1996) is more of a concept book, but it presents information about numbers, money, and coins in an interesting, developmentally appropriate way. The book shows different numbers of jelly beans for sale at one cent each. A chart at the beginning of the book shows the front and back of each coin, its name (e.g., penny, nickel, dime), and the value of each coin in terms of number of cents. On various pages, there are different combinations of coins that face outstretched hands holding the number of jelly beans that the coins are worth. At the back of the book is another chart showing the colors of jelly beans and the flavors each color represents.

- *Literary elements such as character, setting, and theme:* Biographies are books about real people and can introduce vivid characters in descriptive settings much the same as fictionalized stories. Narrative informational books embed information about a topic in a story format, so literary criteria as well as informational text criteria must be applied to them. For example, in *Mouse Paint* (1989) and *Mouse Count* (1991), both by Ellen Stoll Walsh, the concept of primary colors mixing to create secondary colors and the concept of counting up and then back down are both presented through a story about mice. The quality of the story is considered by applying literary criteria while the information is considered through expository text criteria.

Having reviewed the preceding factors that contribute to book quality, we also should point out one more feature for teachers to take into account, no matter what type of book is being considered. It is a feature that is somewhat difficult to name, but, as has been said of certain other phenomena, you know it when you see it. And children know it when they see it: It is a book that is vivid and comes alive when they read. In other words, an informational book may contain accurate and clear information but be deadly dull. Likewise, there are plenty of published stories that are not really engaging to most young children because the plot isn't compelling, the characters aren't interesting, and so forth. Evaluation and selection of any read-aloud book should include close consideration of whether it is a work that will engage children in its story or in the information it offers.

Finally, as part of this discussion of quality, it is useful to consider the place of mass-availability books in the classroom—the types of books sold in supermarkets and by major retailers. Often, these books are not characterized by being of high quality on any of the dimensions just discussed. The mass-availability books based on movies and television shows tend to be especially disappointing in terms of literary quality. Nonetheless, given that many families have easy access to these books and some families have access to *only* such books at home, it makes sense to try to steer children toward the ones that are relatively well written. Books such as the Berenstain Bears series and Golden Books have long been popular. This is particularly important when considering that if children recognize books in the stores that they have seen in the classroom, they will be more likely to choose ones that are relatively well written to have at home.

Applying the quality indicators just discussed for storybooks and informational books thus helps in identifying good works of all types, and getting the best books possible into children's hands in the classroom is always our goal. But we should also remember that although high quality is a necessary criterion, it is not the only criterion for deciding whether to use a book as a read-aloud. In other words, a book may be a good book, even a great book, but may not be a good read-aloud book, as the opening example of Ms. Tatum's use of *That Pesky Rat* illustrated. In addition to literary quality, two more factors should be carefully considered: 1) the book's design features and 2) your curricular reasons for using the book.

Design Features

In addition to the words of the text and the illustrations themselves, a number of elements contribute to the overall design—and thus the effect—of a picture book. Size and shape of the book, the endpapers, font, the amount of white space, whether the illustrations bleed to the edge of the page or not, type of paper— these and other elements contribute to book's design. There are three design features related to a book's read-aloud suitability that are especially important for teachers to consider: illustration-text relationships, illustration size and complexity, and interactive design features.

Illustration-Text Relationships

When we read aloud to a group of children, the illustrations in a book are especially important because they serve as a key focal point of the children's attention. Some books are particularly well suited as read-alouds because of the way that the text and the illustrations work together. In these books, each element contributes something to the effect of the book that the other does not. The text tells part of the overall story the book conveys, and the illustration tells another part. Together, they provide listeners with an experience that is more than either of the two separate parts. For example, the humor in a book such as *Don't Let the Pigeon Drive the Bus!* (Willems, 2003) comes from the illustrations and the way they define and amplify the text. The text moves this story along, but the illustrations give the story its personality. Willems's drawings are done by using limited strokes and muted colors, and his depictions of the pigeon's eyes and body flawlessly capture the range of emotions the pigeon expresses throughout the book.

Some books for young children do not have enough text, or their texts are not engaging enough by themselves. With these books, the illustrations offer opportunities for teachers to engage children in discussing various elements of visual literacy. In situations in which there is limited text, the text can prompt children to offer additional language, or the teacher can use this opportunity to talk about the illustrations and to teach children to be visually attentive.

Illustration Size and Complexity

Children want to see the pictures in a picture book, and because comprehension of a picture book depends on the illustrations as well as the text, children need to be able to see them if a read-aloud is to be successful. Notice that the size and clarity of the illustrations in books such as Robert McCloskey's *Make Way for Ducklings* (1941) or Eric Carle's *The Very Hungry Caterpillar* (1981) are such that even in a large-group setting, children can see and process them. Even the white space in these books is important in helping to make the illustrations more focused and visible from a distance. Compare them with the illustrations in a book such as *The Tale of Peter Rabbit*, designed by author/illustrator Beatrix Potter (1902/1986) to be one of her "little books for little hands," which is clearly intended for individual children to hold and enjoy alone. Or consider a typical Steven Kellogg illustrated book, *The Mysterious Tadpole* (2002), which is a very engaging story to most preschoolers. The illustrations are wonderfully busy, inviting a child or pair of children to pore over the details, yet those same details make the illustrations unclear from a distance. These aforementioned books are all wonderful books for young children, and we highly advocate their use in the preschool classrooms, but when reading to a large or even small group of preschoolers, the clarity of the illustrations and the sheer size of the book make it more or less appropriate for sharing with a group. Of course, a number of children's books are available in a big book format. The more successful of the transitions to this large format are books that are clearly the right books for sharing with a group of children. But many regular-sized books work well for group read-alouds. The task is to identify the books with illustrations appropriate to sharing in a small- or large-group setting.

Interactive Design Features

Many books for preschoolers have features such as pull tabs, flaps, or pop ups built into them that get children to interact physically with the book. Generally speaking, books like these do not make good read-alouds. The reason is that their success with a reader depends on the reader manipulating the book through direct and sustained contact with it. But books with very simple interactive features can work as read-alouds. Think about, for instance, *Where's Spot?* (Hill, 1980), which has simple flaps to be lifted, each answering the question of where the dog might be found. The teacher can readily and effectively lift the flaps in a group setting, or individual children could be given the opportunity to do so. Likewise, the reissued *Dear Zoo* by Rod Campbell (2005) has preschoolers anticipating which animals might be under the flap of each type of container sent to the zoo. Many of Eric Carle's books also have playful features—holes, cut-out shapes, chirping noises, and so forth—and his books have long been among the those most often, and most successfully, used for preschool read-alouds.

CURRICULAR REASONS FOR READING THE BOOK ALOUD

To determine if a book is a good read-aloud book for you and your group of children, it is important to consider your own instructional goals: What do you want students to get out of this? In some cases, you will hope to connect to the content knowledge of the unit or theme being taught. Perhaps you want to develop listening skills. Perhaps you like the ways in which the book supports children's ability to think and discuss. Many teachers find that sharing a good read-aloud together and discussing it develops a sense of community. Other books are best enjoyed purely for pleasure. For example, when there are only 5 minutes left before the end of the school day, reading a purely pleasurable book is a worthwhile experience in and of itself. In other words, not every book must have an instructional goal in order for it to be a good selection. Keeping instructional goals in mind, however, when selecting a book for a read-aloud and following through with an appropriate discussion, and other educational activities that complement the book, to maximize the learning opportunities for children is critically important. Not focusing on instructional goals may lead to lost opportunities when the follow-up to the read-aloud fails to address what the children need to learn and instead focuses only on what is entertaining and fun.

TYPES OF BOOKS TO INCLUDE IN THE READ-ALOUD REPERTOIRE

Just as we strive to provide children's bodies with a balanced diet of food, so should we strive to provide children with a balanced diet of books for their minds. The following are different types of books a teacher can make part of the read-aloud repertoire in order to offer a healthy mix that promotes children's thinking and also considers individual interests and needs.

Narrative and Informational Books

Narratives—stories—are an essential part of what makes us human. Our lives are, in many respects, stories. Stories serve as a means of passing along the traditions, values, and beliefs of various cultures, as well as a way for children to explore issues and interpersonal relationships that help them learn about living with others in the world. Also, stories—whether in the written form or from the oral tradition—are an integral part of every culture.

Stories typically are the foundation of what we read aloud to preschoolers. There are literally thousands of good narrative books available for young children in the United States. These stories originate from many different cultures, countries, and ways of life, and they appear in various forms: traditional literature, fantasy, and realistic fiction. Tried and true favorites such as *Blueberries for Sal* (McCloskey, 1948), *Petunia* (Duvoisin, 1950), *Ask Mr. Bear* (Flack, 1968), and *The Three Billy Goats Gruff* (Galdone, 1979b) still make for great read-alouds. More recent books like *Beautiful Blackbird* (Bryan, 2003), *The Hatseller and the Monkeys* (Diakite, 1999), *A Beasty Story* (Martin, 1999), *The Trip Back Home* (Wong, 2000b), and *How I Became a Pirate* (Long, 2003) are every bit as engaging and appropriate for preschoolers.

In addition to stories, it is important for preschool teachers to include a rich array of informational texts in what is read aloud to preschoolers. Until recently, relatively few informational books appropriate for young children were available. We still do not have as great a number or variety of good information books for preschoolers as we have stories, but at least there is now a good selection of books that present various topics of interest to young children in ways that make the information readily accessible. For example, *Chameleon, Chameleon* (Cowley, 2005) brings chameleons to life through beautiful photographs and simple text, and *Actual Size* (Jenkins, 2004) is engaging to young children because it introduces them to diversity in nature through pictures of various animals or their body parts (e.g., foot of an elephant, face of a tiger) that show their actual size. Other informational books help children learn more about the human experience. Through the simple text and wonderful photographs in *Bread, Bread, Bread* (Morris, 1989), children discover the different kinds of bread people eat around the world, as well as a little bit about how people around the world live. Even some of the early reader (controlled vocabulary) information books make good read-alouds for preschoolers. *A Bed for Winter* (Wallace, 2000), for instance, follows a mouse to the beds of several different animals as they prepare for the change of seasons.

It is important for preschool teachers to be aware that there is a preponderance of narrative informational books available, but that there are still relatively few books with straightforward expository text appropriate for young children. In fact, we found that of the higher quality straight expository texts for preschoolers, many were written prior to 1980. The key thing to remember is this: While engaging children in discussions about informational books, teachers should sort out the discussion about the story from the information that is presented, thus helping children separate fact from fiction.

In addition to books that provide information on a variety of subjects, accounts of people's lives—biographies, autobiographies, and partial biographies—can work well as informational read-alouds for preschoolers. Most young children are very interested in the lives of people—famous people, local celebrities, and even unsung heroes whose deeds are fascinating to learn about. Such books let them think about the choices people make and how they overcome difficulties in trying to accomplish their goals. *Martin's Big Words* (Rappaport, 2001), for instance, introduces young children to one of the major figures of the Civil Rights Movement. Or, in a different realm, children familiar with the picture books of Lois Ehlert will enjoy finding out more about this author and her work in *Under My Nose* (Ehlert, 1996).

Concept Books

Concept books "convey knowledge, answering the question 'What's that?'" (Temple et al., 2006, p. 151). They are written about a wide range of topics—everything from colors and shapes (e.g., *Color Zoo*, Ehlert, 1989) to types of machines (e.g., *Machines at Work*, Barton, 1987) to relative size (e.g., *Is It Larger? Is It Smaller?*, Hoban, 1985) to numbers and the alphabet. Concept books are actually a type of informational book, but we want to encourage including concept books as a specific type in the read-aloud repertoire, especially for younger preschoolers.

There are a number of reasons we believe concept books are especially important to use with young children. Concept books stimulate growth in children's vocabulary and help to enlarge their understanding of the world that surrounds them. And because children are naturally curious about their world, concept books engender conversations that pave the way for the "expository thinking" that will be critical for children's later success in school when they are expected to read a wide variety of informational books. Concept books build the initial foundation that will eventually be central in learning about the world both in and out of school. Think of them as stepping stones into longer and more fully developed informational books.

Alphabet and counting books are types of concept books that play especially important roles in the preschool classroom, but finding the right books to use can be challenging. A major reason to bring alphabet books into the classroom for read-alouds is to teach children to identify letters and learn sounds associated with those letters. The best alphabet books for this purpose are simple ones that, on any given page, prominently display the featured letter and one or two objects beginning with that letter. Many of the recently published alphabet books do not present the alphabet in such a simple, straightforward way; rather, it may be integrated into a storyline, be presented in a very elaborate fashion, or contain highly unusual words and therefore is not as central to the book. To introduce basic alphabet concepts, teachers may want to rely on alphabet books published some years ago such as *John Burningham's ABC* (Burningham, 1964/1999). If the decision is made to use counting books that embed number concepts into a storyline, an example such as *Feast for 10* (Falwell, 1993) presents a model that works well with preschoolers. In this clever story, an African American family goes grocery shopping and then cooks a meal during which they count to 10 twice. The book offers wonderful counting practice for children. To help children in their initial acquisition of the concept of one-to-one correspondence, however, it is probably better to use simpler books such as *Count!* (Fleming, 1992) that, on a single page, present the featured number and items corresponding to that number.

Many concept books have a question–answer format that works especially well with preschoolers. Margaret Miller's *Whose Hat?* (1988) poses a question throughout the book, which is followed by a photo of the hat, and the subsequent double-page spread shows an adult wearing that hat in their roles, and a child playing in that role. In a similar format, Miller has also created *Whose Shoe?* (1991). Books such as these invite young children to participate by guessing, and thus invite them into the read-aloud experience as they make sense of the book.

Some concept books are nearly wordless, such as *Becca Backward, Becca Forward* (McMillan, 1986). They may label the concept itself, but otherwise leave the rest of the language up to the adult and children to create together during the read-aloud. Others are completely wordless. In Tana Hoban's book, *Exactly the Opposite* (1990), there are no labels, only photographs that imply conceptual opposites like open/closed, push/pull, or forward/backward.

Predictable Books

Predictable books are books that have repetitive patterns, either in language (e.g., *The Important Book*, Brown, 1949), structure (e.g., *Mommies Say Shhh!*, Polacco, 2005), or both (e.g., *I Went Walking*, Williams, 1990). Most predictable books are narratives (e.g., *Joseph Had a Little Overcoat*, Taback, 1999; *Bringing the Rain to Kapiti Plain*, Aardema, 1981; *Possum Come a-Knockin'*, Van Laan, 1990), some are informational books (e.g., *My Beak, Your Beak*, Walsh, 2002), and others are simply pattern books (e.g., *Brown Bear, Brown Bear, What Do You See?*, Martin, 1983; *If You Give a Mouse a Cookie*, Numeroff, 1985). Predictable books are especially useful for fostering preschool children's literacy because they offer enough support to enable children to easily participate in the read-aloud by reading along and even engaging in emergent readings of the books on their own.

There are many excellent predictable books that work well as read-alouds. In addition to the examples just mentioned, books such as *It Looked Like Spilt Milk* (Shaw, 1947), *Oh A Hunting We Will Go* (Langstaff, 1974), *The Napping House* (Wood, 1984), *The Chick and the Duckling* (Ginsburg, 1972), and *Over in the Meadow* (Keats, 1971/1999) have long been a staple of preschool teachers' read-aloud repertoires. Newer predictable books that work very well as read-alouds include titles such as *Do Donkeys Dance?* (Walsh, 2000), *I Heard a Little Baa* (MacLeod, 1998), *We Were Tired of Living in a House* (Skorpen, 1999), and *Oh, Look* (Polacco, 2004). Predictable books can be especially appropriate as read-alouds because they make it likely that repeated reading of the book will enhance children's emerging literacy skills as they chant along and engage actively in the repeated readings of the book.

Word Play Books

Books that highlight language are indispensable as part of the read-aloud program. Word play books nurture children's delight in new vocabulary, and they also build an extremely important aspect of young children's early literacy development, phonological awareness (i.e., the ability to hear the individual sounds that make up language). Nursery rhymes and poetry are ideal word play books to feature as read-alouds. *My Very First Mother Goose Rhymes* (Opie, 1996), *Diez Deditos: Ten Little Fingers and Other Play Rhymes and Action Songs from Latin America* (Orozco, 1997), *Play Rhymes* (Brown, 1987), and *Pio Peep* (Ada, 2003) are good examples of nursery and play rhyme collections. Another especially appealing collection is *The Neighborhood Mother Goose* (Crews, 2004), which features the traditional rhymes accompanied by contemporary photographs of children from diverse cultural groups in familiar home and neighborhood settings. Some good collections of poetry for reading aloud to young children include *Days Like This: A Collection of Small Poems* (James, 1999), *A Zooful of Animals* (Cole, 1992), and *Confetti: Poems for Children* (Mora, 1996). Jump rope and street rhymes are other forms of poetry that are always big hits with young children. Joanna Cole has compiled collections of them, such as *Anna Banana: 101 Jump Rope Rhymes for Young Children* (Cole, 1989) and *Miss Mary Mack* (Cole, 1990), which work well. And then there are the shortest poems of all, called terse verse, that are delightful two-word rhymes (e.g., green screen, stuck truck, wet pet). Preschoolers love guessing what the rhymes are when they look at the photographs in Bruce McMillan's books such as *Play Day* (1991) and *One Sun* (1990).

In addition to nursery rhymes and poetry, a wide variety of other books feature word play that stimulates young children's language growth. Some are stories (e.g., *Louella Mae, She's Run Away!*, Alarcón, 1997), others are predictable books (e.g., *Mr. Gumpy's Outing*, Burningham, 1971), and still others just play with language (e.g., *Bein' With You This Way*, Nikola-Lisa, 1994). As child listeners are caught up in the search for the elusive Louella Mae, for example, they discover that the author offers rhyme clues that aid in predicting just where the frantic family will next search for Louella Mae.

Books such as Janet Wong's *Buzz* (2000a), Harriet Ziefert's *Who Said Moo?* (1996), Sandra and Susan Steen's *Car Wash* (2001), Melinda Long's *When Papa Snores* (2000), or Denise Fleming's *Barnyard Banter* (1994) get children paying attention to the different kinds of sounds that occur in the environment such as barnyard animals' mews, honks, and caws or grandpa's and even grandma's snores. In *We're Going on a Bear Hunt* (Rosen, 1989), children delight in performing the characters' actions and the sounds associated with them. Or when you read *The Lady with the Alligator Purse* (Westcott, 1988), invite children to clap along to the rhythm. *Sheep in a Jeep* (Shaw, 1986) is another excellent choice. After having it read to them, one group of Head Start children recreated the words and rhythm of the book as a rap and recorded it for others to listen to. What a performance it was!

Alliteration is another facet of language that children enjoy exploring in read-alouds. Examples well suited to preschoolers are *The Horrendous Hullaballoo* (Mahy, 1992), *Four Famished Foxes and Fosdyke* (Edwards, 1995), and *Big Bear Ball* (Ryder, 2002), which is built around a toe-tapping rhythm and with a lot of alliteration and rhyme.

Perhaps more than any other single factor, what distinguishes capable readers in elementary and even high school from students who struggle with reading is their vocabulary knowledge. Early childhood is a critical time for getting the vocabulary knowledge going, and a thoughtful selection of read-aloud books can make a big contribution. Books such as *I Stink!* (McMullan, 2002), *Toad* (Brown, 1996), and *Mud* (Ray, 1996) have interesting and "fertile" words that describe their subjects, and, as discussed earlier with the example of William Steig, a number of authors include in their stories wonderful literary words that will expand children's vocabulary.

By immersing children in a host of books featuring interesting words, distinctive rhythms, repetitive sounds, and rhyming words, teachers help children discover (and delight in) the words that make up language and the sounds that make up words—the very foundation of vocabulary and phonological awareness that is critical for their later success as beginning readers.

Books with a Range of Topics

Even in a group with only seven or eight children, we know that there are great differences in what interests the individual children who make up the group; therefore, including not only a wide variety of types of books, but also selecting read-aloud books that cover a wide range of topics is important in order to appeal to children's diverse interests. Doing so not only connects to their existing interests but also stimulates them to cultivate new curiosities. It is important to remember that many of the children coming to preschool have limited experience outside of their immediate neighborhoods or what they see on consumer oriented television. Books can take them places they've never been, show them things they've never seen, and introduce them to characters who can enrich their lives. Exposure to a range of topics helps build the background knowledge that is crucial for later success in not only reading, but in all of their academic subjects in school.

The list of what interests young children is endless, but books on the following topics usually have wide appeal as read-alouds:

- Children's everyday challenges and issues

- Animals and nature

- People overcoming odds to succeed

- How things work

- Fun child activities (e.g., sports, games)

- How people live throughout the world

- Community helpers

- Transportation

- Self, family, and community

- Adventures

- Imagination

- Memorable characters in fact and fiction

- How our bodies work (e.g., losing a tooth, early childhood health issues, how parts of the body work)

- Children's emotional and social growth

- Weather

- Plants

It is clear that many of these topics closely connect with typical preschool curriculum units or classroom themes. For example, most young children love both stories and information books about animals and nature. A number of Denise Fleming's books on this topic are usually read-aloud hits. They typically feature both rich language (using minimal text) and interesting information. *In the Small, Small Pond* (Fleming, 1993), for example, introduces young children to the seasonal cycle of pond life, whereas *In the Tall, Tall Grass* (Fleming, 1991) features many of the creatures that make their homes in fields. Lois Ehlert is another author who has written and illustrated excellent books about nature. *Feathers for Lunch* (Ehlert, 1990) is a simple story about a cat trying to catch a bird for lunch. Lois Ehlert, however, makes the book a learning experience by including a wide variety of birds in her illustrations, each of which is labeled. She includes additional information about the various types of birds in an endnote. Animals and nature is also one of the few topics published that contains good information suitable for preschoolers.

Equally important, however, are noncurricular topics and issues that are of tremendous consequence to children, such as children's everyday challenges. Children face a number of challenges and problems, and one way they learn to cope with issues is by seeing how other children, or animals behaving in the role of children, deal with similar problems. Many of Kevin Henkes' books, for instance, speak to this topic. His best works feature mice with very real childlike problems—the arrival of a new baby (*Julius, the Baby of the World*, 1990), needing a special comfort object (*Owen*, 1993), or being teased (*Chrysanthemum*, 1991). Likewise, many books by Ezra Jack Keats address similar issues that are considered everyday challenges for preschoolers. The urban dwelling, multicultural cast of children in his stories deal with realistic childhood anxieties in positive ways as they face jealousy over getting attention around a new baby sibling (*Peter's Chair*, 1980), disappointment over not winning *(Pet Show!*, 1972), or being bullied by older kids in the neighborhood (*Goggles!*, 1969). Other books expertly deal with other daily issues of childhood, such as in David Shannon's *No, David!* (1998), or fear of being too old to be caught sleeping with a stuffed animal, as in Bernard Waber's *Ira Sleeps Over* (1973).

Of course, just about anything can interest the range of young children you teach in a given year. For example, some may be fascinated with how farmers cultivate pumpkins from tiny seeds and how those seeds grow into pumpkins that can be turned into jack-o-lanterns, as is depicted through the photographs in *The Pumpkin Patch* (King, 1990). Other children want to sit through seemingly every story involving dinosaurs and every dinosaur information book on the planet. In *This Is the Way We Go to School* (Baer, 1990), preschoolers discover that children around the world travel to school by foot, by boat, by subway, by horse and buggy, and so forth. The book *Koala Lou* (Fox, 1988) tells the exciting story of what happens to a young koala that enters "Bush Olympics" and loses in her event.

Fortunately, a large number of high-quality books on a range of topics well suited to reading aloud—most of them stories, but with increasing numbers of informational books—are readily available, and additional good books appear each year. To find additional titles, pay attention to people who know children's books. One method is to talk to the staff at a good, independent children's bookstore or to a knowledgeable children's librarian in a public library. Another is to read reviews in publications such as *Book Links*, *Young Children*, and *Childhood Education*. Also, tune in to discussions among knowledgeable teachers in your own setting or in other centers or preschools. And, of course, pay attention to your children and their reactions to books, their book preferences, and their suggestions.

Multicultural Literature

As we strive to include a range of genres and a range of topics in read-alouds, it is also important to ensure that multicultural literature is well represented among the books used. When selecting multicultural books, keep in mind that as listeners, children need opportunities to experience books that serve as "mirrors" of themselves, as well as opportunities to hear about others through books that serve as "windows" to the lives and experiences of people different from themselves. For example, an African American girl who listens to *Amazing Grace* (Hoffman, 1991) may feel a connection to the story in which a girl rises to the challenge when her classmates tell her she can't be Peter Pan in the school musical because she is a girl and she is black. On the other hand, the same African American girl may get a glimpse into a new experience when listening to the story *The Color of Home* (Hoffman, 2002) in which a boy from Somalia struggles to express himself to classmates because he doesn't yet speak the same language as they do. A key thing to remember when reading aloud multicultural literature is that the more different the cultural experiences in the book are from those of the children, the more the children need scaffolding from the teacher. The teacher can lead discussions about experiences that may seem very foreign to children and thus bridge to the unfamiliar situation in an understandable way.

Fortunately, there are many multicultural titles on a variety of topics that are good for reading aloud to preschoolers. Excellent for younger preschoolers is the book *Mung-Mung: A Fold-Out Book of Animal Sounds* (Park, 2004) that depicts how various cultures around the world mimic animal sounds differently. Older children might enjoy *Where Are You Going? To See My Friend!* (Carle & Iwamura, 2003), which is also an interactive book that engages listeners in the "telling" of the story. This book is an especially interesting multicultural book for reading aloud because of its premise. It is written in English in one direction, and in Japanese from the opposite direction (the way Japanese books are traditionally opened). The two sides tell parallel stories about going to see a friend, and the friends meet in a four-page foldout in the center of the book. The text is presented in a format suitable for choral reading, thus engaging listeners in chanting along with the reader.

Chapter Books and Read-Alouds

Chapter books are not appropriate for all preschoolers, but some older children may be ready to listen to their first chapter books when they are read aloud. In particular, children who have had extensive experience listening to books in a read-aloud and who can settle in and listen to read-alouds for relatively long periods are likely to respond well to chapter books. Read-alouds of chapter books promote children's literacy development by giving them experience listening to books without visual support. Special care is needed in selecting these longer books for preschoolers, however, because many are too complex for young children and are conceptually better saved for more mature children. For young children, select relatively short and simply written chapter books such as *The End of the Beginning* (Avi, 2004), *Freckle Juice* (Blume, 1984), or books in the Junie B. Jones series such as *Junie B. Jones Has a Monster Under Her Bed* (Park, 1997). Teachers can help children gain further experience listening to texts without visual support by reading aloud children's magazines and poetry.

CONCLUSION

Attention to the practice of reading aloud as an instructional activity for early childhood classrooms has burgeoned in recent years (Dickinson, 2001; Teale, 2003) as has research on its use and effectiveness (see also van Kleeck, Stahl, & Bauer, 2003). A careful reading of the van Kleeck, Stahl, and Bauer (2003) volume confirms early childhood educators' long-held belief that reading aloud in the classroom has a positive impact on young children's emergent literacy knowledge, strategies, and attitudes. But it is also important for early childhood educators to keep in mind that a variety of factors mediate how much of a difference reading aloud actually makes in a particular classroom. It is known, for instance, that the amount of time teachers spend reading aloud as part of the instructional day can be a positive or negative factor (Meyer, Wardrop, Stahl, & Linn, 1994). We also know that teachers have different read-aloud styles (Dickinson, 2001; Dickinson & Keebler, 1989; Martinez & Teale, 1993) and that the different teacher read-aloud styles are related to differential literacy learning outcomes for children (Beck & McKeown, 2001; Dickinson & Smith, 1994; Martinez & Teale, 1993; Whitehurst, 1994).

On the other hand, studies of the mix of factors that determine how much of a difference reading aloud actually makes have paid comparatively little attention to another factor that figures prominently in understanding the role of reading aloud as an instructional activity: what teachers read to children.

Our experience tells us that the book matters. Teachers have too little time with their children, so it makes sense to share the highest quality books possible during read-alouds.

We have presented, in this chapter, a case for regarding the selection of what to read aloud as a central issue for a preschool teacher to consider. We offered, throughout the chapter, a number of read-aloud recommendations. We encourage use of these titles in the preschool classroom because they exhibit the features of high-quality books and because they represent a range of genres and topics that should appeal to the range of interests and skills typically present among a group of preschoolers. But more important than simply picking the particular books mentioned here is for each teacher to think about the qualities and characteristics of good read-aloud books and to develop his or her own sensibility of how to evaluate and select good books for the classroom.

Thus, raising consciousness about the importance of book selection is one important issue for early childhood education. Enabling teachers to be more purposeful in selecting books is also critical. By becoming aware of criteria for excellent read-aloud books and of an existing body of children's books that historically worked well as read-alouds with preschoolers, teachers will be able to enhance the effects of one of the most important instructional activities in the early childhood classrooms.

REFERENCES

Beck, I., & McKeown, M.G. (2001). Text talk: Capturing the benefits of read-aloud experiences for young children. *The Reading Teacher, 55,* 10–20.

Dickinson, D.K. (2001). Book reading in preschool classrooms: Is "recommended practice" common? In D.K. Dickinson & P.O. Tabors (Eds.), *Beginning literacy with language: Young children learning at home and school* (pp. 175–204). Baltimore: Paul H. Brookes Publishing Co.

Dickinson, D.K., & Keebler, R. (1989). Variations in preschool teachers' storybook reading styles. *Discourse Processes, 12,* 353–376.

Dickinson, D.K., & Smith, M.W. (1994). Long-term effects of preschool teachers' book readings on low-income children's vocabulary, story comprehension, and print skills. *Reading Research Quarterly, 29,* 105–121.

Martinez, M., & Teale, W.H. (1990, December). *The impact of teacher storybook reading style on kindergartners' story comprehension.* Paper presented at the 40th annual meeting of the National Reading Conference, Miami, FL.

Martinez, M., & Teale, W.H. (1993). Teacher storybook reading style: A comparison of six teachers. *Research in the Teaching of English, 27,* 175–199.

Meyer, L.A., Wardrop, J.L., Stahl, S.A., & Linn, R.L. (1994). Effects of reading storybooks aloud to children. *Journal of Educational Research, 88,* 69–85.

Teale, W.H. (2003). Reading aloud to young children as a classroom instructional activity: Insights from research and practice. In A. van Kleeck, S.A. Stahl, & E. Bauer (Eds.), *On reading books to children: Parents and teachers* (pp. 114–139). Mahwah, NJ: Lawrence Erlbaum Associates.

Temple, C., Martinez, M., & Yokota, J. (2006). *Children's books in children's hands: An introduction to their literature* (3rd ed.). Boston: Allyn & Bacon.

van Kleeck, A., Stahl, S., & Bauer, E B. (Eds.). (2003*). On reading to children: Parents and teachers.* Mahwah, NJ: Lawrence Erlbaum Associates.

Whitehurst, G. (1994). A picture book reading intervention in day care and home for children from low-income families. *Developmental Psychology, 30,* 679–689.

CHILDREN'S BOOK REFERENCES

Aardema, V. (1981). *Bringing the rain to Kapiti Plain* (L. Dillon & D. Dillon, Illus.). New York: Dial.

Ada, A.F. (2003). *Pio peep!: Traditional Spanish nursery rhymes* (V. Escriva., Illus.). New York: Rayo.

Alarcón, K.B. (1997). *Louella Mae, she's run away* (R. Litzinger, Illus.). New York: Henry Holt.

Avi, T. (2004). *The end of the beginning.* San Diego: Harcourt.

Baer, E. (1990). *This is the way we go to school* (S. Bjorkman, Illus.). New York: Scholastic.

Barton, B. (1987). *Machines at work.* New York: HarperCollins.

Blume, J. (1984). *Freckle juice.* New York: Simon & Schuster.

Brown, M. (1987). *Play rhymes.* New York: Dutton.

Brown, M.W. (1949). *The important book* (L. Weisgard, Illus.). New York: Harper & Row.

Brown, R. (1996). *Toad.* New York: Dutton.

Bryan, A. (2003). *Beautiful blackbird.* New York: Atheneum.

Burningham, J. (1971). *Mr. Gumpy's outing.* New York: Holt.

Burningham, J. (1999). *John Burningham's ABC.* New York: Crown. (Original work published 1964.)

Campbell, R. (2005). *Dear zoo.* New York: Little Simon.

Carle, E. (1981). *The very hungry caterpillar.* New York: Philomel.

Carle, E., & Iwamura, K. (2003). *Where are you going? To see my friend.* New York: Orchard.

Child, L. (2002). *That pesky rat.* Cambridge, MA: Candlewick.

Clifton, L. (1983). *Everett Anderson's goodbye* (A. Grifalconi, Illus.). New York: Holt.

Clifton, L. (1987). *Some of the days of Everett Anderson* (E. Ness, Illus.). New York: Holt.

Clifton, L. (1992). *Everett Anderson's friend* (A. Grifalconi, Illus.). New York: Holt.

Clifton, L. (2001). *One of the problems of Everett Anderson* (A. Grifalconi, Illus.). New York: Holt.

Cole, J. (1989). *Anna Banana: 101 jump-rope rhymes for young children* (A. Tiegreen, Illus.). New York: Morrow.

Cole, J. (1990). *Miss Mary Mack* (A. Tiegreen, Illus.). New York: HarperTrophy.

Cole, J. (1992). *A zooful of animals* (L. Munsinger, Illus.). Boston: Houghton Mifflin.

Cowley, J. (2005). *Chameleon, chameleon* (N. Bishop, Illus.). New York: Scholastic.

Crews, N. (2004). *The neighborhood Mother Goose.* New York: Greenwillow.

Demi. (1990). *The empty pot.* New York: Holt.

DdePaola, T. (1975). *Strega Nona.* New York: Simon & Schuster.

Diakite, B.W. (1999). *The hatseller and the monkeys.* New York: Scholastic.

Duvoisin, R. (1950). *Petunia.* New York: Knopf.

Edwards, P.D. (1995). *Four famished foxes and Fosdyke* (H. Cole, Illus.). New York: Harper-Collins.

Ehlert, L. (1989). *Color zoo.* New York: HarperCollins.

Ehlert, L. (1990). *Feathers for lunch.* San Diego: Harcourt, Brace, Jovanovich.

Ehlert, L. (1996). *Under my nose* (C. Ontal, Illus.). Katonah, NY: Richard C. Owen.

Falwell, C. (1993). *Feast for 10.* New York: Clarion.

Flack, M. (1968). *Ask Mr. Bear.* New York: Simon & Schuster.

Fleming, D. (1991). *In the tall, tall grass.* New York: Henry Holt.

Fleming, D. (1992). *Count!* New York: Henry Holt.

Fleming, D. (1993). *In the small, small pond.* New York: Henry Holt.

Fleming, D. (1994). *Barnyard banter.* New York: Henry Holt.

Fox, M. (1988). *Koala Lou.* San Diego: Harcourt, Brace, Jovanovich.

Gackenbach, D. (1977). *Harry and the terrible whatzit.* New York: Clarion.

Galdone, P. (1979a). *The little red hen.* New York: Clarion.

Galdone, P. (1979b). *The three billy goats gruff.* New York: Clarion

Ginsburg, M. (1972). *The chick and the duckling* (J. Aruego & A. Aruego, Illus.). New York: Macmillan.

Goldin, A. (1989). *Ducks don't get wet.* New York: HarperCollins. (Original work published 1965)

Grimes, N. (1994). *Meet Danitra Brown* (F. Cooper, Illus.). New York: HarperCollins.

Grimes, N. (2002). *Danitra Brown leaves town* (F. Cooper, Illus.). New York: Amistad.

Henkes, K. (1990). *Julius, the baby of the world.* New York: Greenwillow.

Henkes, K. (1991). *Chrysanthemum.* New York: Greenwillow.

Henkes, K. (1993). *Owen.* New York: Greenwillow.

Henkes, K. (2000). *Wemberly worried.* New York: Greenwillow.

Hill, E. (1980). *Where's Spot?* New York: Putnam.

Hoban, T. (1985). *Is it larger? Is it smaller?* New York: Greenwillow.

Hoban, T. (1990). *Exactly the opposite.* New York: Greenwillow.

Hoffman, M. (1991). *Amazing Grace* (C. Binch, Illus.). New York: Dial.

Hoffman, M. (2002). *The color of home* (K. Littlewood, Illus.). New York: Dial.

James, S. (1999). *Days like this: A collection of small poems.* Cambridge, MA: Candlewick.

Jenkins, S. (2004). *Actual size.* Boston: Houghton Mifflin.

Kasza, K. (1987). *The wolf's chicken stew.* New York: Putnam.

Keats, E.J. (1962). *The snowy day.* New York: Viking.

Keats, E.J. (1969). *Goggles!* New York: Macmillan.

Keats, E.J. (1972). *Pet show!* New York: Macmillan.

Keats, E.J. (1980). *Peter's chair.* New York: Random House.

Keats, E.J. (1999). *Over in the meadow.* New York: Viking. (Original work published 1971)

Kellogg, S. (2002). *The mysterious tadpole (25th anniversary edition).* New York: Dial.

King, R. (1990). *The pumpkin patch.* New York: Dutton.

Langstaff, J. (1974). *Oh a hunting we will go* (N.W. Parker, Illus.). New York: Simon.

Lass, B., & Sturges, P. (2000). *Who took the cookies from the cookie jar?* (A. Wolff, Illus.). New York: Little Brown.

Long, M. (2000). *When Papa snores* (H. Meade, Illus.). New York: Simon & Schuster.

Long, M. (2003). *How I became a pirate* (D. Shannon, Illus.). San Diego: Harcourt.

MacLeod, E. (1998). *I heard a little baa* (L. Phillips, Illus.). Toronto: Kids Can Press.

Mahy, M. (1992). *The horrendous hullaballoo* (P. MacCarthy. Illus.). New York: Viking.

Martin, B., Jr. (1983). *Brown bear, brown bear, what do you see?* New York: Henry Holt.

Martin, B., Jr. (1999). *A beasty story* (S. Kellogg, Illus.). San Diego: Harcourt Brace.

McCloskey, R. (1941). *Make way for ducklings.* New York: Viking.

McCloskey, R. (1948). *Blueberries for Sal.* New York: Viking.

McMillan. B. (1986). *Becca backward, Becca forward.* New York: Lothrop.

McMillan. B. (1990). *One sun.* New York: Holiday House.

McMillan. B. (1991). *Play day.* New York: Holiday House.

McMillan. B. (1996). *Jelly beans for sale.* New York: Scholastic.

McMullan, K. (2002). *I stink* (J. McMullan, Illus.). New York: HarperCollins.

McPhail, D. (1995). *Pigs ahoy!* New York: Dutton.

Miller, M. (1988). *Whose hat?* New York: Greenwillow.

Miller, M. (1991). *Whose shoe?* New York: Greenwillow.

Mora, P. (1996). *Confetti: Poems for children* (E. O. Sanchez, Illus.). New York: Lee & Low.

Morris, A. (1989). *Bread, bread, bread* (K. Heyman, Illus.). New York: HarperTrophy.

Morris, A. (1995). *Houses and homes.* New York: Mulberry Books.

Most, B. (1990). *The cow that went oink.* San Diego: Harcourt.

Nikola-Lisa, W. (1994). *Bein' with you this way* (M. Bryant, Illus.). New York: Lee & Low.

Numeroff, L.J. (1985). *If you give a mouse a cookie.* New York: HarperCollins.

Opie, I. (1996). *My very first Mother Goose* (R. Wells, Illus.). Cambridge, MA: Candlewick.

Orozco, J.L. (1997). *Diez deditos: Ten little fingers and other play rhymes and action songs from Latin America* (E. Kleven, Illus.). New York: Dutton.

Park, B. (1997). *Junie B. Jones has a monster under her bed.* New York: Random House.

Park, L.S. (2004). *Mung-mung: A fold-out book of animal sounds* (D. Bigda, Illus.). Watertown, MA: Charlesbridge.

Polacco, P. (2004). *Oh, look.* New York: Philomel.

Polacco, P. (2005). *Mommies say shhh!* New York: Philomel.

Potter, B. (1986). *The tale of Peter Rabbit.* London: Warne. (Original work published 1902)

Rappaport, D. (2001). *Martin's big words: The life story of Dr. Martin Luther King, Jr.* (B. Collier, Illus.). New York: Hyperion.

Ray, M.L. (1996). *Mud* (L. Stringer, Illus.). San Diego: Harcourt.

Rosen, M. (1989). *We're going on a bear hunt* (H. Oxenbury, Illus.). New York: Margaret A. McElderry.

Ryder, J. (2002). *Big bear ball* (S. Kellogg, Illus.). New York: HarperCollins.

Shannon, D. (1998). *No, David!* New York: Scholastic/Blue Sky Press.

Shaw, C. (1947). *It looked like spilt milk.* New York: Harper & Row.

Shaw, N.E. (1986). *Sheep in a jeep.* Boston: Houghton Mifflin.

Skorpen, L.M. (1999). *We were tired of living in a house* (J. Cepeda, Illus.). New York: G.P. Putnam's Sons.

Steen, S., & Steen, S. (2001). *Car wash* (G. B. Karas, Illus.). New York: G.P. Putnam's Sons.

Steig, W. (1969). *Sylvester and the magic pebble.* New York: Simon & Schuster.

Steig, W. (1982). *Doctor De Soto.* New York: Farrar Straus & Giroux.

Taback, S. (1999). *Joseph had a little overcoat.* New York: Viking.

Van Laan, N. (1990). *Possum come a-knockin'* (G. Booth, Illus.). New York: Knopf.

Waber, B. (1973). *Ira sleeps over.* Boston: Houghton Mifflin.

Wallace, K. (2000). *A bed for winter.* New York: DK Publishing.

Walsh, E.S. (1989). *Mouse paint.* San Diego: Harcourt.

Walsh, E.S. (1991). *Mouse count.* San Diego: Harcourt.

Walsh, M. (2000). *Do donkeys dance?* Boston: Houghton Mifflin.

Walsh, M. (2002). *My beak, your beak.* Boston: Houghton Mifflin.

West, C. (1996). *"I don't care!" said the bear.* Cambridge, MA: Candlewick.

Westcott, N.B. (1988). *The lady with the alligator purse.* New York: Little, Brown.

Willems, M. (2003). *Don't let the pigeon drive the bus!* New York: Hyperion.

Williams, S. (1990). *I went walking.* San Diego: Gulliver Books.

Wong, J. (2000a). *Buzz* (M. Chodos-Irvine, Illus.). San Diego: Harcourt.

Wong, J. (2000b). *The trip back home* (B. Jia, Illus.). San Diego: Harcourt.

Wood, A. (1984). *The napping house* (D. Wood, Illus.). San Diego: Harcourt.

Ziefert, H. (1996). *Who said moo?* (S. Taback, Illus.). New York: HarperCollins.

Early Reading First and Its Role in Defining High-Quality Professional Development

Lea M. McGee

Reading instruction in the United States has undoubtedly been altered by the requirements of the No Child Left Behind Act of 2001 (PL 107-110). Through this law, Reading First (RF) provided local districts with more than $1 billion to improve the reading instruction in low-performing schools with large percentages of low-income children. Its sister, Early Reading First (ERF), though not providing as many dollars as RF, has had a significant impact on preschools. ERF is also a grant program authorized under Subpart 2, Part B, Title I of the Elementary and Secondary Education Act of 1965 (PL 89-10). The purpose of ERF grants is to provide funds to local preschool programs so that the administrators can prepare children to enter kindergarten with the foundational early language and literacy concepts, skills, and strategies that will prevent future reading failure. This program is also intended to primarily serve children who reside in low-income families. Organizations that receive ERF grants are required to use scientifically based reading research to create classroom environments that are rich in age-appropriate print, including having the alphabet displayed where it is visible to the children, having many books available, and having ample materials to encourage writing. Teachers must deliver "intentional and explicit, contextualized, and scaffolded instruction" (U.S. Department of Education, 2007, p. 5) and use activities that will ensure the age-appropriate development of "oral language (i.e., vocabulary, expressive language, listening comprehension) phonological awareness (i.e., rhyming, blending, segmenting) print awareness, and alphabet knowledge (i.e., letter recognition)" (U.S. Department of Education, 2007, p. 5). Program administrators are required to provide intensive and ongoing professional development that includes mentoring and coaching teachers in their own classrooms. Grantees are expected to use effective coaching strategies that include providing demonstrations in classrooms in which teachers observe, and then subsequently discuss and reflect on methods of improving instruction and learning.

In this grant program, the notion of transformation is critical. Guidance for ERF specifies that projects must transform early education programs into centers of excellence (U.S. Department of Education, 2007). Thus, grantees must transform the existing classroom environment, curriculum, instruction, assessment, and professional development as well as children's achievement. Through this guidance, ERF is intended to target organizations that are willing and able to take on the task of transforming effective teachers in ordinary classrooms into highly effective, exemplary teachers in extraordinary classrooms. The key to all of the transformations expected in ERF lies in professional development. Current systems must change in order to allow teachers to change.

EARLY READING FIRST AND PROFESSIONAL DEVELOPMENT

It was not surprising to me that ERF Guidance provides only minimal information about the kinds of professional development necessary to transform ordinary classrooms and teachers into exemplary classrooms and teachers. Over the 30 years I have been teaching (mostly at the university level), change has proven to be an elusive goal for individual teachers, schools, and systems (Fullan, 2001; Fullan & Hargreaves, 1992; Hargreaves, 1994). ERF thus provided a new challenge for most professionals in early literacy. On the one hand, the grant clearly called upon professional knowledge and creativity. Grants would be awarded to groups with leadership in early literacy to craft a unique vision of how to transform early childhood classrooms into extraordinary classrooms. On the other hand, we were going to need expertise in a new arena: leadership for change. Having worked with similar projects, some successful and some dismal failures, I was aware of the pitfalls in crafting a vision and then actually getting teachers to buy into the vision and do the work. Although there are dozens of books that describe change, leadership, and coaching, there are far fewer stories of actual teacher change that identify supports instrumental in affecting that change. However, three components of change are outlined in most professional recommendations:

- Teachers are more likely to change their instruction when they perceive that their students will learn more effectively using new strategies or when they find that teaching is easier.

- Teachers are more likely to change their instruction when they perceive that they will get the support they need (e.g., appropriate materials, demonstrations, clear guidelines, consistent expectations about when and how to use the instruction, positive feedback rather than criticism).

- Teachers are more likely to change the appearance, arrangement, and contents of their classroom when they have consistent guidelines and expectations and they perceive a rationale for doing so.

PROFESSIONAL DEVELOPMENT IN PROJECT EX EL AND CORE

In 2002, I was instrumental in writing the ERF grant awarded to Alabama's Department of Children's Affairs. Project Ex El started in four classrooms in the first year, grew into 10 classrooms in the second year, and shrank to eight classrooms in the third year (one teacher left because of pregnancy and another classroom did not receive funds to continue). These classrooms were in two locations more than 120 miles apart within the state of Alabama. The majority of classrooms were in public schools, but two classrooms were in a Head Start center. I developed a model of professional development in this grant that I transferred to a second 2004 ERF awarded to The University of Alabama. Project Community of Reading Excellence (CORE) started in five classrooms in a small town in rural Mississippi and grew to seven classrooms in the following 2 years. This project included two child care centers, four Head Start centers, and one prekindergarten public school classroom. The original model of professional development changed over time as I observed teachers' responses to each of the different kinds of learning opportunities with which we experimented. I implemented these changes within the 2002 grant and later refined them in the 2004 grant.

In the 2002 grant, we began professional development with a typical 2-week summer institute for teachers in which I presented some materials, but mainly relied on outside expert consultants. Both of the two consultants were well respected in their fields, had published in the areas they shared with us, and were experienced university professors. We met daily for 5 or 6 hours for 5 days in a location closer to one of the preschool sites, and for the next 5 days in another location closer to the other preschool site. I coordinated with the consultants on the content they were going to present, the timing of presentations, and the handouts and materials that we would need. We addressed, among many topics, how to change the classroom environment, interactions that would enhance children's language development, how to read aloud to children to build vocabulary, the nature of phonemic awareness and how to teach for it, and the need to address confusable letters in alphabet instruction.

After the first few weeks of school, it became clear that our summer professional workshop was not successful in helping teachers modify their classroom environments or change the intensity and effectiveness of their instruction. I realized in hindsight that I should have arranged for outside evaluators to conduct interviews with the teachers and assistants after the summer workshops. These interviews could have provided a more objective assessment of what the teachers learned and did not learn. As I visited the sites at the beginning of the second month of the project with the project reading coach, I concluded that the teachers had actually implemented only a few ideas discussed in our summer workshop. All of the teachers had rearranged their schedules as required to have one small-group literacy lesson each day. All of the teachers had placed more books in their book centers and set up a writing center; however, these represented minimal changes in the classroom environment.

The reading coach and I established a schedule for me to accompany her on classroom visits each month to discuss all of the teachers' progress in changing their classroom environments and instruction. We prioritized two immediate problems: The teachers were not transforming their classroom environments beyond making minor adjustments, and they were not using powerful small-group language or literacy activities even when they had established a routine for small-group instruction. We decided we needed to make two changes to our approach to professional development: We needed to establish criteria for defining a print-rich environment, and we needed to help the teachers plan effective small-group lessons in literacy.

We had already planned on using the Early Language & Literacy Classroom (ELLCO) Observation Toolkit (Smith & Dickinson, 2002) as the assessment of our classroom environment. (In 2002, ERF projects were required to assess the quality of the language and literacy environments.) We decided to use only a portion of that tool, the Literacy Environment Checklist, to measure our classroom environments. We decided to use these criteria as a definition of a print-rich environment; therefore, in early October we explained to the teachers that the grant required us, by the end of October, to have each classroom included in the grant receive a perfect score on the Literacy Environment Checklist. Further, we explained that the grant required us to maintain a perfect score throughout the 3 years of the project. The reading coach evaluated each classroom, shared the results with the teachers, discussed with the teachers the changes each classroom needed, and made dates to help teachers physically change their classrooms. We had professional development meetings in the afternoons to help the teachers learn to create shared writing charts, a necessary display expected in a "perfect" environment.

We also told teachers that the grant required each classroom to have a second dramatic play center (e.g., grocery store, barber shop, fire station, flower shop). We conducted a short professional development session on how to set up this center, and the reading coach worked with each teacher to rearrange the classrooms to provide space for this new center. We provided digital cameras and required that teachers take 10 photographs of children playing in the dramatic play centers. We provided each teacher with five books related to their second dramatic play center, suggested reading and writing props, and visited the classroom to demonstrate how to play along with children in these centers.

We invited one of our consultants to return to the project to demonstrate read-alouds in the whole group and to share with us several activities appropriate for small-group lessons. At that point we made a critical decision: All consultants would be expected to teach the children as we observed and to lead follow-up reflective discussions. We would no longer have workshops in which experts would tell us what to do. Instead, they would show us how to do the activities in several different classrooms. As the consultants taught the children, we were able to see them perform many activities we previously had not realized they could perform. The children were eager to participate, and the teachers saw the value of two of our key instructional activities for the first time: whole-group interactive read-alouds and small-group alphabet instruction. I began scheduling demonstration lessons with the teachers, and the reading coach and I led the teachers in reflective discussions. The reading coach scheduled specific days with each teacher to observe them as they taught using the activities I had just demonstrated or had been demonstrated by the experts.

This cycle of observation—identifying priorities for professional development, bringing in consultants to demonstrate specific strategies and lead reflective discussion, and providing follow-up classroom coaching by our reading coach—became our model of professional development. Through the first year of the project, the teachers were introduced to the seven key instructional activities that were included in our grant through demonstration in their classrooms with follow up coaching. We interviewed the teachers and found that they preferred to have consultants teach in their classrooms and have me present information during summer school workshops to bring consistency to the project.

We imported this model of professional development to Project CORE. We were required to launch this project in January rather than wait for the summer; therefore, we began the project with only two Saturday workshops focused on changing the environment, making shared writing charts, and reading aloud. We focused on only these three aspects of the project during the implementation year, and we used consultants who taught demonstration lessons with the children in the project and led reflective discussions. The reading coach followed up with classroom demonstrations and observations. The following summer, we had 4 workshop days in which we focused on effective alphabet instruction in small groups, vocabulary activities in small groups as follow-ups to interactive read-alouds, and drama and retelling. I conducted these summer sessions to set expectations and establish consistency. Later in the year, we added phonemic awareness instruction and used fingerpoint reading to develop concepts about print. Again, we used expert consultants who provided demonstrations of these activities with the children. Each lesson the consultants taught became the focus of classroom coaching for the following month.

In both projects, our teachers changed. The proof of their new effectiveness is reflected in the child outcome data: The children in Project Ex El and CORE outperformed control children. Most importantly, children who were in project classrooms after the implementation of the project scored significantly higher than children who were in the same classrooms prior to the project. With the same teacher, the children performed better after the teacher participated in professional development projects.

CONCLUSION

As I reflected on the professional development provided in Project Ex El and CORE, I realized that it met the three criteria I outlined earlier in this chapter. Teachers bought into the second dramatic play center and other aspects of their transformed classroom environment because they observed their children playing with joy, pretending to read and write in exciting new ways, and using language they had not heard of before. The behaviors of their children showed teachers the value of this center and of littering the classroom with books and writing materials. Data collected during the project were also convincing. Monitoring data collected in December of the first year revealed that many of the children had already learned as many as 15 or more alphabet letters. Some teachers previously had not had any children learn this many letters across the entire year; therefore, it was not surprising that in January we noticed a new commitment to the project after all the teachers reviewed the results of this monitoring assessment. The teachers also embraced the notion of coaching. Teachers began to seek me out when I was in their building, and they spontaneously arranged for me to teach demonstration lessons on the spot with their children. It was obvious that all of the teachers heavily relied on the reading coach to provide much needed encouragement and suggestions for solving tricky problems with individual children. Our professional development was successful because it met the needs of teachers, produced convincing results, and was delivered in classrooms.

REFERENCES

Elementary and Secondary Education Act of 1965, PL 89-10, 20 U.S.C. §§ 241 *et seq.*

Fullan, M. (2001). *Leading in a culture of change.* San Francisco: Jossey-Bass.

Fullan, M., & Hargreaves, A. (1992). *What's worth fighting for in your school?* New York: Teachers College Press.

Hargreaves, A. (1994). *Changing teachers, changing times: Teachers' work and culture in the postmodern age.* New York: Teachers College Press.

No Child Left Behind Act of 2001, PL 107-110, 115 Stat. 1425, 20 U.S.C. §§ 6301 *et seq.*

Smith, M.W., & Dickinson, D.D. (with Sangeorge, A., & Anastasopoulos, L.). (2002). *Early Language and Literacy Classroom Observation (ELLCO) Toolkit* (Research ed.). Baltimore: Paul H. Brookes Publishing Co.

U.S. Department of Education. (2007). *Guidance for the Early Reading First Program.* Washington, DC: Author.

Developing an Early Literacy Professional Development Program

ROSEANN RINEAR

On my first morning visiting the Guppy class at the preschool in which I was the new project director for the federally funded Early Reading First (ERF) grant, I found a shocking scene: The room and the children were in total disarray. Children were fighting with each other or just wandering around, the learning centers were devoid of interesting literacy materials such as books and environmental print, and there weren't any themed dramatic play props, listening centers, or writing centers. All the room had were some blocks, a few books, crayons, three pieces of furniture in housekeeping, tables, chairs, a record player, assorted manipulatives, and toys. These classroom items could not meet the ERF or the Early Language and Literacy Classroom Observation (ELLCO; Smith & Dickinson, 2002) standards. There were not enough interest centers, and the centers that existed had few items to entice children to explore and learn. The shelves were not labeled or organized. The dramatic play area did not have the extra items needed to extend the children's play. The only items that were there were a stove, table, chairs, and a refrigerator. To extend and expand play, items are needed to bring language and literacy alive. Creating a dramatic play theme (and providing materials to support that theme) promotes language and literacy. I explained to the teacher that an example of this would be setting up the area as a veterinary hospital. The children could have paper, pencils, folders, books on animals, signs that show the costs of treatment, a stethoscope, bandages, an operating table, and a place to bill the customers. Children could write down information on the pet and owner. The doctor could write down the diagnosis of the pet and the office clerk could bill the customer. Posters and signs assist in language development and help children expand their vocabularies. As the author Owocki (1999) stated

Children become literate as they explore the functions and features of written language. A function is a reason or purpose for using print. Exploration of function is a natural part of play because children need written language to support their play themes. Play provides a natural and meaningful context for exploring the many functions of written language. (p. 24)

The teacher told me that the children were bored and would not listen to her. I asked her if she had been to any trainings on ELLCO or on the Early Childhood Environment Rating Scale (ECERS; Harms, Clifford, & Cryer, 2005). Much to my chagrin, she had not been to any ELLCO training sessions, only to ECERS. I knew my new position was going to be more of a training position and less of a director. I promptly explained the use of each tool. The ELLCO is a field-tested observation toolkit, utilized to address the environmental factors in classroom early literacy and language development. This tool acts as a guide to help administrators, trainers, and teachers find the strengths and weaknesses in their literacy and language program. Once weaknesses are identified, the trainer can work with the teacher to improve the areas. The ECERS is also a field-tested observation tool that provides an overall view of the environment, including use of space, materials, and experiences to enhance children's development, daily schedule, and supervision. This scale consists of 43 items divided into seven categories: Personal Care Routines, Space and Furnishings, Language Reasoning, Activities, Interactions, Program Structure, and Parents and Staff.

As a leader, supervisor, or trainer, one of the most rewarding tasks is working with teachers to improve their skills and their understanding of how children learn. It is imperative that all child development organizations have plans for training teachers and staff. To be effective, these programs must provide tools for ongoing evaluations to ensure the continuous production of positive effects in the classroom (Epstein, 1993). Most importantly, any new teacher training must have a clearly defined connection between meaning, logic, and individual validation. The teachers in my centers needed training in understanding language and literacy in the classroom and using observational assessment tools to strengthen the classroom environment. The ELLCO and ECERS would be utilized as self-directed learning techniques. Such techniques must come to the forefront of any training, and of equal importance, the retraining of teachers needs to take place within a democratic, open-minded community of thinkers.

Several years ago, I worked with 12 preschools to understand effective training and its impact on children's learning environments. These schools had similar issues to those of the ERF schools with which I was working. The major concern I had was why teachers were not utilizing the training they had received throughout the years. Supervisors and trainers observed a failure to provide child-centered, developmentally appropriate and adequately prepared language and literacy learning experiences and environments, which often resulted in behavior problems that interfered with the learning process.

Teachers were frustrated because of difficulties with fully engaging children in planned activities. The children were bored, often started fights, and acted negatively toward each other. Teachers were spending the majority of their time redirecting or disciplining their students, and experienced difficulty following their scheduled curriculum plans. An additional observation was that teachers struggled to create and implement opportunities to support children's language and literacy. In most of the classrooms, developmentally appropriate materials, print-rich environments, and learning centers were nonexistent. Children were not interested in using the provided play equipment, and teachers could not provide meaningful learning experiences for extended time periods. The existing activities were teacher directed rather than child directed, and they did not demonstrate a conceptual understanding of how to utilize and incorporate developmentally appropriate language and literacy into the learning centers.

These teachers, like the ERF teachers, had participated in numerous workshops over the years, but these training opportunities neither improved the learning environment nor the way in which the teachers approached planning or implementing language and literacy in developmentally appropriate curriculum.

In the classrooms, supervisors, trainers, and teachers reported frustration and helplessness due to the absence of specific strategies to address their staff's performance and the children's behavior. After many discussions with members of all of the groups, I discovered that in most cases teachers had no previous experience or knowledge of best practices to plan and implement appropriate activities in language and literacy within prepared learning environments. The only information teachers possessed came from previous in-service trainings that did not include hands-on, adult-modeled child development theory.

Another issue was that the classroom training activities presented were primarily teacher directed as opposed to child directed. Teacher training, therefore, never demonstrated the concept of child-centered learning. The teachers and trainers did not understand the concept of planning and implementing learning centers that were based on developmentally appropriate practices (DAP), nor did they believe this process would make a difference in the children's learning. These environments were not designed to adequately support the children's individual learning, group learning, or language and literacy. The typical school environment did not encourage experimentation, self-esteem, self-control, relationships, language, or positive self-image. These centers failed to support and encourage the physical, intellectual, emotional, and social growth of all the children in the program. Teachers planned, prepared, and implemented learning centers without regard for the children's needs, levels of development, literacy, interests, and individuality. Learning centers did not allow children to make choices when engaging in individual or group activities, so the children were not developing discretionary time-management skills. The majority of the observed classrooms did not provide for an effective learning environment that employed five or more interest centers designed to help children have a variety of learning, language, and literacy experiences. Most of the classrooms had minimal child-related displays or print-rich environments. The two most compelling pieces of evidence were from the ECERS and the ELLCO scores. The results of these measures pointed to a poorly designed environment that did not support language and literacy. Research has shown that environment directly impacts children's behavior in the classroom. To create effective language and literacy environments, the classroom needs print-rich materials, alphabetic systems, and books to encourage children to incorporate words into their everyday play, art, music, and outside play. These tools are the foundation of reading and writing. After reviewing the ELLCO, teachers needed training in the following areas: 1) creating a print-rich environment, 2) establishing a writing center, 3) providing materials for supporting and extending written work in the dramatic play and block areas, 4) utilizing open-ended activities and materials to explore, 5) establishing a dramatic play area that reflects real life, 6) enriching the library area, and 7) inserting books into all learning areas.

After the investigation was completed, supervisors and trainers were compelled to ask three questions that shaped the development of new training: 1) Were the trainers using appropriate methods of training? 2) Could more in-service change the teachers' behavior? and 3) Could the results from this new training improve language and literacy?

First, there needed to be an examination of in-service training and the methods used to train teachers. After careful consideration, it became obvious that, despite numerous sessions on creating classroom environments, the teachers failed to utilize the training. Research of best practices revealed the main cause was inappropriate training information rather than lack of workshops. It also became obvious that fault resided within the methodology of the trainings and not with the teachers themselves. Supervisors and presenters reviewed previous training outlines. Several issues became apparent that hindered effective training of the teachers. All of the training experiences were how-to workshops, with little thought or planning as to how adults effectively learn. Best practices review suggested many plausible solutions. Trainers incorporated opportunities for teachers to brainstorm with their co-workers, reflecting on or about concepts that were learned during the session. Ann Epstein (1993) wrote five lessons for training that make a difference in teaching practices: 1) be continuous and constant, 2) be based on coherent concepts of teaching and learning, 3) train teachers in the way they teach, 4) address teachers' ideas, beliefs, and dispositions as well as their skills and techniques, and 5) address not only the developmental needs of children, but other needs as well.

Supervisors found that many of the trainings were not grounded in child development principles. As Kathleen Glascott (1994) explained, "Training has to be more than a 'how to do' workshop. Education must be grounded in a child-centered philosophy" (p. 131). The majority of the teachers had no training that emphasized the essential importance of the child's environment. The next glaring problem was that most teacher workshops implemented only one modality of learning: direct instruction or lecture. Methods of hands-on training and examples were not observed in any of the outlines. These deficits were highly detrimental to any training program. Often, supervisors heard from staff that the workshop was ineffective, but no one had ever taken the time to investigate strategies utilized by the trainer as a possible reason.

It was discovered that teachers were never provided with information that linked developmentally appropriate practices, language and literacy, or child development theories to current trainings. Teachers had been taught child development theories during their time in college. They were provided with information on school rules and regulations and emergency procedures. They were told how to fill out and process administrative forms. It was the lack of theoretical information that created an insurmountable gap, leaving teachers incapable of connecting theory to application in the classroom. This, in turn, resulted in classroom environments that lacked quality, equipment, print-rich materials, language, literacy, and age-appropriate learning centers.

A further concern involved training teachers to structure effective learning environments through the use of developmentally appropriate practices. Feng (1994) wrote that when training teachers to use learning centers effectively, it is vital that those teachers understand developmentally appropriate practices. According to Feng, the term *developmental practices* means knowing how children develop and learn, approaching children as unique individuals, and treating children with respect. In his article for the National Association for the Education of Young Children's Guide of 1994, Feng reported, "A growing body of research has emerged recently, affirming that children learn more effectively through a concrete, play-oriented approach to early childhood education" (p. 26). Kantrowitz and Wingert (1989) advocated teaching with developmentally appropriate practices, which are based on curriculum that utilizes scientific knowledge regarding how young children learn.

Best practices have shown that several components are needed to ensure a quality program. Teachers must understand the meaning of quality and how it affects the program. Koralek, Colker, and Dodge (1993) wrote that "a quality program is individualized to meet the needs of every child" (p. 2). Buysse, Wesley, Bryant, and Gardner (1999) stated that the "quality of a program is directly proportional to the degree of the teacher's knowledge and skill in the area of typical child development" (p. 2).

Dunn and Kontos (1997) explored the importance of utilizing theories and principles of child development. They found that very few early childhood education classrooms exemplify developmentally appropriate practice. The research showed that "as little as one third to one fifth of the programs studied were using the appropriate practices in the classroom" (p. 8). This was clearly evidenced by the authors when previous training outlines were examined and found to be devoid of developmentally appropriate training practices instruction.

Teachers were unfamiliar with the research on children's knowledge in language and literacy. Research from Lomax and McGee (1987) showed that children's knowledge about print follows a loose developmental sequence. The first developmental stage includes formations of general concepts about the purpose and functions of print. The second stage is having the ability to visually recognize environmental print, letters, and words. The third stage is understanding phonemic awareness that words consist of a sequence of spoken sounds (phonemes). The last stage of development is understanding the letter–sound relationships of phonics.

Besides experiencing a lack of information on language and literacy, these teachers had never taken or allocated the time for reflection and dialogue with other early childhood professionals. The directors and trainers never recognized reflection and dialogue as effective tools for training adults. Adults have many experiences upon which to build, and these experiences can be the foundation for their learning. Adults greatly benefit from reflection, sharing, and communicating their ideas and insights with others (Alexander, 1999).

The environment at the schools did not encourage experimentation, foster curiosity, promote language development, or challenge the children's ability. Elements previously discussed, varying learning modalities, child development theories, time for reflection and dialogue, and application of developmentally appropriate practices were noted as critical in an effectual training program. However, the quintessential element needed was teachers' knowledge of planning then implementing a quality classroom environment. Teachers often talked about a quality preschool, but most teachers had a difficult time defining its true meaning.

Another deficit that was exposed during my time with the supervisors was the lack of a mentoring program. Looking at best practices, training is enhanced through a mentorship program because more experienced staff members can draw on current skills and past experiences to encourage growth in newer staff members.

Furthermore, it was learned that supervisors had not encouraged teachers to continue their education or to improve the program. Teachers had not been motivated by administration to seek further education or to learn new strategies to evaluate their classrooms.

When implementing training, one must also address three factors that can critically impact teachers' morale and motivation. First, a trainer must utilize a staff survey to discover the learning gaps that need filling in the classroom. By employing the ELLCO, more gaps on language and literacy will be exposed in their classrooms than utilizing the ECERS alone. In addition, staff and teachers should develop an individual professional growth plan to serve as a guide for future training. Most importantly for trainers, the learner must see the value of changing a behavior, learning a new skill, or increasing knowledge. Best practices states that effective training sessions help to empower teachers.

The successful training must include the principles of being a change agent. This requires an understanding of not only the strengths and weaknesses of the organization, but also of the culture in which the intervention will take place. As a change agent, the focal point becomes leading organizations away from traditional ideals and methodologies and encouraging adaptation of new ideals and methodologies. In order to be successful in the role of a change agent, one must have the ability to successfully lead and encourage others. Several researchers have studied leadership skills, with the results providing a listing of the characteristics and traits of successful leaders.

Drucker, Hesselbein, Goldsmith, and Beckhard (1966) outlined five strategies for effective leaders in *The Leaders of the Future*. Drucker's contention was that the leader, or change agent, must utilize these strategies in order to be successful in the implementation of their studies. These concepts were echoed by Senge's *The Fifth Discipline* (1990), wherein strategies for those who wished to affect change could find information on the processes needing development in order to achieve that change in management goals.

First, the change agent must create and articulate a compelling vision that will capture the attention of the organization, its employees, and its customers. This vision must speak not only of the past, but of the present and the future as well. Providing a clear progression of possible outcomes to the employment of change will help to encourage organizations to undertake and embrace change, by not only the leader, but also by the employees and the organization as a whole.

Second, the change agent must have the ability to clearly and concisely communicate with the key players in the organization, in essence, to win them over. In order to be successful in the future, it is of vital importance that support for the vision is provided before one implements any type of change.

Third, the change agent must become comfortable, tenacious, consistent, and focused on the vision and the tasks needed to effect a positive change. This is by far the most difficult, due to the energy needed to produce the organizational change.

The fourth role of the change agent is to encourage employee empowerment to implement the change techniques and methodologies to allow for a successful culmination of the program. This step requires the change agent to recognize talents and various other tools that are readily available to help achieve success.

The fifth and final role of the change agent is having the ability to find effective tools to provide empirical data in addition to having the courage to admit the fallibility of the study. Accepting success or defeat must be part of the scenario.

The last critical factor that a trainer must be aware of to understand cultural approaches to creativity is another issue worthy of examination. Carter (1992) stated that when training teachers to understand creativity, it is important to help them first understand how their personal culture influences their behavior toward creativity. It is necessary for teachers to make connections between the experiences that they value and the influence this has on experimentation, trust, and venturing into the pursuit of their own interests. It is also important for these teachers to understand their feelings about making a mess. Children must be encouraged to be creative with language if they are ever to become truly literate. They often make a mess learning a new skill before they master it.

Creating bridges between cultures is another essential area of focus. Jones (1993) claimed that in bicultural settings, mutual learning is an essential part of effective training. The facilitator, who is a respectful learner, can assist in creating bridges between cultures. The early childhood teacher who gains skills in crossing bridges can become a "cultural broker" for children, parents, and other teachers in the community. A supplementary example is found in Shareef and Gonzalez-Mena(1997), who stated that trainers need to use transformative education when training teachers. According to the authors

> Transformative education is a process that allows us to see the enormity of human experience. It allows for the roles of teachers and learners to be fluid and reciprocal, because it is a process that searches for the missing voices rather than assume one voice speaks for all. (Gonzalez-Mena, p. 8)

After 25 years of training teachers, I have several recommendations to ensure effective trainings that will increase effective language growth in the classroom. My first recommendation is to utilize the ELLCO and ECERS to measure environment–teacher interaction and language with children. This will assist teachers to further their understanding of what makes up an effective learning environment and the correlation between environment and the child's ability to learn. The introduction of new concepts is beneficial only insofar as teachers believe that progress will be made. In order to facilitate teachers wanting to continue with this type of training program, it would be necessary to show graphic evidence of their improvement resulting from participation in the training (i.e., ECERS, ELLCO).

My second recommendation is that from the first day of training, the trainer should limit the number of participants in each class to approximately 12. Research has shown an observed and identified positive result in behavioral and attitudinal shifts when class sizes are reduced. The teachers increased their level of class participation during discussions and asked well directed questions.

The third recommendation is to pay attention to possible incidences of the Hawthorne Effect, which may occur in any situation in which the experimental conditions are such that the participants are aware that they are taking part in an experiment, are aware of the hypothesis, or are receiving special attention that improves their performance (Gall, Borg, & Gall, 1996, p. 475).

Finally, ensuring continuation of the techniques brought forward by instruction, there needs to be ongoing training to allow new teachers to learn the techniques and be able to expand their teaching skills. Perhaps the best way for this to be accomplished is by implementing a model classroom wherein individuals can view the techniques, train on those techniques, and then implement the techniques within a specialized learning environment. This type of training classroom would allow teachers to spend concentrated time over several weeks to learn how to create a language- and literacy-rich learning environment for their students. The model classroom and training will help new teachers understand the literacy-rich environments and language-filled learning centers that make up a quality center.

There is no mystery to creating and maintaining a schedule for effective teacher–staff training. Utilizing the best practice that has been proven will ensure the success of the training program. Taking into consideration the needs of staff must be the most critical component when planning. Remember when training teachers to utilize the adult model, a hands-on approach, and use all the modalities. Training must be constant and continuous. Growth is necessary and should be mapped out for the year on a training calendar. The creation of this calendar keeps the need for ongoing training at the forefront of everyone's mind. It is paramount to include appropriate practices and child development theories. Provide master teachers and/or mentors to work with new teachers to help them grow and learn. Train master teachers and/or mentors for the model classrooms to understand and value the concept of being mentors. It is imperative that teachers reflect and engage in dialogue during training. They need to discuss how training impacts their teaching, the children's behavior, and changes in their classroom. Preschool teachers must view themselves as professional by creating a personal growth plan for themselves. Many times teachers are trained in a specific area and there is no follow-up by administration or the instructor. This inattentiveness sends the message that the information is not important to the quality of the program. Show teachers and staff that all training is important by following up afterward to ensure new concepts or modalities are being applied in the classroom. The director or trainer should point out the positive behavior that occurs from the classroom changes suggested by the training. For example, show that a newly print-rich environment has fostered the growth of the children's vocabulary. Assist teachers and staff to understand subtle changes in the classroom shown by implementation of the appropriate instrument to measure change in environment, language and literacy, or interaction between teachers and children.

During the course of the year, have teachers conduct a monthly literacy checklist. Every 6 months, allow teachers and staff to conduct evaluation on their classroom. The results of the ELLCO utilized for environment/interaction and language/literacy of teachers with children should be shared with the administration to determine the need for future training. During staff meetings, the results need to be discussed with all classroom personnel to encourage continuation of child-centered literacy and language-learning environments. Teachers must understand and know that literacy and language starts with the ability to listen and express ideas. This is first accomplished when children can express their needs to both peers and adults. Later, more details emerge and the child begins to share more information. Children receive pleasure from establishing friendships, telling jokes, answering questions, posing questions, and playing cooperatively. Children learn to understand their world and the importance of language through shared cultural experiences, rituals, and activities. They gain the knowledge that oral and written language are connected and related. Children know the difference between letters, words, and sentences. Children start to comprehend punctuation, capital letters, and that reading moves from left to right and from top to bottom. They can write their names and convey messages through print. Children see themselves as readers and writers and develop a joy for language and reading.

Creating a learning community at school is vital to a quality program. The teaching staff needs to meet monthly to discuss innovations, problems, or other situations arising from this new environment. Sharing information will promote teacher growth and encourage further knowledge.

Many administrators imagine training teachers as an arduous task and view training as an annual event. I view training as a continuous, everchanging, and fun adventure. When training is offered frequently, it signals that teachers are worthy of new learning and the organizations are interested in their professional development. Administrators must remember that the teachers' education and training has a direct impact on the children's experiences, which, in turn, affect their cognitive, social, and emotional growth.

The hardest concept for new administrators and/or trainers to grasp is how to effectively teach or train teachers from theory to practice. Many people convey knowledge to the teachers and feel the training has been effective. These same people will declare that teachers can easily recognize a quality program. Most will be disappointed in the results that follow in the classrooms. Administrators and/or trainers then assume that teachers and staff were inattentive during the workshop. But the crux of the matter is that, while the attendees understand the meaning of quality, these same teachers do not understand how to apply this new knowledge in the classroom.

Training is the most important task an administrator can accomplish in the program. As the leader of your program, create a learning community with your teachers and staff. Be an example to the group by reading new materials and sharing them. Encourage all teachers and staff members to continue their education and share their knowledge with the children and parents. Lastly, make your training fun, meaningful, provide an open environment for questions, and introduce new ways to look at old problems. Training should always inspire teachers and staff to utilize innovative activities in the classrooms.

Visiting the Guppies now, after effective training with the teachers, is an awesome sight that would make any ERF director ecstatic. The room is orderly, neat, and clean. It is print-rich, and each learning center has books related to that center (e.g., science books in the science area, books about buildings in the block area, animals in the veterinarian's clinic in the dramatic play area, art picture books in the art area). Everywhere one looks there are environmental print and labels on the shelves. Child-created journals in the science area tell about observing the new baby finches. Pictures and print are meaningful to the children, and there is a new vocabulary word wall. The book center is a cozy and inviting place for children to check out a vast variety of books (e.g., storybooks, chapter books, picture books, history books, art books, cultural books, Spanish books, fairy tales, rhymes, alphabet books). The dramatic play center reflects one of the themes the children are interested in for the month. The children have decided to turn the dramatic play center into a post office next week when they will be learning about writing and mailing letters. During circle time they are encouraged to ask questions during the book reading. The teacher works hard at remembering to ask children to predict, inquire, and tell what they learned during the story. After school, the children are encouraged to take books home to share with their families.

The teacher is very eager to discuss with me all the new language and vocabulary the children are learning. She is proud of her room and the skills she is using to help children in language and literacy. This teacher understands the importance of language and literacy and how this knowledge will help her children be ready for kindergarten next year.

REFERENCES

Adams, M.J. (1990). *Beginning to read: Thinking and learning about print.* Cambridge, MA: MIT Press.

Buysse, V., Wesley, P.W., Bryant, D.G., & Gardner, D. (1999, Spring). Quality of early childhood programs in inclusive and non-inclusive settings. *Exceptional Children, 19*(4), 301–314.

Carter, M. (1992). Training teachers for creative learning experiences. *Child Care Information Exchange, 85,* 38–42.

Drucker, P.F., Hesselbein, F., Goldsmith, M., & Beckhard, R. (1966). *The leaders of the future.* New York: Peter F. Drucker Foundation for Nonprofit Management.

Dunn, L., & Kontos, S. (1997, July). What have we learned about developmentally appropriate practice? *Young Children, 52,* 4–13.

Epstein, A.S. (1993). *Training for quality: Improving early childhood programs through systematic in-service training.* Ypsilanti, MI: High/Scope Research Foundation.

Feng, J. (1994). Issues and trends in early childhood education. *Viewpoints (Opinion/Position Papers, Essays, etc.),* 2–26.

Gall, M., Borg, W., & Gall, J. (1996). *Educational research.* New York: Longman Publishers.

Glascott, K. (1994, Spring). A problem of theory for early childhood professionals. *Childhood Education, 70,* 131–132.

Harms, T., Clifford, R.M., & Cryer, D. (2005). *Early Childhood Environment Ratings Scale (ECERS).* New York: Teachers College Press.

Jones, E. (1993). *Growing teachers: Partnerships on staff development.* Washington, DC: National Association Education of Young of Children.

Kantrowitz, B., & Wingert, P. (1989, April). How kids learn. *Newsweek,* 50–56.

Koralek, D.G., Colker, L.J., & Dodge, T.D. (1993). *The what, why, and how of high-quality early childhood education.* Washington, DC: National Association for the Education of Young Children.

Lomax, R., & McGee, L. (1987). Young children's concept about print and reading: Toward a model of word reading acquisition. *Reading Research Quarterly, 22,* 237–256.

Morrow, L.M. (2001). *Literacy development in the early years: Helping children read and write* (4th ed.). Needham Heights, MA: Allyn & Bacon.

Owocki, G. (1999). *Literacy through play.* Portsmouth, NH: Heinemann.

Senge, P.M. (1990). *The fifth discipline.* New York: Bantam Doubleday Dell Publishing Group, Inc.

Smith, M.W., & Dickinson, D.D. (with Sangeorge, A., & Anastasopoulos, L.). (2002). *Early Language and Literacy Classroom Observation (ELLCO) Toolkit* (Research ed.). Baltimore: Paul H. Brookes Publishing Co.

Shareef, I., & Gonzalez-Mena, J. (1997, May/June). Beneath the veneers of resistance and professionalism. *Child Care Information Exchange, 115,* 6–8.

CASE STUDY 2

Creative
Contexts for Literacy

A Reggio Emilia Approach
Using Art and Documentation

CYNTHIA P. GEHRIE, ELIZABETH LANDERHOLM, AND GEORGINA VALVERDE

In the summer of 2005, a graphic artist, a documenter, and an early childhood education (ECE) professor co-created a summer workshop. The child care teachers work at early childhood centers from Roots of Literacy and Reading, an Early Reading First (ERF) project designed to develop centers of excellence. A workshop was designed based on three signature principles in the Reggio Emilia approach (Edwards, Gandini, & Forman, 1998): 1) art, 2) co-creative teaching, and 3) documentation (Albrecht, 1996).

The Reggio Emilia approach promotes a view of children that supports children's own investigations into learning about the world. Such inquiries can lead to complex projects in which new environments are created by the children to achieve an authentic purpose.

The Reggio Emilia approach uses graphic art to investigate questions and represents knowledge as it is accumulated and organized. This workshop offered teachers hands-on experience with art. In addition to providing an experience of making art in a studio atmosphere, elements of representation such as 3-D construction, symbol making, and visual narrative were used. To create a context for

The workshop described in this chapter is part of a series of professional development workshops prepared for the Roots of Language and Literacy (ROLL) Project. Project ROLL is an Early Reading First project developed by Northeastern Illinois University's (NEIU) Early Childhood Program and the Chicago Teachers' Center. ROLL provides professional development training in early literacy for early childhood teachers at the NEIU Child Care Center and the Children's Centers of Cicero-Berwyn. These childcare centers all have a high percentage of children and families living in poverty and children whose first language is Spanish (other English language learners include those who speak Korean, Arabic, and various Eastern European languages).

this work, we asked the participants to create representations of a personal space, and then donate these to the class to use in group projects in which they combined their individual personal spaces to create new environments as a group.

The Reggio Emilia approach uses documentation, such as photography and narrative text, to describe the actions, language, and thinking of children as they work. These descriptions build a group resource from which new learning emerges. We documented the workshop sessions and returned to the documentation when we reflected upon the learning process. We also explored ways to use documentation to support oral language practice and vocabulary building. The structure is similar to what we used with the graphic arts. First, participants generated vocabulary from personal experience. Then they contributed their words and concepts to form a texture (touch), sound, and smell database. The database was used to create poems and to enrich the new environments created using visual art.

THE CLASSROOM CONTEXT: EARLY LANGUAGE AND LITERACY CLASSROOM OBSERVATION TOOLKIT, RESEARCH EDITION

In the spring of 2005, the documenter in this project conducted an assessment of the literacy environment in classrooms at two sites of the Children's Centers of Cicero-Berwyn. The Early Language and Literacy Classroom Observation (ELLCO) Toolkit, Research Edition (Smith & Dickinson, 2002) is comprised of three parts: 1) Literacy Environment Checklist, 2) Classroom Observation and Teacher Interview, and 3) Literacy Activity Rating Scale. The Classroom Observation is used to score the organization of the classroom, contents of the classroom, presence and use of technology, opportunities for child choice and initiative, classroom management strategies, classroom climate, oral language facilitation, presence of books, approaches to book reading, reading instruction, approaches to children's writing, approaches to curriculum integration, recognition of diversity in the classroom, facilitation of home support for literacy, and approaches to assessment. Using the ELLCO Toolkit, Research Edition, we found that Project ROLL teachers were strong in a variety of the areas on the instrument but, in particular, needed to learn ways to develop the literacy environment and their teaching strategies to encourage children's independent investigation. This was true for both individual and small-group teaching strategies.

A common thread across the classrooms was that there were many missed opportunities because teachers did not respond when children began to explore materials and questioned the teacher about areas rich in potential for investigation. Oral language and literacy instruction generally took place with the whole class during circle time. There was little vocabulary building, oral language, and writing in the activity classroom areas such as the block area or housekeeping area. Teachers were not working with small groups of children nor were they engaging them in conversations that might lead to follow-up investigation. The workshop needed to provide authentic experiences for the teaching staff as learners so that they might discover principles of group process and authentic investigation that could be incorporated into their teaching.

To help teachers begin to explore using more small-group work in their classrooms, we focused on two qualities of group work.

1. *Group process brings forward multiple perspectives.* We wanted participants to have the experience of starting a project from their own perspective, and then working with others to combine perspectives to create a new collaborative point of view. We wanted them to experience an environment in which it is normal to borrow or "piggyback" ideas and expressions from the other participants. The insight that everyone contributes to the whole, and everyone can use materials from the whole, is an essential concept to comprehending the utility of a collaboratively created idea database. Putting data together in this way and sharing it hands on without the technical layer of a computer, acquaints participants with a core element of modern technology.

2. *Group process offers a context to compile words, practice vocabulary building, and participate in oral language expression.* We wanted participants to explore using group process to generate lists of vocabulary derived through group activities. We wanted them to have the experience of practicing oral language as a natural part of learning in small groups.

The values inherent in these two experiences were mirrored in the design of the workshop. Three professionals with strong backgrounds in three different areas facilitated the workshop. Their participation in the workshop grew out of their professional skills, and the goal of the workshop was not to attempt to blend these perspectives into a single, homogenized viewpoint. Adapting the professional structure used at Reggio Emilia, we wanted the participants to experience the value of different perspectives and to reach their own synthesis of ideas.

INTRODUCING THE REGGIO EMILIA EXPERIENCE USING CLASSROOM LITERACY AND TECHNOLOGY

A Reggio Emilia approach to professional development emphasizes the "belief that adults as well as children need opportunities for sharing, experimenting, revolting, building theory, and constructing knowledge about the world in which they work" (New, 1994, p. 34). A goal of this workshop was to provide investigative instruction from three points of view so that participants would experience the tools of the investigative process for themselves. We hoped they might begin to form their own understanding of inquiry-based instruction by using observation, representation, and by developing databases for organizing and documenting information. They would thereby gain insight into learning theory that supports the co-construction of learning and project-based teaching methodology.

Italian educators at Reggio Emilia advise visitors not to copy Italian schools. Instead, visitors are urged to adapt the Reggio Emilia approach to their local situation. In this project, The Children's Centers of Cicero-Berwyn (CCCB) child care centers were working on areas of literacy and technology. Our workshop worked in these areas using a Reggio Emilia approach to staff development. We worked with Reggio Emilia concepts of documentation, collaboration, utilization of stimulating materials, supportive and provocative teacher role, and reflection (Fraser & Gestwicki, 2000). The facilitator roles of documenter, artist, and ECE professor approximate the Reggio Emilia elements of the documenter, artist, and professor.

In the workshop, the Reggio Emilia approach to working with children emphasized

1. The viewpoint of the artist, or atelierista—to develop the learning environment by sharing pictures and ideas.

2. The viewpoint of the ECE professor, or pedagogista—to develop ways of helping children develop inquiry question-asking.

3. The documenter's viewpoint—which in Reggio Emilia is both the pedagogista's and the atelierista's—in which teachers learn to observe, record, and develop from children's investigative learning.

Our approach was to

1. Model documentation as the documenter created a running narrative of each workshop on a computer, photographed each step of the process, and shared these narratives and photos with the class. The photos also served as prompts for reflection during the evaluation session on the last day.

2. Co-develop a sensory database of participants' contributions and ideas as scaffolding for collaboration, group learning, co-construction of knowledge, and the construction of new knowledge.

3. Model the use of multiple materials by using art to construct various representations of experience. We also brought participants through a process in which they translated these representations from one format to another.

4. Model the use of a facilitative role that offers critique, support, and asks provocative questions to push the learner to higher levels of understanding and problem-solving. The artist modeled this during one-on-one critique sessions and group exhibit critique discussions.

5. Reflection on the implication of these experiences for teachers in the context of the American preschool environment. The ECE professor led reflection on the use of this approach within the framework of schedules and lesson plans required in the American system and by those funding the system, such as Head Start. The group reflected on ways to build skill sets for teaching with

group process, ways to structure independent projects, and ways to arrange the classroom to represent experience using 3-D constructions and 2-D graphic formats.

The development of sensory description in a database offers a framework for vocabulary development and practice and scaffolding for group work in the co-construction of knowledge. Because the scaffolding leads to the construction of a multimedia database, it supports CCCB's goal to develop the use of technology in instruction.

The Reggio Emilia approach leads to a rich literacy environment by providing support for teacher–student conversation, oral language within the framework of group work, and independent investigation. Current literature on the context for teaching and learning literacy supports this focus. For example, essential early literacy teaching strategies identified by the National Association for the Education of Young Children include "rich teacher talk" and "integrated, content-focused activities" (Roskos, Christie, & Richgels, 2003). Rich teacher talk is described as the practice to "engage children in rich conversations in large-group, small-group, and one-to-one settings." When teaching with integrated, content-focused activities, teachers will "provide opportunities for children to investigate topics that are of interest to them. The objective is for children to use oral language, reading, and writing to learn about the world" (pp. 2–4).

The use of art and multiple forms of representation has long been recognized as the core of investigative instruction. Children pursue self-directed new learning when teachers

> Provide many opportunities for children to plan, anticipate, reflect on, and revisit their own learning experiences. They engage children in discussion and representation activities [e.g., writing, drawing, or constructing models] to help children refine their own concepts and thinking and help themselves understand children's thinking. (Bredekamp & Copple, 1997, p. 167)

Here are some examples of research supporting the importance of early oral language and vocabulary development to success in literacy:

1. Measures of preschool teacher discourse significantly enhance vocabulary and language development for children entering kindergarten with lasting effects through fourth grade (Dickinson & Tabors, 2001). Developing a classroom structure that supports complex and purposeful student–teacher discourse was one of the purposes of this workshop.

2. A characteristic of successful literacy development is the ability "to attend to difficult tasks, and to develop the motivation that helps one become a self-sustaining learner" (Dickenson & Neuman, 2006, p. 13). Investigative projects, such as those at Reggio Emilia, provide scaffolding for sustained learning projects.

3. Vocabulary skill in kindergarten is found to correlate with seventh-grade reading skills (Tabors, Snow, & Dickinson, 2001). The database exercise in the workshop links observation to emergent vocabulary, which is practiced and applied in subsequent activities.

4. A 1995 study by Hart and Risely found that children from poorer families are less likely to hear rich models of oral language. In their first 4 years, children from professional-class homes hear 11 million words. Children from working-class homes hear 6 million words. Children from welfare homes hear 3 million words. The children in the CCCB childcare centers come from populations most in need of focused work to develop their vocabulary (Hart & Risely, 1995).

5. Cooperative learning allows students to learn while being engaged in the learning process with other students. In one research study, small groups of students translated content material from "teacher talk" to "kid talk" and showed gains in reading comprehension (Klinger, Vaughn, & Schumm, 1998). This workshop is designed to help participants transition from teacher-led classroom organization to small-group work, by providing the experience of learning in small collaborative groups.

THE ACTUAL WORKSHOP

The workshop is described here day by day. Descriptions are presented using the voices of the ECE professor, the artist, and the documenter. Some additional material created by the participants is presented in table form.

Day 1

The Early Childhood Education Professor: We opened the workshop with a description of the Reggio Emilia model of early childhood education. The focus was on key ideas at Reggio Emilia (Albrecht, 1996) that I call the 4 C's of the Reggio Emilia approach: 1) a *community commitment* to each child's right to learn in a functional, beautiful environment; 2) a belief in the *competent child* with a focus on potential instead of problems in classroom design; 3) a recognition of the need for *communication and documentation* (both visual and verbal) among all members of the community, including children, teachers, parents, and the larger network of community resources; and 4) a system of *collaboration* in learning, and co-creating with teachers, children, parents, and community members. We gave teachers several articles on the Reggio Emilia approach to review for the second day. With this as a background, we were able to connect practice to theory.

The Artist: We asked participants to identify, in their minds, a personal place to use in an extended exercise. We used a visualization experience to help them identify their place. Then I presented a variety of examples of how artists have represented *place*. One artist documented his daily walks and plotted them according to a map of Chicago. A second used photographs and paintings to create collages that depicted the demolition of the infamous Chicago housing projects. A third created dream-like images that incorporated bits of pottery, architectural details, and religious imagery to investigate historical themes. A fourth artist depicted cyborgs in his studio to meditate on the artist's role in the technological era. After discussing the various art examples, the participants created a representation of their personal place using a wide range of materials: tape, markers, glue, hole punchers, felt, erasers, pencils, exacto knives, white bond paper, novelty paper with embossed designs, pastel chalks, permanent marker pens, many colors of tissue paper, wire hangers, popsicle sticks, paint brushes, and India ink.

From the onset, we identified the importance of enlarging the definitions of literacy to include visual culture and multiple modes of representation. We wanted participants to consider the notion of place from many vantage points, not simply from a personal and familiar perspective. To open up these meanings, we showed participants photographs, postcards, maps, catalogues, entries from encyclopedias, and exhibition records demonstrating different conceptions and representations of place. We considered how different media and genres affect particular aspects of space.

Translation was another key idea in this project. We wanted teachers to consider multiple ways in which impressions and experiences are identified, and how these representations are all forms of literacy. For example, in visual literacy, sound can be translated into color and temperature. The sound of a screeching car can be red hot. Comprehension includes the capacity to recognize these translations from the literal to the figurative.

We introduced the idea of using a database to collect individual experiences into a common resource (see Day 2 sidebar). Sensory impressions of their personal place were to be recorded in simple descriptive terms describing texture, sound, and smell. These were entered in a table and then combined into a matrix on Day 2. Once gathered in the matrix, language could be used to generate sounds, images, smells, and tactile representations.

Generally, teachers recognize the important role drawings play in supporting children's self-expression. The potential drawing has on helping in the development of analytical skills, however, is largely untapped. By the time children enter elementary school, drawing is limited to art class or as a free-choice activity to fill in downtime. Not surprisingly, by the time they reach adulthood, most people experience great anxiety and feelings of inadequacy in relation to drawing. To encourage open-ended approaches to drawing and to free up experimentation, we introduced a variety of materials and techniques. Materials included different textures of paper, felt squares, fabric scraps, and cardboard. We presented a variety of tools: pencils, markers, ink, oil pastels, scissors, cutters, glue, and glue sticks. The wealth of choices proved liberating to the majority of participants.

Day 2—Exhibit Discussions

The Artist steers the discussion toward the variety of visual representations, although most students needed to share the story of their special place. The group singles out an exquisite collage representing a childhood memory.

Participant: I grew up in Palestine, and I liked to climb up in the apple trees. We have evergreens that grow straight up. These are cherry trees.

Artist: There are three [cherries], which is magical. It might come from your culture, because the visual representations are generally symmetrical with things radiating from the center."

Throughout the discussion, the artist pushes participants to go beyond narration and retelling, and to examine instead their motivations or problems encountered in the process of representation.

Participant: I was trying to give the pleasure of my place, but it was difficult to do.

Artist: You are identifying a problem. It does not meet your expectations. There is a lot in this place and you have not found a way to translate it.

We provided a short ink drawing demonstration in which we showed participants how to use correction fluid to fix any "mistakes." We also gave them the option of cutting and pasting to fix mistakes rather than throwing their paper away. These processes are analogous to digital processes of text and image manipulation that use copy or cut-and-paste functions in word processing software. We encouraged experimentation by using tools other than brushes to enhance the process rather than focusing on results. Throughout the work session, the artist supported participants' attempts by pointing out their strengths: the delicacy of a gesture, attention to detail, compositional strength, or sensibility to color. In this context, participants began to develop familiarity with the technical language of the visual arts, which is the 25th goal of the Illinois Learning Standards for Fine Arts.

A surprising outcome of the first day was the predominance of 3-D representations that resembled architectural models. In hindsight, it was a natural consequence resulting from the abundance of materials. Only a few students chose to draw with ink.

The Documenter: After building graphic constructions of a personal, special place, I instructed participants to visualize this place in the evening to complete their homework assignment, and if possible, physically visit that place.

They were given pages of blank tables to complete, which would be made into a paper database the next day. The boxes in the tables were analogous to data fields in computer software in which database records are compiled. This was a hands-on experience that introduced basic concepts in information formatting, storage, and retrieval. In their special place, participants completed a table on the sounds they heard, the textures they could see or feel, and the aromas or scents they could smell (see Tables CS.1, CS.2, and CS.3).

Participants were also instructed to bring an object from their particular place to the classroom on the second day. The object would be used in producing a sound, using an artifact from their special place. These database activities, which were built into the Reggio Workshop, were designed to develop awareness that learning activities can be a source of meaningful data for extended work. By co-constructing a database out of participants' exploratory activities in the classroom and from homework, the class co-generated its own resource vocabulary for use in extended projects. The development and use of the database for extending projects can provide scaffolding for individual and self-generated inquiry. Through these activities, the teachers might generate their own understanding of many principles.

The construction of a database from learning activities enriches the literacy environment by creating data files embedded in the context of personal experience. The creation of a database is a natural process that emerges in collaborative activity. Whenever participants pool information and then share the pool to go beyond the work of individuals, they are working with a database. Developing skills in generating, formatting, accessing, and using data for the production of new work is a key component in developing rich group productivity.

In this exercise, learners co-constructed several database "threads" (e.g., sound, smell, texture [touch]) out of a single formative project that includes individual and group activities. The first stage of this project included frontloading that prepared students for extended inquiry. The term *frontloading* refers to the practice of providing students the information, experience, or demonstration they will need to succeed in a hands-on activity. Frontloading prepares students to understand and become comfortable with the context of the experience. Frontloading during this workshop included providing visual examples of graphic

Table CS.1. Data matrix on sounds from special places: Samples

Description of sound	Qualities	What does it sound like?
Dove cooing	Rhythmic, high tone followed by lower tone	Rhroo, Rhroo
Hose (water) running	N/A	Tsssssssss tsssssssss ploop
Dog walking on sidewalk	Short, quick steps	Tick, tick, tick, tick
Airplane flying	Low, quiet rumble	rrrrrrrrrr
Door squeaking open	High pitch	nnnnnnnnnn

Table CS.2. Data matrix on smells from special places: Samples

Description of smell	Qualities	What does it smell like?
Charcoal barbeque	Offensive, eyes burning	Lighter fuel, then onions
Gas grill	N/A	Chicken, sauce
Aftershave	Strong, textured	N/A
Fish	Strong colored	N/A

representation such as photographs, journals, and paintings that showed the different ways several artists portrayed a sense of place. The students portrayed a sense of place by exploring maps and their systems of coding and notation; demonstrating the use of materials, such as applying ink with brushes and water washes; and using visualization exercises to set up the landscape of their special place for a series of activities within the formative project.

Data for the database are drawn from activities using several senses: sight, sound, smell, and touch. The database is used for new expression and inquiry. Small-group products during the workshop on the third day were created as examples of co-constructed knowledge artifacts.

Day 2

We began Day 2 by examining the graphic constructions of participants' special places created on the first day. The work was displayed as an exhibit, placed on tables, and hung on the walls. The transcripts of the conversation are valuable in identifying personal and collective inquiries, a key component of the Reggio Emilia approach.

After the discussion, participants were asked to create a 2-D drawing of their special place from a bird's-eye view, and to incorporate a texture from their database. This time they were limited to white paper and black felt-tip markers of var-

Table CS.3. Data matrix on texture (touch) from special places: Sample

Description of texture	Sample
Glass-textured table top	Rubbing (even smooth texture)
Grass: green and straw color, some short and some long strands	Drawing (like lines of scribble up and down)
Sunflower: yellow almond shaped petals, yellow dots curled inside petals, green center, green leaves and stems, fuzzy stems	Drawing (flower on long stem and leaves branching from stem)
Wooden Indian: carved from tree trunk, rough splitting wood	Drawing (head, shoulders to waist, long hair with headband)
Hose: smooth green, snakelike, rubbery	Drawing (long tube in "figure 8" shape with nozzle on one end)

ious widths. As in the previous session, the exercise of conceptualizing real space on a flat surface was extremely frustrating for some because they were not familiar with drawing objects in perspective, a technique that makes objects look 3-D on a piece of paper. The documenter collected homework data tables that were combined into a classroom database of text descriptions using sound, touch (texture), and smell. There were also rubbings of texture.

Participants introduced the object they brought from their special place and demonstrated how it could be used to produce a sound. Working in pairs, they combined their two sounds into a short rhythm sequence using both sounds, which they then presented to the class. To begin an audio database, a video camera was used to record audio segments of both individual sounds and paired rhythm sequences. In this exercise, participants moved from individual products of a single sound to blended phrases that combine several sounds. This morphing from personal to small-group production served as frontloading for the convergence exercise on the third day.

Day 3

Copies of the class's "smell database"—made from combined tables of smell recorded during the first day's homework assignment—were distributed. Participants were asked to talk in small groups about the smells listed in the database, to look for common categories, and to make observations.

The Artist: I observed that this generates a discussion of the words that were used to describe smell, and the difficulty of describing smell directly through its qualities, instead of by materializing it by describing smell through visual terms (e.g., cheeseburgers smell juicy), and describing its origins or locations (e.g., fruit smells like honeydew or honeysuckle flowers). This is a rich discussion of the nature of language and how we use it to create meaning and description.

The descriptions were also personalized, as participants explored the links between smell and its role in their memory of past experience. There was also discussion of "value"—which smells were pleasant or unpleasant, which were associated with high or low values in scales of importance.

Linkages of smell to process were also explored. Different stages of production or decay have their own associated smells. All of these discussions build vocabulary and expressive skills for describing experience.

The Documenter: In addition to the data fields produced from the sensory charts, the bird's-eye drawings of the special place were converted into a visual, symbolic database. The drawings made on the second day were photocopied. Participants divided into groups, and each group received a set of photocopies to use in the next exercise. Each group constructed a new "created place" from the photocopies by cutting and pasting and re-photocopying the individual drawings to provide as much volume of an image as the new environment required. As they worked in groups they made comments, such as

"I want the tree from hers."
"I want my chair."
"I want the cobblestones."

This is convergent authoring, a kind of writing that now forms the basis of media writing. For example, reporters use multiple sources such as a computer, books, radio, and television to assist them in writing their stories.

The exercise moves the participants from working as individuals to having the participants come together to create a database in a collaborative learning style, and then using the information in the database as a springboard for new activities. This experience of working together on the database to enrich the resources for the group is an example of the dynamic power of individuals all contributing their ideas and insights in the process of constructing a database.

The Early Childhood Education Professor: I introduced a lesson plan format used in the ECE program and assigned homework to the teachers. The lesson was to write up one of the experiences of the first 3 days, list the state goals for one area, and translate the experience into lesson plan format. The goal of this exercise was for the teachers to be able to translate their experiences into the format required by the state so that teachers can see that they can use these experiences with children and still complete the funding requirements and the state requirements of their schools and/or agencies.

Day 4

This day began with an exhibit of the converged environments from the previous day. These were group representations assembled from a shared, co-constructed database of visual symbols such as cobblestones, trees, chairs, a hot tub, and buildings taken from the 2-D representations of special places. Both the facilitators and the participants commented about the process of co-creating a new artifact out of a co-constructed database. The ECE professor commented by saying

"The idea of photocopying is that it opens up possibilities for cutting out images, borrowing one another's symbols—it made the process so much freer."

A participant added

"We all had the same pictures, but each group did their own design. Each has different ideas."

The Documenter: As documenter, I find that these comments demonstrate the sense of new freedom that can be experienced when options are expanded as participants discover that it is okay to use one another's work to extend new work. It makes clear a shift in the culture of the classroom in which students are supporting one another's development, instead of competing and hoarding knowledge.

The Artist: I brought in a zoning map of the town of Cicero. I wanted participants to consider it as a point of reference when discussing their final drawings. Cicero is originally a manufacturing town. It is bordered by numerous railroad tracks that isolate the community from the main street that houses the town hall and a lively commercial strip. The manufacturing areas are designated in green. Many participants misread this coding as standing for parks and were shocked to learn otherwise. We discussed the use of a legend on our collective maps. The students suggested designating areas for recreation, businesses, residential, imagination/dreams, and green spaces.

In a second activity, pairs of participants used the database of sound, smell, and texture to write a poem. Then the poems were read to the class. Here is an example of a poem: "Fish, splash-splash/ Tight weave, smooth, rough,/ Colorful."

The poems created from the database were surprisingly fresh. The database helped us distance ourselves from the mandate to "be creative." With this open-ended approach, participants were able to consider the poetic potential of language culled from everyday situations.

At the end of Day 4, time was set aside to review photos from each day using a projection screen. Participants were asked to write their responses to the photos. Then, each day was briefly discussed. This created a database of open-ended responses, including written data and verbal data.

Verbal Discussion and Review of the Workshop

The Documenter: In the review of verbal comments, two themes emerge. First, there is discussion of the adjustment the teachers made to this kind of learning, particularly the challenge of doing a creative project with a multitude of materials. These activities were a challenge for the participants, and when they succeeded in creating their projects there was a feeling of accomplishment. Second, they verbalized their response to working in small groups. One of the challenges was the development of skill in working within small groups.

The Early Childhood Education Professor: This experience with collaboration was particularly important for teachers because this was an area on the ELLCO Toolkit, Research Edition, that the teachers needed work on. They said that group work supported creative expression and was stimulating. Teachers verbalized their response to the experience of using a co-created database.

Participants began to understand how to use a database to extend learning through small-group projects. They verbalized the idea that they can create new expressions using the database and share resources with everyone. The database is a way of sharing, stimulating, and making resources available to everyone.

The Artist: An important goal of this workshop was to push participants to participate in a creative process without basing their efforts on a predetermined model. We hope that this experience will be a baseline for future classroom projects. The experimentation with materials and techniques allows for multiple translations of experiences. The database is a starting point for organizing meaning culled from everyday life (see Table CS.4).

Written Reflections on the Workshop

Each member of the workshop compiled written reflections individually, and compiled one reflection for each of the workshop days. Time should be set aside so that the members may share their reflections, or copies of the reflections should be made and passed to all workshop members.

Written Evaluations for Day 1

The Documenter: Written evaluation revealed deeper reflection on the process of approaching a creative assignment with open-ended materials that stimulate individual approaches.

Table CS.4.   Verbal discussion and review of workshop

Summary observation	Participants' comments
At first, participants did not know how to approach a creative task with open-ended, supportive materials.	"There were a multitude of materials. It was intimidating. In the end I was proud of what I came up with."
Participants said that small group projects were a good learning method.	"It is nice to work in a group; I would like to do more projects like this."
Participants were developing the communication, collaboration, and co-creation of the Reggio approach.	"At first, people listened about Reggio, then we chose materials and were busy making it. We were working together and asking each other what we wanted to do. We were working together as a group to get success. Communication. Group process."
They expressed that everyone contributed to the process.	"We brought something to make a noise from our special place. Making the sounds was important."
The database supports creative activity.	"Good idea on how to write a poem, use a database."
"It was easier to write out of others' creations."

The Artist: The most successful outcome of this day was the participants' positive experience with a variety of materials and tools. Although this
abundance was overwhelming for a few students, it is hard to say what their
experience would have been if the opposite had been the case.

The Early Childhood Education Professor: Teachers expressed a wide
variety of feelings about the creation. Reviewing the documentation later will
help them remember that children also respond in diverse ways to an experience. Some teachers loved having so many materials, whereas others were intim-
idated (see Table CS.5).

Written Evaluations for Day 2

The Documenter: Most of the evaluation statements for Day 2 focused
on the process of converting the original 3-D construction of the special place
into a 2-D, black and white, bird's-eye view.

There were also some descriptive comments on the use of the sound object
and experimentation with sounds that were linked to the special place. This experience with sound was intended to frontload the idea of moving from individual
work to combining one's own work with others to make new work products.

The Artist: Day 2 included an introduction to the idea of constraint. By
limiting the media, we were able to focus instead on perspective and design. The

Table CS.5. Day 1: Written reflections of the workshop

Summary observation	Participants' comments
Participants were willing to try some-thing new, and soon after, a momentum was created as they moved into the activity.	"A day to create a special place, a familiar place, or a place we frequent. Many ideas and materials are in the room as people are busy at work and taking pride in their place."
	"Not sure where to start. Not a creative per-son, but had fun once I thought about how to create my special place."
Participants lacked skills of represen-tation, although they knew what it was they wanted to express.	"I was very intimidated and overwhelmed because I knew it would be difficult to repre-sent my special place, but I started and used the materials the best I could which I didn't totally achieve."
Everyone approached the assign-ment in their own way, and every-one was finding individual solutions to the problem of representation.	"There were many materials to choose from to design my special place. Individuals creat-ing, and constructing in a variety of ways."
Participants were realizing that the open-ended use of materials is bal-anced by an assignment that is grounded in personal experience that builds on prior knowledge (a theory breakthrough).	"Materials. Confusion. What do I create? Con-fidence of knowing my special place."

black and white drawings "translated" the richness of the previous day's 3-D models into line, pattern, and texture.

The experiments with sound were analogous. We restricted participants to exploring the sound potential of the objects they brought in from their special place. In this way, we were able to focus on the subtleties of the materials and were challenged to exploit each object's potential for sound-making.

The Early Childhood Education Professor: The teachers worked individually on their creations and began to co-create with the sound experimentation (see Table CS.6).

Written Evaluation for Day 3

The Documenter: On Day 3, participants worked in small groups to create a new space using the symbolic representation developed from their 2-D, birds'-eye drawings of their special place. As participants gained experience in working with a database in groups, they came to value the process (see Table CS.7).

The Artist: When we examined the database fields on smell, I noticed that many of the descriptions were visual, or physical words. Is this the difficulty of describing smell, or is it our visual dominance?

The documenter had said at the end of Day 2, "Something is missing: a larger question, a real inquiry that galvanizes the group's energies toward a common purpose." The created space and the database approach proved to be the missing piece.

To build the created space, I instructed the group to break out into small groups of four or five. Then each group was asked to take their drawings and use the copy machine to duplicate, enlarge, and reduce details of each person's drawing. After photocopying, they were to cut and paste these elements to co-create a space.

This activity took less than 20 minutes, but the results were impressive. The groups were able to quickly zero-in on different elements that each member

Table CS.6.   Day 2: Written reflections of the workshop

Summary observation	Participants' comments
Participants began to combine sounds and build on one another's sound from their personal space.	"We also brought something that makes sounds from our special place. Everyone made a sound using rocks, water, wooden spoons, etc." "We brought something from our special place and we made the sound." "We teamed up and combined sounds and sound experiment: cup and saucer, water. I slowly poured water, tap with the saucer on the cup. Different tone of sound. Water affects sound."

Table CS.7. Day 3: Written reflections of the workshop

Summary observation	Participants' comments
Participants were developing a sense of how to participate together, drawing on everyone's ideas.	"We were working in groups to create a place that was special and desirable to all of us. It was fun to take pieces from all of the works and combine them into one. I found my group very open and easy to work with. Ideas were taken or left—but no one felt like their ideas were unimportant or bad."
Participants were learning how to combine items from a database into a new construction.	"We were working in groups to come together and make an aerial view. We used views from all places to make one environment."
Participants were developing a sense of being part of a team and of engaging in teamwork.	"After looking at each other's black and white view, we decided to photocopy each others' papers and began to group together and pool our ideas and work together as a real team— some cutting, some photocopying, some placing the items on the paper trying to see where they would fit the best. We exchanged our ideas and began to paste our map together— I think we did a great job together."
Participants were seeing that collaborative projects could reflect the contributions of all.	"It was interesting to see how working as a team we could combine everyone's individual project and come out with really nice maps."
Participants were discovering that a database could be used to create new projects, not simply replicate previous work.	"We teamed up and made a bigger space by creating a whole new idea without projects— putting them together to get a new space idea."
Participants discovered that the collaborative spirit has its own energy and context.	"Magic movement. Convergence of place. A sense that everyone contributed." (Note the use of the vocabulary introduced in the workshop—convergence.)
Participants discovered that a group activity can create a sense of mutuality and support for creative work.	"We looked at our air view projects. We shared our thoughts and ideas. We made copies of our work and used them to come up with a group project. It was a nice activity. Great support between us."
Participants realized that co-created database projects support cut-and-paste authoring, which is central to computer-based authoring applications.	They refer to "cooperation, sharing images, using the photocopier, cutting and pasting, organizing, and creating together."
Participants declared that the creative group process was enjoyable.	"It was fun creating new spaces. It was fun collaborating others' special spaces with what we had." It was a "fun, creative time for the team."

brought to the project. The cobblestone pattern from the student who had drawn a memory of an orchard in Palestine was a prized item. Almost every group duplicated it to create walkways and included it in garden areas in their collective maps.

Teachers rarely exploit the photocopier's potential as a drawing aide. Duplication was used to extend patterns, multiply elements, and play with scale. The duplicates freed participants to experiment with each other's ideas instead of holding on to their individual products. The participants expressed the following statements:

"Magic movement. Convergence of place. A sense that everyone contributed."
"We teamed up and made a bigger space by creating a whole new idea with our projects, putting them together to get a new space idea."
"It was a nice activity. Great support between us."

The collaboration with environmental spaces provided experience with the Reggio theories on the importance of the environment as well as the importance of communication, collaboration, and co-creation and the focus on how children enjoy learning together.

The Artist: Day 3 exemplified the challenges of the creative process. Sometimes we reach an impasse. We work through these moments by being flexible and trusting that a cohesive story will evolve if we keep mining the group's impressions collected in the database. At the day's end we have achieved a "Eureka moment" when individual drawings come together in the collective mappings.

Written Evaluation for Day 4

The Documenter: Participants worked in pairs to write a poem using the database vocabulary on touch (texture), sound, and smell.

The Artist: The highlight of this day was creating poetry out of words compiled in the sensory database. The detachment achieved through the semi-scientific model of the database allowed for a fresh approach to language. The idea for this activity emerged out of our examination on the nature of smell. The database suggested unusual juxtapositions of words with great poetic potential: *soft tones, even, like a wind-up toy, clean, strong,* and so forth. The database format imposed a rigor to the language and opened up its descriptive potential.

The Early Childhood Education Professor: Documentation is an important tool for reflection. The teachers remembered more when they reviewed the photos and the artwork from the day before (see Table CS.8).

Concluding Workshop Remarks

The Documenter: In the workshop, participants gained experience in using a co-created database to extend learning activities. They experienced group process in the use of database in project development, and felt the supportive stimulation of this way of learning. They mentioned on several occasions

Table CS.8.   Day 4: Written reflections of the workshop

Summary observations	Participants' comments
Capacity to work from a database was growing.	"Writing the poem in that format was fun—it seemed limiting at first, but when you started putting the words together you really could have continued on." "It makes you view your subject in a different or more abstract way." "Poem—wonderful idea for creating poem—using a database." "Great to see final projects and share ideas and poems with database."
There was growing comfort in co-creative projects.	"We talked about poems—light, airy, sweet, invisible—and teamed up to write a poem of our own."
There was an overall sense that this is a good way to learn.	"I worked with Jackie on a poem. It was a beautiful poem. I really enjoyed the pictures and the review. It was a good experience for me." "Light hearted. Relaxing. I liked writing the poems. Loved the picture documentation."

that they wanted to introduce these methods in their classrooms to promote self-directed learning and literacy projects for authentic purposes.

The Artist: The database was a useful instrument to help participants detach themselves from results and gain a more objective view of process. The coded impressions offer a wealth of opportunities for translation and interpretation and lend themselves to such experimental techniques of contemporary art practice as concrete poetry, collage, and pastiche (an art that imitates the style of previous work or imitates work from multiple sources). The co-constructed product challenges notions of individual authorship and materializes important paradigm shifts brought about by technology in the conception of literacy.

The Early Childhood Education Professor: Having the experiences of representing a favorite place first, then going to that place and collecting data on sounds, textures, smells, and sights started the teachers off as adults having to really look, listen, smell, and feel in a place they felt they already knew. The culmination of the following experiences led to a deeply satisfying learning experience:

- Having the help of the artist to look at other art works and styles of representation

- The challenge of drawing in black and white with no color

- The experience of viewing each other's work

- Collaboration and co-creating

- Communicating and combining ideas

- Using the resources of the community database of words for sounds, sights, smells, and touch (textures)

This learning experience/practice led to an understanding of some of the values infused in the Reggio Emilia approach and ELLCO Toolkit, Research Edition. These included the importance of working in a small group, the importance of investigating sounds, sights, (touch) textures, and smells, the importance of representing visually and verbally, and, finally, the importance of promoting their thinking toward translating these experiences into lesson plans that can be developed with children.

REFERENCES

Albrecht, K. (1996). Reggio Emilia: Four key ideas. *Texas Child Care, 10,* 2–9.

Bredekamp, S., & Copple, C. (1997). *Developmentally appropriate practice in early childhood programs.* Washington, DC: National Association for the Education of Young Children.

Dickinson, D.K., & Tabors, P.O. (2001). (Eds.) *Beginning literacy with language: Young children learning at home and school.* Baltimore: Paul H. Brookes Publishing Co.

Edwards, C., Gandini, L., & Forman, G. (1998). *The hundred languages of children— Advanced reflections.* Greenwich, CT: Ablex.

Fraser, S., & Gestwicki, C. (2000). *Authentic childhood: Exploring Reggio Emilia in the classroom.* Ontario, Canada: Delmar.

Hart, B., & Risley, T.R. (1995). *Meaningful differences in the everyday experience of young American children.* Baltimore: Paul H. Brookes Publishing Co.

Klinger, J.K., Vaughn, S., & Schumm, J.S. (1998). Collaborative strategic reading during social studies in heterogeneous fourth-grade classrooms. *Elementary School Journal, 99,* 3–22.

New, R.(1994). Reggio Emilia: Its Visions and its Challenges for Educators in the United States. In L. Katz and B. Cesarone, *Reflections on the Reggio Emilia Approach* (pp. 31–36). Urbana, Illinois: Clearinghouse on Early Education and Parenting.

Roskos, K., Christie, J.F., & Richgels, D.J. (2003). *The Essentials of Early Literacy Instruction,* Washington DC: National Association for the Education of Young Children.

Smith, M.W., & Dickinson, D.D. (with Sangeorge, A., & Anastasopoulos, L.). (2002). *Early Language and Literacy Classroom Observation (ELLCO) Toolkit* (Research ed.). Baltimore: Paul H. Brookes Publishing Co.

Tabors, P.O., Snow, C.E., & Dickinson, D.K. (2001). Homes and schools together: Supporting language and literacy development. In D.K. Dickinson & P.O. Tabors (Eds.), *Beginning literacy with language: Young children learning at home and school.* Baltimore: Paul H. Brookes Publishing Co.

Index

Page references to figures, tables, and footnotes are indicated by *f, t,* and *n,* respectively.